The Content of Reading

Proceedings of the twelfth annual course and conference of the
United Kingdom Reading Association
Owens Park, University of Manchester 1975

Editor Asher Cashdan

Ward Lock Educational

ISBN 0 7062 3570 3

First published 1976

Set in 11 on 12 point Garamond
and printed by Robert MacLehose and Company Limited, Glasgow
for Ward Lock Educational
116 Baker Street, London W1M 2BB
Made in Great Britain

Contents

Foreword

The twelfth annual course and conference of the United Kingdom
Reading Association was held at Owens Park, the University of
Manchester, in the summer of 1975. In the year of publication of the
Bullock Report on *Reading and the other uses of English*, it was fitting that
the conference took as its major theme *The content of reading*. It was
proposed to examine not just how children and adults learn to read
effectively, but rather the material they are given to read, its purposes,
how it comes to be created and published and how it may be
evaluated. It is hoped that this selection of conference papers makes
a useful contribution to the consideration of these issues – and of
many more besides. There are no easy answers; the important
thing is to go on asking the relevant questions.

   This book is the work of the contributors, who have given
gladly of their time, knowledge and experience. But I should also
like to thank Roy Blackman, Margaret Rockall and Sheila Waters
for the background help without which it would never have appeared
at all.

Asher Cashdan

Part 1
The content of reading

1 The content of reading

Asher Cashdan

The publication of the Bullock Report (DES 1975) provides an undeniable opportunity for a determined effort to raise standards of literacy in both children and adults. As the established organization in this field, the United Kingdom Reading Association is well placed to play its part. Growth in membership will lead to a broader range of publications and services and to a considerable increase in impact upon both professional educators and the community in general.

The need is undoubted. There has indeed been some controversy over recent trends, centring upon the NFER report (Start and Wells 1972) and the suggestion made in it that the post-war rise in literacy levels could now be dropping away. This suggestion is challenged by Burke and Lewis (1975), who state that there is 'no justification . . . for a belief that standards are declining'. But the whole issue pales into insignificance beside the certainty that a high proportion of school leavers do not at present reach an acceptable level of literacy, whatever the trend. The Bullock Report (page 11) quotes researches showing that the reading ability required to cope with ordinary newspaper articles, tax forms, the Highway Code and other common reading material is not attained by anything up to a third of the population. It goes on to claim that 'as society becomes more complex and makes higher demands . . . the criteria of literacy will rise'. So the question is not just whether we have laboriously regained the ground lost in our schools in the Second World War, but whether we can consolidate our present position and then go much further forward. Or to put it in a different form, something radical must clearly be done, when in a highly advanced industrial society of some sixty million people, our best estimate is that some two million adults are not functionally literate. This must at the least mean that our educational system may not be even potentially adequate to its task.

Learning language skills

However, though we have nothing to be complacent about in any department, it is not in the improvement of technical teaching skills that the main solution is likely to lie. Hence the *Black Paper* 'Basics' (Cox and Boyson 1975) are somewhat wide of the mark. For instance, two of these principles run as follows:

> Children are not naturally good. They need firm, tactful discipline from parents and teachers with clear standards . . .
> *and*
> The best way to help children in deprived areas is to teach them to be literate and numerate, and to develop all their potential abilities.

These are but recipes for pushing harder in the same old way as before. But both sociological argument and empirical research suggest that children have the ability to learn, but that they often fail to see the need or relevance of either school in general, or literacy skills in particular. If this is so, then pushing harder may merely lead to stouter resistance.

Thus, Bernstein (1971) now stresses that the working-class child has access to his 'elaborated code', but that he is rarely able to deploy it in the school context. Joan Tough (1973), again, sees children as at a disadvantage at school 'more because of what they have learned to do with their language than because of some deficiency in their knowledge of language'. And Cazden (1970) has reviewed four studies which all indicate that young children acquire language structures quite efficiently even if they do not come from advantaged homes. The problem in these terms is one of performance, not of competence. Indeed, if the notorious 'Language Acquisition Device' means anything, it is that relatively little input is needed for successful language learning, much less formal teaching. Of course, without language experience no language will come. But we are much less confident than we were only a few years ago, in claiming that only 'privileged' homes can produce competent children. Recent research on babies, too, shows how much of the learning initiative comes from the child himself, as he engages with the social environment off his own bat (see Trevarthen 1974).

The problem of motivation

In effect, I want to argue that children *are* naturally good, that they start off both wanting to learn and making a success of learning. So the question to ask is not how can we teach them better, so much as what can we be doing to stop them learning. In this light, we can see that many children, adolescents and, indeed, adults lack academic motivation because they see no personal relevance in school, or are made to feel positively inadequate by the way the school treats them. In particular, many children encounter a 'cultural gap' between their home background and that of the school, between the language, expectations, relationships and values of their parents and those of their teachers. Bridging (or circumventing) this gap is the major educational task.

Nor is this purely a question of social class. As the Plowden follow-up research shows (see Bynner 1972), the important thing seems to be that parents and schools should have aims that are congruent. If they do, the child prospers, irrespective of his social class background. Besides, social class is too indirect and multiple a concept to help us understand a child's home life and how this shapes his attitudes in school, in anything but the crudest terms (see Swift 1968).

Even if we were satisfied that our problem was to produce materials and situations that were right for working-class children, the solution would not be much nearer, as those teachers who have used such literature have found. Alan Davies (1973) in fact suggests that such 'working-class literature . . . is not plausible . . . the problem for most children is that, since they are not speaking the standard language, they are forced to switch both dialect and values when they read the written language'. And most working-class writers who attempt to write for the working class are, he suggests, no longer working class, almost by definition, in writing down what 'tends to be oral and not written'.

Some perspective

Are we then attempting an impossible task or, equally undesirably, trying to impose an alien culture on many of our children? I think we often are doing both of these and that we need therefore to stand back and consider our position, before attempting any quick solutions. In an essay first published in 1942, Margaret Mead (in Keddie, 1973) seems to me to make many of the important points. She compares 'primitive' education in the South Seas, as she studied it, with present-day education in countries such as Britain and the United States, and finds an important difference, which she describes as follows: '. . . the shift from the need for an individual to learn something which everyone agrees he would wish to know, to the will of some individual to teach something which it is not agreed that anyone has any desire to know'. Moreover, she associates this shift with 'the breakdown of self-contained and self-respecting cultural homogeneity' – that is, with a class system! In other words, we have moved away from a model in which what the child needs to know is what the adults around him know: a set of self-evidently necessary occupational and social skills. To learn these, the child (or even adult) goes for the knowledge and instruction he is in need of to a relative, a craftsman, even to a teacher. But no one has to construct a suitable curriculum, or persuade him to learn. Seen this way, Margaret Mead is right to stress the significance of our culture's acceptance of 'discontinuity between parents and children'. As she says: 'Modern education includes a heavy emphasis upon the function of education to create discontinuities – to turn the child of the peasant into a clerk, of the farmer into a lawyer . . . of the illiterate into the literate.'

Clearly, we do not live in a society where it is possible, or even desirable, to avoid such discontinuities. In fact, we are always having to stress the need to learn new skills – skills which often no one has had to practise before. But we do have to come to terms with the problem that if we attempt to impose knowledge on pupils simply because *we* want them to have it, this will hardly be education. The pupil must have the need, or it must be created in him. Otherwise, he will either not learn at all, learn reluctantly – or even learn successfully, but put his knowledge to little use.

There is, however, an even worse danger in the attempt to impose knowledge, skills or even values on children that are not even the teachers' own. How many 'non-readers' teach their pupils to read? And how many teach other subjects, too, in which they have little intrinsic interest, pushing their pupils through standards and public examinations, not for the use of literature, mathematics or whatever, but simply to improve their occupational prospects – to provide them with passports?

The child's purpose

What I am suggesting, then, is that the most dangerous teacher is the one who considers reading as 'an end in itself'. For this implies an abdication from any wider considerations than immediate success. It is this kind of attitude that allows teachers, in infant schools in particular, to offer children year after year the most vacuous material. Readers of the 'Dick and Janet' ilk are justified on the grounds that, even if they do not contain anything very worthwhile, they are well constructed for learning purposes. Their vocabulary gradients and controls are good, or their introduction of phonic rules is well controlled, and so on. It is frequently pointed out also that the children like them. What is often not realized is that this 'liking' is more a matter of being obliging to the teacher, or of enjoying the decoding exercise, than of any commitment to the book's content.

The trouble with relying on such extrinsic motivation is that not only is it a tremendous waste of opportunity to give children rubbish, when even the first reader could be a worthwhile and educative experience, but that such means are unlikely to be justified by the end – they will actually prevent it being attained. For if the chance to convince the child of the worthwhileness of reading material is lost right from the start, it is unlikely ever to be regained. The children who are most vulnerable are, of course, those who encounter no reading material outside the school. The more fortunate at least can tolerate 'Flip and Nuff' because they can see that they make some contribution to learning to read other material, which they know *is* worthwhile.

Where do 'advantaged' children get this insight? It has been traditional for educationists to say that it is because they come from families where there are books, and where they see that adults enjoy and get benefit from reading. However, this only takes the argument half way. In the 'reading family' the important point is not that the children feel the need to learn to read because the family demonstrates the good example of doing some reading. Though this would provide some important reinforcement, it would be of the same kind that the school teacher provides in the classroom. What is crucial is that the child at home discovers the intrinsic value of reading for members of his family. He learns what they read for, what it is they are enjoying and why – partly by sharing it with them. So the parents' reasons for reading emerge and become the child's own intrinsic motivation. The classroom moral of this is that the child of whatever background has to see the teacher reading, not just to help the pupil but for the teacher's own profit and enjoyment. Teachers of children of all ages should be reading aloud constantly. And teachers should select 'reading aloud' material at least as much on the basis of their own preferences as on that of what they expect their pupils to like. There are enough books about to satisfy both criteria!

The hidden content

We cannot leave early reading material, however, without drawing attention to a further and grave danger. This lies in the teacher's frequent abdication, in the attempt to 'get on with the job', from examining the context of what is being offered the child, often incidentally and indeed unintentionally. This is the hidden curriculum – what Peter Dickinson is after when he says that 'everything means something'. For the children's reader can be racist, sexist, or class-biased, often without even the authors knowing it (*cf* The Open University 1976). Mum washing the dishes helped by daughter, while Dad mends the car helped by small son, may seem a neutral situation, even to the point of vacuity. But the stereotype is clear and reinforcing, whether the author meant it to be so or not: girls help mothers about the house, while boys do mechanical things with Dads. Blom *et al* (1972) examined a national sample of commonly-used readers in the United States. They report on their typical content in these terms:

> The activities are neutral and redundant without much content significance and variation. They are happy-family-centered and tend to be ambiguous as to sex role. A child is most always with other children and is seldom alone. Older children are siblings and peers rarely appear. In contrast, there tends to be a regressive pull through the emphasis on family attachment and younger siblings, animal stories, anthropomorphized figures, and ambiguity in sex role. The setting is most typically in the suburbs, rarely in the city and usually in and around a home. Pets are amusing, cute, frustrating nuisances.

By contrast, they point out some of the realities of life for the children who will be given these readers:

> Most children live in cities and are in contact with other children of different racial and national backgrounds. Family life is not so exclusively child centered, nor is it constantly happy and smiling. Parents punish and children display a range of emotions. It is most unusual to find fraternal twins in the same family (i.e., boy and girl of age six) and it is more typical to find older siblings and peers in greater frequency than the first grade readers demonstrate. Pets have various meanings to children – they can be companions in adventure, exploration, and rough play, they can be the means of learning about biology (pregnancy, birth, infancy, growth, weaning, toilet training, old age, death, illness, and injury). The stories obviously do not deal with these issues.

In the same vein, how many readers for small children present them as dirty, hungry or in trouble, except in a cosy, half-joking way? And even without the authors' unconscious biases, the sheer emptiness has a further danger. Busch (1972) draws our attention to the possibility that the child will see his reading primer as something very different from a real book: 'By teaching the child with material of little interest or with an emphasis on mechanics, we would seem to be clearly delineating between work and play, school and non-school experiences.' Here may lie the establishment in the child's mind, right from the beginning of his school career, that learning is a school thing which has nothing to do with real life experience.

An ideological scanner?
The Bullock Report certainly shows concern for this problem. The reader's attention is drawn to the effect of content on children's attitudes on page 105. The Committee suggests that:

> Any reading scheme should stand up to questions about how parental roles, sex roles, attitudes to authority, etc., are represented. . . . We do not suggest that reading schemes should be passed through a kind of ideological or ethical scanner . . . it is never too soon to start thinking about the ways in which attitudes may be influenced by reading.

In fact, I think we do have to use a scanner of some kind. Bullock avoids this issue, I suspect, because of its overtones of censorship and because of the impossibility of getting completely general agreement. Clearly, we would not all agree as to what was desirable or undesirable. On the other hand, there are choices to be made and we cannot entirely shirk them.

The teacher in the classroom
It we are to criticize the material we are offered to use with children and its taken-for-granted attitudes, we must also learn to be more sophisticated about ourselves. One of the most significant lessons we can draw from the classroom interaction work of the last few years is that very few of us teachers know how we actually behave. For instance, researches using Flanders' (1970) techniques show the typical teacher talking for something like two-thirds of the time, with pupil talk a relative rarity. A pilot study in the nursery school by Philips and Cashdan (1975) shows most teachers talking far

more with 'advantaged' children, though many probably thought they concentrated on those who needed help most! Garner and Bing (1973) found teachers talking more with boys of one personality type than with girls of another! Again, although many reading teachers would describe their methods in terms of the reading scheme they use, Southgate and Lewis (1973) found that the proportion of 'language arts' time spent working on the reading scheme was less than one-sixth! Other interesting recent research includes that of Barbara Tizard (1975), in which she shows that adults in the nursery setting behave quite differently towards children according to whether they see themselves as in charge, or only as assistants. Paul Gump (1975) also, has carried out interesting analyses of teacher behaviour in open classrooms, which by judicious moving of furniture and partitions gradually became more and more closed! But many of the teachers in these rooms would not have thought that they had abandoned open-plan teaching.

Researches such as these – and there are many more – all suggest to me that a sensitivity to the reading material we provide for children needs to be only part of a much wider sensitivity to our relationships with children and the learning context we provide for them in our classrooms. Without a general examination of our classroom practice, even the best books will make little difference.

Some roads to follow

In conclusion, I would stress that literacy is not an end in itself. It is, however, a most powerful weapon in the armoury of the adult who wishes to be independent and to go on growing, both emotionally and intellectually. Furthermore, although we have seen the other communication media grow immeasurably in the last few years, literacy still has a place which needs no defence. If we accept this and we wish to educate a generation of children who are literate and wish to be, then I would pick out four roads in particular along which we have to travel.

First, we need a new relationship between the trio of child, parent and teacher. The Bullock Committee have asked for this, as have other previous government reports. But it needs to go further than most people have realized. We need not just to enlist parents by explaining modern methods to them, or by being less formidably distant. We need to be a little humbler: to get together, in Margaret Mead's terms, and develop truly shared aims and purposes, so that education can move back into a closer relationship with the community.

Next, we need much more open discussion of social and political issues. Education is not apolitical; it never has been. Teachers have to question the books they are given, the authors who write for their children and the publishers who publish the material. If this can be done in direct discussion, so much the better. This is part of the purpose of the current UKRA Study Course. If not, it has to be done indirectly by letter and other forms of communication. And finally, if necessary, it has to be done with the purse-strings. In the last analysis, publishers will not publish what teachers will not buy.

Political discussion may lead to disagreement. I am arguing that this is unavoidable and that it is probably a good thing. Schools may have to disagree with each other; even within a school, teachers may disagree. But if they feel strongly enough to disagree, and if their disagreement is worked through and shared with parents and others concerned, then I feel that the outcome will always be healthier than the wishy-washy pretence at a consensus view which is so often our preferred alternative – and which at best does nothing more than preserve an unexamined status quo.

Thirdly, Bullock argues strongly for a vertical integration of education and I should like to endorse this concern. To take but one aspect of our current failure, we really must do more about the differences in social and academic attitudes between teachers of young children and those who work in the secondary school. Some of these differences are good and inevitable; others merely reflect lack of thought. If we had an integrated policy, we would not find the sort of thing which is still all too prevalent. I mean the tendency in early education to focus, often very successfully, on the teacher–child relationship, while not bothering very much about the learning material. As I have argued, there is too much teaching of skills without thinking of the hidden curriculum carried along by the material read. Meanwhile, in the secondary school, careful thought often goes into the content of the literature programme, but much less into the learning context. We still have what Bernstein (1971) has called a 'collection curriculum', where knowledge is carved up into tiny 'specialist' subjects and 'transmitted' to an unanalysed (often unreceptive) audience! I should like to see the United Kingdom Reading Association giving a real lead to policy-making in this field and joining together with other bodies such as the National Association of Teachers of English – and other specialist associations too – with the hope that out of creative argument better policies may develop.

Finally, it would be a mistake to think that any of the foregoing arguments were meant to denigrate the activity of teaching. If everyone had to teach himself from the beginning, we would make little progress. Teachers are needed to organize material, to make curriculum choices, to transmit as well as to guide. In learning to read, there does have to be some focus on technique. What I am arguing is that that is far from enough. We have to focus on content. Or, as Joan Tough (1972) has aptly put it in the title to her book, we need a real *Focus on Meaning* – and this I hope will prove a fruitful theme for the rest of this volume.

References

BERNSTEIN, B. (1971) *Class, Codes and Control, Volume 1* Routledge and Kegan Paul

BLOM, G. E. *et al* (1972) 'What the story world is like' in S. G. Zimet (Ed) *What Children Read in School* New York: Grune and Stratton

BURKE, E. and LEWIS, D. G. (1975) Standards of reading: a critical review of some recent studies *Educational Research* 17, 163–74

BUSCH, F. (1972) 'Interest, relevance and learning to read' in S. G. Zimet (Ed) *What Children Read in School* New York: Grune and Stratton

BYNNER, J. (1972) *Parents' Attitudes to Education* HMSO

CAZDEN, C. B. (1970) 'The neglected situation in child language and education' in F. Williams (Ed) *Language and Poverty* Chicago: Markham

COX, C. B. and BOYSON, R. (1975) *Black Paper: Fight for Education* Dent

DAVIES, A. (1973) *Literature for Children* (Unit 2 of Reading Development, PE261) The Open University Press

DES (1975) *A Language for Life* (Bullock Report) HMSO

FLANDERS, N. A. (1970) *Analyzing Teaching Behavior* New York: Addison-Wesley

GARNER, J. and BING, M. (1973) Inequalities of teacher–pupil contacts *British Journal of Educational Psychology* 43, 234–43

GUMP, P. V. and ROSS, R. (1975) 'Problems and possibilities in measurement of school environments.' Paper presented to The International Society for the Study of Behavioral Development, Guildford, Surrey

MEAD, M. (1973) 'Our educational emphases in primitive perspective' in N. Keddie (Ed) *Tinker, Tailor . . .* Penguin

OPEN UNIVERSITY (1976) *Cultural Bias in Children's Books* Radio Programme 24 of *Personality and Learning* (E201)

PHILPS, J. and CASHDAN, A. (1975) 'Nursery teachers' classroom behaviour in the light of their constructs of pupils: an exploratory study.' Paper presented to the International Society for the Study of Behavioral Development, Guildford, Surrey

SOUTHGATE, V. and LEWIS, C. Y. (1973) How important is the infant reading scheme? *Reading* 7, 2, 4–13

START, K. B. and WELLS, B. K. (1972) *The Trend of Reading Standards* NFER

SWIFT, D. F. (1968) 'Social class and educational adaptation' in H. J. Butcher (Ed) *Educational Research in Britain, Volume 1* University of London Press

TIZARD, B. (1975) *Early Childhood Education* NFER

TOUGH, J. (1972) *Focus on Meaning* Allen and Unwin

TOUGH, J. (1973) 'The language of young children: the implications for the education of the young disadvantaged child' in M. Chazan (Ed) *Education in the Early Years* Swansea: Faculty of Education, University College of Swansea

TREVARTHEN, C. (1974) Conversations with a two-month old *New Scientist* 5 May

2 Myth and meaning, or everything means something

Peter Dickinson

My brief is to discuss how and why what a writer puts into his book matters to the reader. As these are questions which I do not often think about, and which in fact I had never thought about coherently until very recently, I shall be telling myself as much as the reader while I attempt to answer them. We will all be starting together from scratch.

I think first I had better present my credentials for tackling this at all. I support my family almost entirely by writing novels of two sorts. First, I write rather donnish detective stories; I specialize in closed situations – a tribe, a religion, a charity. Myself I think of them as science fiction with the science left out.

Secondly, I write children's books – again rather donnish, I think, but quite exciting, and set on the fringe between fantasy and realism. The more fantastic the basic notion the harder I work at making it seem solid and everyday. In fact, one of them was an historical novel, which I treated in exactly the same way – that's to say I regarded Byzantium, where the story was set, as if it were an alien planet. I don't say I made all the history up, but I certainly imagined it all.

My adult books take longer to write than my children's books, but otherwise I write both kinds as well as lies within me. If for some reason I were forced to give up one kind, I would give up the adult books, not for any altruistic reasons about kids being deprived of their ration of Peter Dickinson – they can get on well enough without it – but for the typically writer's reason that I have more freedom to write what I want in children's books.

Well, those are my credentials, and now I must set about answering the questions. How and why does what a writer puts into his book matter to the reader?

I am going to have to go a very long way round in order to answer these questions. There is of course a short way, which is simply to say that I have no idea, and that it doesn't matter to me. When I write a book I am solely concerned with the needs of that book which I judge not by analysable reasons but by what I feel in my intellectual guts to be right. Whether I judge right depends on whether I'm on form.

So that is the short way to an answer. The long way is much, much longer, because of course it's the ancient, endlessly analysed question of what makes art art. I hope it will not spoil your fun if I now answer it. I'll tell you the way we are going in advance, so that you don't spend all your time puzzling out the map and have no eyes to spare for a glance at the beauty spots.

First I am going to deal with the relationship between art and culture, and to do this I will go into some detail about a concept which I call myth. It's got nothing to do with gods and heroes – it's just a piece of jargon I have invented to explain things to myself. Then, still in some detail, I am going to compare American and English myths working in three very lowly forms of art – comics, detective stories and (a bit further up the scale) children's books. After that I will point out two or three ways in which the concept which I call myth affects your own interests – what material you choose for helping people learn to read. And finally we will get round to how and why what I put into a book matters to the reader, and the answer will be that I still don't know, but at least we may have a clearer idea of why I not only don't but can't.

Right. The relationship between art and culture. This bit would really sound much better in German – Der Kunst-Kultur Nexus – only I don't speak the language. The first and vital point is that art is not culture and culture is not art. Furthermore, they overlap much less than we tend to think. Culture is what makes one society different from another. It includes such things as the status of women, the colour of buses, the belief in a God or Gods, the reasons for workmen going on strike, the way in which people gamble, the shape of wax models in shop windows, the ideal holiday, almost everything you can think of except those aspects of living which are entirely governed by reason, and in which therefore there is an optimum solution to which all sensible societies will closely conform.

'. . . those aspects of living in society which are entirely governed by reason . . .'. Think about it, and you will see that it doesn't include very much. There is an enormous amount in all our lives which is governed by something other than reason – things which we are prepared ultimately to die for, things in which two viable societies can behave so opposedly that when they meet each thinks the other must be a bunch of blasphemous savages, things which can be of central importance to one generation and meaningless to the next. These are the things which distinguish one type of society from another, and it is the causes of these differences to which I have given the quite arbitrary name 'myth'.

A myth, in my jargon, is a belief or idea or world-picture which is widely held in a particular society, or section of society, but which that society is not prepared to submit to rational analysis. This doesn't mean it's against reason, or wrong. There can be a whole number of causes that keep a myth in its mythic status. I will outline a few, so as to make my meaning clear.

For instance, you may get a situation where two myths are logically incompatible. Some primitive tribes – the Azande, for instance – believed two things about witches; (a) that they were enormously powerful, and (b) that almost everybody might be one. Either of these destroys the other, but if you keep them at the level of myth you can believe them both. You may think we are too sophisticated nowadays to follow this sort of line, but it's not long since I heard a chap on the radio demanding, almost in one breath, (a) free collective bargaining, and (b) a fully planned economy. I admit that it is possible that the speaker had reconciled these two ideals at a rational level, but most of those who seek them both hold at least one in terms of myth, and I dare say you and I, in our own fields, can be equally blind – necessarily blind, from our own point of view.

Or there is the type of myth which has to be held in that form because, if fully formulated, we would see that it is morally intolerable. The Nazis invented such a myth about the Jews. I was very alarmed not long ago to hear a gentle and saintly friend using the myth of structural violence to justify ordinary violent violence; he didn't go as far as to say that when a school bus is blown up by a mine it's OK because the children in it were guilty of structural violence, but he was a long way down that road. I expect my own rejection of his ideas was based on myths equally ignoble. On cosier ground, the now-defunct belief in the Imperial role of the British nation was a myth of this sort.

Then there are myths which deal with concepts too vague to formulate. Patriotism is a good example. I am a patriot. I admire and cherish England – but what do I mean by that, because there are many aspects of England that I hate and despise? It's an ideal England I love and would die for, a myth. You could construct a situation in which a patriot might feel compelled to betray his country – in fact you could say that Alexander Solzhenitsyn was such a man.

I won't elaborate any further. But remember that the opposite of myth is not truth, or even reality. A myth may of course be false, but it can equally well represent an ungraspable truth. And while a myth is held it is real, as real as the human mind.

Myths are necessary to our sanity. We cannot live by reason alone. Culture, then, is the outer manifestation by which one society distinguishes itself from another. Myths are the inner drive which cause it to produce that culture. Culture is what shows we are different. Myths are what make us different.

Right, that's the first section of the mystery tour. Those who have brought sandwiches can now eat them, while the rest of us consider the ruined castle of art.

Art. I believe art is the means by which a society celebrates its own myths. It does this unconsciously, because that is the nature of myth. It does not analyse or describe, it celebrates. Some myths are so deep and enduring that the society whose myths they celebrate is really all humankind in all the ages. There is, for instance, a mythic element in the relationship between two people which distinguishes love from the sex-drive, and this has been celebrated in love poetry which can speak to us through the garblings of translation and across the static of the centuries. And, to go even outside humankind, didn't Jane Goodall see her chimpanzees welcoming the change of seasons with a rain dance?

But other myths have been so remote, or transient, or private that we can gaze and gaze at the art which celebrated them and still have no inkling of how or why these things mattered.

I have seen in my own lifetime a whole new art-form spring into being to celebrate the myths of a new culture. I mean the pop revolution, which was born to let the first free generation make hay with its own freedom, and rejoice. That's what it was there for. That's why it works.

Now, before we come to the comics I'd like to make a couple of points. The first I half covered when I said that art is not culture. I believe that we are living in a society which, for a number of necessary reasons, has discarded a lot of outworn myths, and some which may not be outworn but which it has discarded anyway – things like the need for a structured society, and the existence of a loving God, and there being a purpose in life beyond life itself, and the sanctity of work, and so on. This has left a vacuum, and in order to fill it we have tried to elevate art to the status of myth. We have said man is of central importance. Man's highest endeavour is to produce works of art. Therefore art matters more than anything. So, more and more, art tends to celebrate art. Abstract painting is painting about painting, unconcerned with anything else. The films which critics most admire cannot really be appreciated by somebody who hasn't already seen all that director's previous films. A composer who produces a work called 'Four minutes twenty-three seconds' during which not a note is played is making a point not about silence but about the absence of music. And so on. Perhaps this state of affairs was inevitable, but it still won't do. Art is like a vast cathedral, full of alcoves and side-chapels. We can worship there many different Gods in many different ways, and perhaps they will answer. But if we try to worship the cathedral itself we shall find that all the shrines are empty and all the Gods gone.

The second point is that it's a mistake to discuss the function of myth in terms of the work of great artists, because great artists have such power over their material that they are able, consciously or unconsciously, to alter the nature of the myths they celebrate. Dickens, for instance, changed the way in which the Victorian middle classes – the most powerful society in the world at that time – thought about themselves. Even somebody who is only a near-great writer – Kipling is a good example – may acquire what greatness he has by his ability to create and manipulate myths.

It is for this reason that I want to talk about American superhero comics for a bit, and compare them with their pallid English counterparts. As art they are trivial – but still art – but the myth they celebrate is very potent. In case some of you are readers of more serious literature than me, I'll remind you of what they are like. There are two sorts of superhero, the invincible and the vincible. The vincible always have henchmen and tend to have glass jaws too, so that they can be laid out and lashed to a passing killer whale by the villain, but they get out of it by luck, superior technology, and the villain having to go off and attend to some other part of his villainy. Spiderman and Batman are examples. I'm more interested in the invincible superhero – Superman himself, Thor, The Silver Surfer, the Hulk and so on. They work alone. Their biggest problem – at least their scriptwriters' biggest problem – is their invincibility. There are two classic ways round this. Either they have an Achilles' heel – for instance Superman loses his strength in the presence of a mysterious metal found only on his native planet, and the Hulk has a tendency to turn into a mild-mannered scientist at the wrong moment, I've never found out why – or else there's somebody still more invincible to overrule them, as Galactos overrules the Silver Surfer and Wotan banishes Thor to wander America in the guise of a hamburger chef, with his invincible hammer turned into a ketchup ladle. They wrestle with moral problems – quite simple ones but still genuinely moral – such as, 'Must I save the human race from the dreaded Rhumarrhoids even if it means acting in such a way that Anne will hate me for ever?' They do their wrestling, and also their vaunting, when they struggle with supervillains, in gloriously purple prose. Though their scriptwriters may put in the odd mocking aside they take themselves extremely seriously. And they last for ever, or for fifty years, whichever is the longer.

There are also two sorts of English superhero. The first sort is the real thing, the solid article, the native son. He is the comic villain – Billy Bunter with his heroic greed or the Blots with their heroic unteachability. (I expect you've all got Blots were you come from.) But if you compare the English invincible superhero with the American he is copied from, interesting differences emerge: first he's got no staying power – a couple of years at best; second, he's almost always accompanied by a comic henchman, whose role is essentially deflationary; third, very often the mainspring of the plot is his search to get back to his own time and planet and lay down his invincibility; fourth, he wouldn't know a moral problem if he saw one, and fifth, he simply doesn't work. All this, I believe, because the superhero has no place in our mythology. Behind the American superhero one can sense, however dimly, huge tides acting invisible between the galaxies. Behind the English one there is only the mocking tangle of society as it is. It's as though the American myth said, 'OK, superheroes don't really exist, but they ought to', and the English answer was, 'Certainly superheroes don't exist, but if they did it would be a pretty kettle of fish.'

The superhero is a celebration of a myth about the relationship between man and society. This has often been discussed; the John Henry figure, who said, 'A man ain't nothin' but a man.' He is totally free, master of his own destiny and therefore morally invincible. He does not only occur in comics, of course, or in such obvious places as westerns and Disney films. You found the myth recelebrated in the film *Easy Rider*, and it was no accident that that saga of two totally free young men on bikes should have been shot against a lyric evocation of the great American landscape, nor that the mainspring of the plot should have been the wholly antisocial act of peddling heroin. It doesn't even only occur in art – it breaks out into life. President Kennedy's famous charisma fed on it, for instance, and he wore a rather chic version of the Superman haircut. The Presidential system seems to demand supermen, above and outside normal moral constraints – Kennedy, Johnson, Nixon – even the mild-mannered President Ford is showing ominous signs that he may suddenly change into the invincible Hulk.

But we have a different myth of the relationship between man and society, and it's this I want to move on to. I'm sure it has often struck you what a very rum phenomenon it was that the standard reading of intelligent men between the wars was the classic detective story – very often it was the only thing they read. We tend to judge these now by the few that have survived – a few Dorothy Sayers, three Marjorie Allinghams, one or two Christies and, say, half a dozen others. But there were thousands of them, and the majority were very bad indeed. Not merely bad, but boringly bad, trivial, imperceptive and usually cheating over the one solid talent they were supposed to display. What was their appeal?

It seems to me important that their heyday was the period after the first world war, and their readership was almost exclusively drawn from the class that had been destroyed, one way or another, by that war – either destroyed in the trenches or undermined by the social, economic and political upheavals that followed it. Furthermore, this class had been exclusively educated in the old public school belief (or in my terms myth) that the trained mind can solve any problem, and its fellow-myth, potent but seldom stated, that the trained mind is not guilty of having messy emotions.

So consider the following as a parable of this state of affairs. There is an idyllic setting, a closed, rich world, probably a country house. Very often the only fly in the ointment about this world is that its wealth, which most of the cast so comfortably wallow in, comes from a very unpleasant character who is not quite a gentlemen but has broken into the gentry class by making a pot of money in some rather despicable way. Into this golden world bursts the one irredeemably ugly act – murder. The millionaire is found dead on the carpet of his library, surrounded by the very books – those tokens of high civilization – which he is unworthy of. Perhaps the library is locked, in a useless longing to close the ugliness off from the rest of the idyll, but to no avail. All those beautiful, idle people are involved, suspected, questioned. The idyll will never be the same. But lo! into the middle of this shambles steps the one being who can put everything to rights, the embodiment of the trained public school mind – the amateur detective. Usually he is rich. Often he keeps up a flow of badinage to show he has no emotions. But, by God, he puts everything to rights with his trained intellect. By demonstrating in a final shocking denouement that it was the butler who did it, he proves that the working classes are to blame. So, in expiation the butler takes the eight o'clock walk and the idyll settles back into its longed-for calm.

I think that all works, only I've been a bit unfair about the butler. In my terms, the classic whodunit is a celebration of a myth about man and society, which says at its simplest that we are all members of that society, and the society must be ruled by reason, and that reason demands that we should all know our place in that society and let's not have any horrid revolutions, if you please. It is an infinitely banal version of the Shakespearean hive.

Now, if we may cross the Atlantic once more, it's interesting to compare with this the classic American whodunit. There are two sorts, opposite sides of the same coin. The first was invented by Dashiell Hammett and Raymond Chandler, and in it the mystery does not typically take place in a closed world but in an open city, an untamed wild. And it is solved not by the trained intellect but by the man of guts and integrity, the man who, however often he is hit on the head, will still get up and go on being himself – the moral superman, all over again. Then there is a sort of novel which I think the Americans do particularly well, which is the police precinct mystery. Here the murder is solved not by the intellect, or by guts, but by a machine – a machine composed of people. The myth is that a big enough machine will solve any problem. You see it celebrated in a quite different fashion in American football in the extraordinarily elaborate plays dictated by the coach on the touchline. And you see the myth in action in the real world in the fleets of bombers thundering out over Vietnam to solve the problem with another 20,000 tons of high explosive.

We'd better get back to children's books. We're now on our way home, via the ideal good place. I haven't read as many children's books as I have comics and whodunits, so what I am going to say now is based on sketchier knowledge. Anyway, the ideal good place is a very potent myth. It's the place to which all satisfactory stories bring the hero and/or heroine at last. And it's my impression that the classic ending in English children's books has the hero coming home, whereas the classic ending in American children's books has him setting out. For us, the ideal good place is the place were we belong, or ought to belong. It may be Number

14 Railway Cuttings with Mum opening the *Weetabix* packet with the breadknife as usual, while the 8.32 rattles the windows as it drums up to town, dead on time. Probably we've spent the previous ten chapters saving the 8.32 from train-robbers, or preventing the line being closed, or simply running away. But we've come home. Alternatively, home may be the battlemented keep which our ancestors have held by cunning and courage against generations of tyrannical kings, and to which we have at last proved our right as the true heirs. (I love that sort of story, but it's hard to get away with writing them these days.) In that case it's where we belong. It's the ideal good place.

But in the American myth the ideal good place is somewhere else. It's beyond the horizon. It's a valley with timber to fell, land to break, grizzlies to shoot. It's the Big Rock Candy Mountain. It's over there, not yet but soon. It's manhood. This, like the superhero myth, is an expression of the difference between a nomadic culture and a sedentary one.

Well, those are my three examples of myth in action and in art. There are two things to notice; first that they are involuntary, and second that they are powerful. The writer doesn't put them in on purpose, and the reader is not aware that he is being affected by them. But they are there, and working. I would venture to suggest that whenever you find a lump in your throat over something which you know to be trash you are in the presence of myth. So how does this affect us?

I'll start with how it affects you, which is impertinent of me. But there! Let's start with very small children. A child grows into an immensely complex and totally inexplicable world. If you accept my terms, it makes sense to say that at first a child views everything he deals with as if it were myth, and that the process of learning his way in the society he deals with consists of learning which matters belong in the realm of certainty and which in the realm of myth. And I believe that books, stories, songs, rhymes and games all play an essential part in testing and discovering what's myth and what's not. Take those two awesome giants which rule the adult world, whose names are Cause-and-Effect and Time. You all know that children have no real idea of how either of these giants works. You've seen them try to mend a broken toy with plasticine or wool. You've seen them stretch a few minutes of boredom into a measure-less desert, or compress a whole morning's happy absorption into one gold instant. Now, why do children need stories – stories with real plots, in which one thing happens because of another and follows it under the iron rule of time? Because it is a way of testing the powers of those giants, without actually submitting to their rule – and ultimately of discovering that they are not giants at all, but inescapable solid facts, unchanging from age to age and tribe to tribe. They are not myths at all. That is why a good, solid, water-tight plot-line is essential in a story for children. It's also why it is a mistake to regard children's literature as being in the same continuum as adult literature: children's use of myth is rather different. Children use books and stories not to celebrate myths but to learn them, to discover which ones are right for them, to discover their context and focus in the society they are part of. I think I must emphasize again that this is, and has to be, an un-conscious process.

That brings me to my second point. If the response to myth is an unconscious process who's to tell which celebrations of what myths are going to click with the reader? In the teacher's case, how are you to know what reading matter will so engage the attention of the unwilling reader that he will actually forget his unwillingness and long to plough on. My advice here can only be negative, and is probably contradicted by your own experience, but even so I feel that there must be something in it. I am suspicious of the trend towards books and stories about things which the child knows and understands. I'm not suspicious of the books themselves, because they may be very good. The existence of bad John and Jane readers doesn't necessarily mean that these brand new Terry and Sandra readers *must* be good. They may or may not be, and to a large extent it will depend not on surface realism and relevance, but on the myths they embody and explore – and this is something which is outside anyone's control except the writers'. What matters is not theory, or social conscience, or even intelligence. It's the existence of a writer with the knack of telling a story which children want to read, and if it's a real writer that matters more – infinitely more – than whether the story's about Dad's new car breaking down or the dragon with hiccups or the boy who owned all Birmingham.

The reason why I say I'm against the trend, but not against the books, is that once the trend is established and accepted you'll get writers who haven't the knack trying to cash in, and their books will look OK and have OK illustrations (by the way, were any illustrations ever less OK than Richard Scarry's, and were any ever more success-ful?) and they'll be promoted like billy-ho by their publisher's publicity branch, which probably calls itself So-and-So Educational, and they won't work, because they lack the underlying element of myth.

So, then, finally, how is that underlying element achieved and recognized? Or to put it another way, how do I – let's assume for the moment and without prejudice, as the lawyers say, that I'm a writer who has the knack – how do I write books in such a way that the reader will want to read them? I still don't know the answer to this, but I know a few bits of it. First and most important, since the faculty in us which is in contact with myth is not reason but, in a very broad sense, imagination, everything that I write must be fully imagined. Every page, every sentence, every tick of a clock or stir of a dawn bird. It's not enough for it to sound right and look right and smell right – it must feel right. This is not as difficult as it sounds. In a way it's only a matter of plain honesty with yourself and your book. After all, you are going to spend at least half a year of your life writing it, and if it doesn't interest you enough to make you, so to speak, live it, then that's half a year spent doing something in which you are not very interested. Nobody can be honest, even at the privacy of his desk, all the time, of course, but you learn to recognize the danger signs. 'My God I'm writing well' is one and, 'It's time somebody said something funny' is another. You learn too that easy writing may not be inspired, and that hard slog isn't necessarily lifeless. In effect you do the best you can, not for your own pride as a writer, nor to keep your bank manager happy, but for the sake of the myth which you are celebrating.

You don't think in those terms, of course, not while you're writing. If you're on form, you don't think in any terms at all: you may worry, but if you do it's about idiotic things like does a door open on its left- or right-hand side and do small children still say 'So sucks to you'. The book, meanwhile, emerges at your fingertips, and all the things you need – images, vocabulary, speech rhythms, scenes, gestures – are there waiting for you and you pick them out just like an old-fashioned typesetter picking letters out of a forme, without even having to look because his fingers know where they are.

> There was a young lady of Wantage
> Of whom the town clerk took advantage.
>> Said the borough surveyor
>> 'Indeed you must pay her –
> You've altered the line of her frontage'.

Whoever wrote that was bang on form. You can see that no part of it necessarily came before any other part – it fits together as though Apollo had glided down and whispered it in his ear. Don't let's go into what particular myth it celebrates.

I think I ought not to have made, a paragraph or two ago, the hypothetical assumption that I'm a good writer, because it's irrelevant. As you'll have seen from my earlier examples, it can be, and very often is, quite lowly examples of art which actually tap these strange impulses. The difference between good writers and the rest of us is that they celebrate deeper and more long-lasting myths – what I have called the myths of common humanity. We twang the cord of now, but they set up reverberations and harmonics that will wake sounds along very distant wires. But the lowliest writer wakes some echoes. In the words of the subtitle of this talk, everything means something. And the important thing is that that meaning doesn't lie on the surface, cannot be analysed or discussed, can only be responded to or not responded to.

So the question remains – how can a writer know whether readers very different from himself are going to respond to his work? How do teachers and librarians, choosing books for people very different from themselves, know whether those people are going to respond to the books they choose? The answer lies in the imagination – the faculty which is in touch with myth. It does not lie in any theory, in any rule of thumb, in any following of previously successful examples. It lies, in effect, in our common humanity.

3 Creating more than a basic reading scheme

Joyce M. Morris

From conception to publication, the creation of a basic reading scheme is a large, complex and lengthy operation. In consequence, publishers do not seriously consider embarking on such a venture until they are reasonably assured that a new scheme would be generally welcomed by the teaching profession. Even then, they usually proceed with extreme caution because so much depends on their choice of senior author and the conceptual framework he or she proposes.

Seven years ago, I accepted an invitation from a major publishing company to discuss the possiblity of designing a new type of basic reading scheme. That is, a scheme to meet the needs of teachers and pupils as indicated by the publishers' own experience, and by investigations such as those I had conducted on behalf of the National Foundation for Educational Research. Even more important and concomitant with those needs, it would be a scheme whose guiding principles and recommended practices were soundly based on scholarly knowledge of the English language and linguistic processes as well as facts about how children learn.

My first meeting with the publishers revealed that, if necessary, they were willing to take considerable calculated risks in order to make a significant contribution to the cause of literacy. This was evident, for example, from the way in which they were prepared to discard 'traditional' ideas about basic reading schemes, and consider a developmental language programme incorporating listening, speaking, reading and writing. Accordingly, in sympathy with their aspirations and after further discussions, I agreed to write a 60,000 word rationale for the creation of much more than a basic reading scheme in terms of general scope and specific innovation. In other words, I agreed to be the architect and, subsequently, the director of what is now known as *The Language Project* (Morris *et al* 1974) with its two principal elements *Language in Action* and a series of *Language Guides*.

In line with the conference theme, the main purpose of this paper is to give some idea of the conceptual and practical aspects of creating that part of *The Language Project* intended primarily for use with and by children; that is, *Language in Action*. However, before doing so, I must point out that the *Language Guides* complement the pupils' materials and, conceptually, should not be regarded as a separate entity. Indeed, they are an integral part of a publishing programme whose basic philosophy, though formulated several years ago, supports the one general summarizing conclusions of the Bullock Report (DES 1975) that, 'there is nothing to equal in importance the quality and achievement of the individual teacher'.

Thus, improving teacher quality is a central aim of the *Language Guides* as it is of *Language in Action*. The difference is that, among other things, the latter is essentially a 'teacher-training instrument' designed to help busy teachers acquire a special brand of *explicit* knowledge about language development while they are actually at work with children. The *Language Guides*, on the other hand, provide student and practising teachers with a broad background of knowledge and knowhow which is all the more valuable for being presented by authors with different kinds of expertise and viewpoint. In short, the two elements constitute a dual approach to enhancing the quality of teaching what the Bullock Committee so aptly calls 'a language for life'. They also cater for individual differences within a structural framework, and support the thesis that, although good teachers matter more than materials, good materials help to make good teachers and, hence, good learners.

Conceptual aspects

Concentrating now on the materials for children, it is difficult to decide which conceptual aspects to discuss in the limited space available. Omissions could lead to misunderstandings and, obviously, one cannot assume prior study of the children's materials already published or the *Resource Books* (Morris 1974, 1975a) for teachers that go with them. In the circumstances, therefore, it is probably best to state briefly why and how *Language in Action* is conceptually very different from a 'traditional' reading scheme.

A language arts approach

First of all, it is not conceived solely, or even mainly, as resource material for teaching and learning reading. This is graphically illustrated by the 'Language Project symbol' which represents all four language arts, namely listening, speaking, reading and writing.

The vital importance of consciously developing *oracy* as a foundation for literacy is stressed, and all constituent materials are specifically designed to develop oracy at various linguistic levels, from the auditory discrimination of speech sounds to more complex listening and speaking skills. For example, some pre-literacy books are devised on the 'I spy' principle, to help children distinguish the initial sounds in words and link them with their corresponding letters, which are raised in nylon flocking on the front covers to provide kinaesthetic experience too. Picture story books of various kinds develop general and specialized vocabularies, and all are vividly illustrated to stimulate dynamic oral discussion. Moreover, the books with verbal content make extensive use of alliteration, onomatopoeia, rhyme and other forms of word play so that when, as intended, they are read aloud many times, they train the ear as well as the eye and, in doing so, forge the link between spoken and written English.

Unlike 'traditional' reading schemes, *Language in Action* is conceived as a developmental programme for the acquisition of *literacy*; that is, writing as well as reading, with special attention to spelling. This is a fundamental difference which cannot be emphasized too strongly. Indeed, I would go so far as to say that, because of this difference alone, *Language in Action* should never be thought of or referred to simply as a 'reading' scheme.

Naturally, because reading is basically a *decoding* process and both writing and spelling are *encoding* processes, these significant differences are reflected in the construction of the children's materials. For instance, the reading books for language levels 1 to 3 inclusive incorporate a unique system of spelling pattern progression derived from my own detailed analyses of English in spoken and written form. Briefly, this system relates forty-four phonemes to 396 graphemic possibilities in words, which are then classified into major sets of spelling patterns. These are incorporated in the books in a way which makes learning to spell a relatively easy, enjoyable procedure, not least because it is linked with story reading. What is more, the book titles constantly remind children (and teachers) of English spelling patterns, and act as mnemonics when they are learning to internalize a model of the orthography. A book called *King Dan, the Dane,* for example, draws their attention to the effect of 'marker', 'modifying' or 'magic' *e*. It also reminds teachers of two major sets of spelling patterns, sets A and B (Morris System), and that they are highlighted by the 'linguistic method of contrast' which is a 'natural' learning strategy inasmuch as it is used by pre-school children when learning to speak, without formal teaching.

The language of literacy

There is a wide diversity in the way children speak English when they start school. Hence, I think that publishers should not be expected to attempt the well-nigh impossible task of producing basal texts which cater for this diversity. In my view, as I have pointed out at previous conferences (Morris 1975b, 1975c), only the individual teacher is able, through a language-experience approach to literacy, to provide resource materials which take account of children's own speech and dialects. These, of course, may be in their 'purest' form as described by Goddard (1974), or in their 'most contrived form' as exemplified by *Breakthrough to Literacy* (Mackay *et al* 1970).

All this is not to say that I do not appreciate the importance of children using published materials such as *Link-Up* (Reid and Low 1973) which, in the early stages, uses syntactic patterns found to be common in the speech of five or six year olds and omits those found to be rare or absent; that is, structures belonging to the language of books. What I am saying is that the nature of English is such that its major disadvantage is at the level of phoneme-grapheme correspondence. Therefore, children need didactic materials which help them get to grips with this problem and yet are conceived with the language of literacy in mind; that is, language which is different in manifold ways from spoken language.

Language in Action is so conceived, and this partly accounts for the fact that the stories are by professional children's writers. It also accounts for some characteristics of its verbal content which, unlike *Breakthrough to Literacy* and *Link-Up*, follows the normal convention with regard to capital letters and punctuation marks right from the start. This is because capitalization provides clues to (a) word recognition (perception and meaning) and (b) intonation and, hence, meaning. Punctuation marks are also clues to intonation and meaning in that they are graphic signals to remind the tongue and ear of the inherent melodies and rhythms of speech.

A diagnostic instrument

Another important feature of *Language in Action* is that it is a diagnostic instrument in itself. It was conceived as such because diagnostic teaching and learning is a very important principle, but difficult to follow, especially with traditional materials, large classes and in the context of progressive education.

When teachers 'hear' children read the books, on-the-spot diagnosis is a comparatively easy procedure. This is because the verbal content is so constructed as to draw their attention to what a child cannot do, does not know, or is confused about. For example, it draws attention to whether individuals have articulation, auditory and/or visual problems. It also indicates any sentence construction and/or comprehension difficulties. What is more, treatment can speedily follow diagnosis because the teacher knows that there is a *Language in Action* book which highlights what the child has to learn.

Story books versus primers

At this point, you may be wondering whether *Language in Action* is conceived as some 'linguistic jack-of-all-trades' with the intention of making redundant even the most recently-published reading schemes. This is certainly not the case, for children will always need a variety of published materials, and even relatively 'old' schemes such as the Beacon Readers (1922) have much to offer the modern generation. In fact, today's children usually love Books 4, 5 and 6 as much as my pupils did in days gone by.

This brings me to the last conceptual aspect I have space to mention before turning to the practical aspects of creating materials for children. I especially mentioned the later Beacon Readers because it was my former pupils' delight in them which first fostered the idea of bridging the gap between primers and children's literature. These pupils were very retarded and could not read the books themselves, but they enjoyed looking at them whilst I read the stories aloud. They pointed out that the books were so interesting compared with the dull, banal primerese of the material allocated to me for teaching purposes. 'If only', they said, 'we could start learning to read with "real" stories like these, or with comics which have exciting words such as Splash! Splosh! Slam! Bang!' Why not?, I reflected, as through the years I heard virtually the same refrain in countless classrooms and, as a research worker, observed other teachers trying to breathe life into endlessly repetitious sentences with no hope for their pupils of a 'real' story at the end of all the sweat, toil and tears.

Needless to say, by the time I came to write the rationale for *The Language Project*, my experiences had led me to conclude that the material provided for teaching the early stages of reading left much to be desired. It generally favoured pupils with retentive memories who often passed for fluent readers and yet, on closer examination, revealed that they had simply learnt their basal readers off by heart, and had virtually no ability to read other books.

Accordingly I decided that, come what may, *Language in Action*, though resource material of didactic nature, would be specifically designed to bridge the gap between the world of primers and children's literature. Moreover, it would be such as to encourage children to learn to read (and spell) rather than pretend to read.

Practical aspects

Contributing authors and artists

The next step was to select authors and artists to contribute illustrated material which would not only bridge the gap between primers and children's literature, but which would translate all the other basic principles into practice.

Finding the right artists proved relatively easy and, right from the start, the team was confident that, working in full colour and using modern techniques, it would be possible to provide children with the wide variety of aesthetic experiences that had been planned. By contrast, finding the right authors was difficult, because professional children's writers normally create stories to be read *to* children, and there are comparatively few experienced in writing stories for beginning readers. However, after a diligent search, a nucleus of talented writers was formed for the first thirty-four books, to be published in March 1974.

All contributing authors work to detailed briefs set by me as project director. These explain the objectives of each book, for whom it is primarily intended, the type of verbal content it should contain in terms of vocabulary illustrating specific spelling patterns, structure (or 'function') words, phrases and sentence patterns, prose or verse style, idiomatic expressions, forms of word play such as alliteration, onomatopoeia, rhyme and so on. Artists are given different types of detailed brief, according to whether they are creating a picture story for the pre-literacy stage, or simply illustrating a book for a contributing author.

The authors and artists discuss their respective briefs at meetings attended by me, the design consultant, and key staff members of the publishing company from the editorial and art departments. All are members of the project team, which also includes advisers representing various kinds of academic and practical expertise relevant to the production of a developmental language programme.

As director of this team project, I am involved in much organization, consultation, writing and editing. The ongoing creative nature of the work with so many different contributors also involves me in continuous analyses to make sure that the total structure, design and detailed plans are being adhered to. The authors and artists accept the challenge of my briefs with enthusiasm, and are pleasantly surprised to discover how much freedom they give for imaginative experiment. Sometimes, however, they get a little carried away, with the result that their first drafts or sketches, as the case may be, contain too much of one thing and too little of another. Then it is my job to suggest how a better balance could be achieved even though it might mean getting rid of yet another 'doggy' character or whatever. In this job, as with all practical aspects of the project, I am ably assisted by other team members.

Evaluation

Before the illustrated texts are finally approved for production, they are made into 'dummy' books and tried out with children, mostly in schools. So far, we have reason to be very grateful to many helpful teachers for their constructive comments. But, obviously, amendments were and can only be made in the light of teachers' comments provided that they do not conflict with the basic principles and conceptual framework of the project.

This brings me to a very important practical issue. The evaluation of children's materials is virtually an insoluble problem. For obvious reasons, it cannot be properly attempted until the materials are published. Then, it is too late to effect any real changes, even in the rare event of an evaluation producing sufficiently conclusive results to suggest that such changes are necessary. As for evaluation in the pre-publication period, in my experience this is mainly useful for giving insights into likely trouble spots.

Resource books

One valuable insight our first school trials gave me was what teachers needed by way of a practical manual if they were to use Language in Action to maximum effect. In general, their written reports revealed that they had misunderstood the purposes of some of the materials because, understandably, they were judging them in the light of their own experience, particularly of 'traditional' reading schemes. They were also unaware of how much each of the pupils' books contained as a resource for teaching and learning.

This largely accounts for the fact that the Language in Action Resource Book is more detailed than British teachers have come to expect of manuals accompanying basal materials. Whilst preparing it, I wondered whether I was giving too many suggestions for teaching/learning strategies to achieve the purposes of each of the first thirty-four pupils' books to be published. But the response to this unusual manual gives good reason to believe that the converse is true. In fact, although the first Supplement to it was published only three months ago, already teachers are asking me to write a book which gives even more detailed suggestions. At the same time, others are urging publication of the detailed rationale, to be called *Background Book: a Foundation for Teachers*.

Publication schedule

This brings me to the last practical aspect I have space to mention. Teachers do not always appreciate that it is impossible to publish all the materials for a large-scale project at one and the same time. Naturally, this creates problems for them, and, in the case of *Language in Action*, I have every sympathy with teachers who are using the fifty-five pupils' books already published, and are anxiously awaiting the rest of the materials to complete the foundation programme.

I also regret the necessity to have production 'waves', not only because it complicates my various tasks, but because misunderstandings can so easily arise until the last vital part of the structure is in place. For example, although priority in publication has been given to materials for the pre-literacy and early literacy levels, there are still gaps to be filled at those levels, which experienced teachers would consider serious omissions in the conceptual framework until they see them filled in according to plan.

Thus, the creation of *more* than a basic reading scheme is, indeed, a large, complex and lengthy operation. It is also extremely hard work for the key people involved, and I have simply not had space to describe all the research that was done before authors and artists were recruited, including that which went into the attractive new typeface for the children's materials called Modified Futura. However, I hope I have said enough to give some idea of the conceptual and practical aspects of creating the materials. I also hope you will have gathered that it is not all a matter of sweat, toil and tears. On the contrary, it has been, and I am sure will continue to be, a joyful experience, and I think you will agree that this shines through the materials we have created for children and their teachers.

References

BEACON READERS (1922) *Original Approach* Ginn

DES (1975) *A Language for Life* (Bullock Report) HMSO

GODDARD, N. (1974) *Literacy: Language-Experience Approaches* Macmillan Education

MACKAY, D. *et al* (1970) *Breakthrough to Literacy* Longman

MORRIS, J. M. (1974) *Language in Action Resource Book* Macmillan Education

MORRIS, J. M. (1975a) *Language in Action Resource Book* Supplement 1. Macmillan Education

MORRIS, J. M. (1975b) 'Building a sound foundation for literacy' in W. Latham (Ed) *The Road to Effective Reading* Ward Lock Educational

MORRIS, J. M. (1975c) 'Language and literacy: spontaneity and contrivance in the learning-teaching situation' in D. Moyle (Ed) *Reading: What of the future?* Ward Lock Educational

MORRIS, J. M. *et al* (1974) *The Language Project; Language in Action; Language Guides* Macmillan Education

REID, J. F. and Low, J. (1973) *Link-Up. An Infant Reading Programme* Holmes McDougall

4 Behind the scenes: some issues in the production of a reading programme

Jessie F. Reid

This paper is not so much about a reading programme as about the experience of constructing and producing one, as well as about some of the issues raised by the undertaking. It is about principles, about decisions, about dilemmas and about compromises. But in the course of the discussion, I shall, as I must, draw to a great extent on my own experience, and shall make a number of references to the production of *Link-Up*.

Constructing, producing and publishing any body of educational material is a very complex business, with a complexity which the simplicity of the end-product can belie, particularly when that end-product is material for beginners. The process involves, for one thing, several separate but interconnected personal relationships. It involves, obviously, a great deal of thought and planning. It involves working to some kind of schedule, and meeting deadlines. It involves the need to be constantly self-critical and open to new insights, while at the same time keeping a firm grip on principles which one has accepted as basic.

What I have said so far makes the operation sound very much a managerial, almost a political, operation (and I mean obviously 'political' with a small 'p'). I think this is true; and I think it has one important corollary: simply because the operation is so complex and so many-sided, authors of educational material must be very clear about what their principles are, so that in the midst of the minutiae of production they do not lose sight of these principles and find themselves led, perhaps under pressure of time, into decisions which may run counter to what they deeply believe.

The circumstances in which our particular scheme was initiated and carried through have a bearing on what I have just been saying. Authors may find themselves in one of three situations. They may devise and write a fairly complete manuscript which they then submit to the publisher of their choice. Or they may produce a synopsis and some sample material and submit this before involving themselves in further work. If a publisher is interested, he may then take an active part in the subsequent development of the material. On the other hand, the publisher may take the initiative and approach the authors with an invitation to submit sample material, or to consider the undertaking of some specified work. This is what happened to Joan Low and myself; and I am mentioning it because of the set of working conditions which it produces. Conditions in which publishers, in the person of their editors, are actively involved, are different from those which obtain when authors are working on their own. We have come to believe that these working conditions are immensely important in terms of the final outcome. Although there may be some restrictions in working along with an editor from the initiation of a piece of work, these are in the end greatly outweighed by the advantages, especially if those on the editorial staff of the publishing house concerned have a truly informed interest in the content and the educational aims of the material being created. It is true that the conditions can give rise to situations where different criteria are being applied by the two sides, and where therefore the need for clarity over principles, which I have mentioned, becomes particularly great. But this in turn can make both sides re-examine their assumptions, which is a very educative process.

The invitation to us to submit proposals for a new basal reading scheme was based on the belief that there was an educational need for one and that the market was ready for it. The publishers were quite clear that what they wanted was material which would have as its core a set of books, though they naturally did not want the material to be limited to books alone. Another point on which they were clear was that they wanted the material to make use of the insights into language and language learning which has been provided over the last twenty years or so by the disciplines of linguistics and psycholinguistics. And they wanted the situational content to reflect aspects of urban life which would be meaningful to children and would provide a fruitful source of classroom interest and activity. They had in mind, therefore, an amalgam of tradition and innovation.

These were all principles which my colleague Joan Low and I found acceptable. The second principle – that of making use of insights from linguistics and psycholinguistics – fitted in closely with my own recent research work and with much other work with which we were both in sympathy. The third principle – that of making the situational content relevant to contemporary urban society and contemporary classroom practice – was one which particularly interested Joan Low. The matter of our agreement on the format of the reading programme was perhaps less predictable in terms of our previous work. In the course of my evaluation of *Breakthrough to Literacy*, which I conducted between the summer of 1969 and the autumn of 1971 (Reid 1974), I had become aware of the fact that it was possible to produce viable infant reading material of which books did not form the core. But both Joan Low and I found ourselves attracted to the notion of a new book-based scheme, and indeed it seemed to me that some of the things I wanted to try to do could only be done through the medium of book material. I think that it is necessary for authors to believe in and approve of the basic ideas out of which their material is going to grow, and that they cannot effectively write just to please others or respond to a need.

The situation in which we and the publishers now found ourselves was one which, interestingly, gives both sides very high motivation. If a work is commissioned, then although the publishers will reserve the right to make editorial suggestions and even impose certain conditions, they know that they will in the end accept the manuscript. Authors who have accepted a commission feel a security which they otherwise might not feel in devoting an immense amount of time and thought to the production of a substantial body of material. This matter of continuing motivation is very important, especially when the first flush of excitement over an enterprise has abated. Times can come when one runs temporarily out of steam, and at such a point it can be someone on the editorial side who keeps the enterprise going, even if only by sending a reminder that a certain piece of manuscript, or a corrected proof, is due back – at the latest – by a given date!

In his book *Now, Barabbas* William Jovanovitch (1965) makes these very points, adding a *caveat* for the editor (page 80):

Writing is the loneliest of professions, and the writer, like all artists, tends to exhaust his personal resources: in the dialogue between the writer and the reader there is an uneven exchange, for what enriches the one has depleted the other . . . if a writer must borrow assistance, or merely encouragement, then it would seem natural that he turn to an editor . . . for the editor, this is flattering but dangerous, for he must decide at what point assistance becomes interference.

Acceptance of a commission is normally followed by the production of a synopsis for approval. It is not possible here to give a running account of the changes and modifications through which our synopsis went. Rather, I will make one or two general points about this aspect of the construction of a reading programme such as ours. Firstly, ideas do not all come at once, so producing a synopsis is not easy. The process is a creative one and so, as in other creative processes, ideas evolve, or are modified, or discarded, or changed finally out of all recognition; and the various people participating in the enterprise interact with one another in a variety of ways to produce these changes. For example, the publishers' insistence that the content should reflect urban life set us thinking about those aspects of urban life which we might use as a situational starting point for the first book – always a most difficult thing to decide about. Book 1 was very much harder to write, and went through many more changes, than Books 6, 7 and 8. This was partly because of the knowledge that once the beginning was settled and built on, it would be almost impossible to change. But out of thoughts about busy streets and vehicles and shops, the idea arose that these situations presented us with a superb opportunity for realizing one of our specific teaching aims – that of teaching about the nature and some of the uses of written language. These concepts form part of the early learning that has to take place (Reid 1966; Downing 1970; Hardy 1973). So 'public print', or 'print in the environment' became one of the features of the early material. It proved, fortunately, to be a fruitful idea, which we were able to diversify in a great many ways. But had it not, then the painful task of discarding everything and starting again would have had to be faced.

A second point about this planning stage is that views on what is educationally optimal and on what is commercially viable or expedient clearly cannot always coincide. It is obviously no use publishing material which teachers will not be persuaded to buy. It is equally, of course, questionable whether you should publish something which teachers may well buy but which you do not think is educationally sound; and I think that you reach here one of the crucial areas of decision-making both for publisher and author. How far is the publisher a public servant, a guardian of standards, or a missionary? How far is the author 'in business'? When, for either, does conviction become dogma?

Two examples from our own experience will illustrate these points. We were originally in favour of having a plan based on a fairly large number of small books. We produced an outline which had a number of levels with six books at each level, and in addition a number of bridging books. The publishers would not accept this proposal because, they said, if we produced a scheme with a very large number of books many schools would not buy them all. We would then find elements of the scheme being used piecemeal and it would simply fail to have an impact as a mainstream body of learning and teaching equipment. This was, of course, an argument on educational as well as on business grounds. They proposed instead a different plan: to have a core of books spaced so that they could be used in succession with more able children, but with provision to fill in the steps between the core books with additional steps. This was the outline which we in fact adopted. The advantage of the plan turned out to be that it was possible to let people see, fairly quickly, the overall structure of the proposed work, and to make material available for use at different stages at a reasonably early point in production. This was an example of a compromise successfully reached on a major issue. The second example of conflict between educational and commercial criteria concerned a piece of ancillary material. For a variety of reasons, neither Joan Low nor I think that the use of the flash card technique as an initial teaching device is desirable. So in spite of the fact that we knew many schools would buy them we decided not to include large single word cards as part of the programme. But there is ground here for serious debate – not about flash cards, but about the principle of publishing only something in which you believe.

An outline is however only schematic, and has to be given substance. I should like to say something in detail about this stage, in order to emphasize how much work can go into the task of realizing theory in practice. Firstly, as I have already mentioned, we used in as many ways as possible the notions of print in the environment, and of the written word in everyday life (cf. Reid 1966; Downing 1970; Hardy 1973) and we used them not only in the text but in the illustrations, of which more shortly. Secondly, working from studies of children's speech (Strickland 1962; O'Donnell *et al* 1967; Menyuk 1969; Chomsky 1970), studies of reading errors (Goodman 1967; Clay 1969; Weber 1970) and studies of the analysis of language in existing primers and extension readers (Strickland 1962; Reid 1970, 1972), we produced a working scale of ascending order of syntactic complexity which was to serve us as a framework for the sentence structures in our books. We also had regard to recent thinking on the relationship of readability to skills of syntax processing, as shown in studies of intermediate skills (Merritt 1969) and of readability (Bormuth 1966). Thirdly, in the early situational content we tried to put a kind of cross-section of urban child life, as socially neutral as we could make it, mixed in with some fun and fantasy, and with some problems and mishaps.

In addition to decisions on major features such as these, one has to make many others, all interrelated: innumerable further decisions about vocabulary; about the grading of numerous features of written text, such as punctuation marks; about the handling of spelling patterns. These are authors' decisions, and I consider that they should be again based as far as possible on observation and research findings. Other decisions are arrived at with much editorial guidance. In our case it was the editors who suggested the typeface, the page size, the placing of illustrations, the choice of artists, the placing of page numbers, the material for and the design of the covers.

Here I want to consider at some length the problem of the role and the nature of illustration in a reading scheme. Some aspects of the illustration of books can present great difficulties. For example, we had decided that because of our use of public print as a means of teaching about the concepts of reading and of written language, the illustrations must form a particularly important part of the teaching medium, especially in the early books. But it proved rather difficult to communicate effectively with the artists, especially in cases where this was done through the editor. I might take as an instance the matter of the avoidance of capital letters in public print. We wanted the child to see the match between words as they appeared in the illustration and as they were being presented in the text, as for example in the case of 'bus stop'; which meant representing the 'bus stop' sign, in the picture, in lower case lettering. Getting this right involved sending the artwork back and forth several times, a process which produced quite a long delay in production. The tradition of keeping artists and authors apart is a strongly established one, but there is much to be said for direct discussion between them.

The relationship of illustrations to text, in books from which children are learning to read, raises other problems. It is, I think, a much more precisely definable relationship than that in most books for children who already can read. I would for this reason defend the right of the authors to approve, and in some cases to specify, certain features of the illustrations, on the grounds that they are part of the content. It would seem a sound principle that, at first, illustrations should be very fully informative, and that as the books progress illustrations should tell the child less and less so that the print has to tell him more and more. This is, after all, what learning to read is all about. It is learning to get information from printed words instead of from real life situations, oral language and pictures. But deciding, at the stage of weaning from high dependence, what to represent in the picture is a difficult matter, involving judgments about those features of the text which need most contextual support: judgments which are, in fact, pedagogical as opposed to artistic.

I want now to turn to the matter of trying material out. I think it is important both from the point of view of satisfying oneself and of giving one's work credibility that some form of trying out should take place and that there should be feedback from teachers. We were very fortunate in having the earlier parts of our material, which were the most problematic in many ways, tried out very thoroughly. We did not have to work with duplicated handprinted material, nor with blown-up typescript: our publishers set the material up in the typeface which was going to be used in the final version and provided black and white illustrations of a high quality. The tryout material was accompanied by a brief questionnaire to the teachers using it. Tryouts were done unobtrusively and as part of everyday classroom work. I have come to believe that this is probably, on balance, a better method than one which is accompanied by a great deal of sense of occasion. I am not going to say that a sense of occasion will invalidate the results. It is bound to occur to some extent every time new material is introduced into a school, and when it produces what Vera Southgate (1965) has called a 'reading drive' this can be a most desirable thing. But a highly organized tryout not only produces a sense of heightened enthusiasm and expectation; it is also normally accompanied by a good deal of back-up support from those involved in the construction of the curriculum. Just how much these circumstances may distort the picture of a scheme's success it would be impossible to say, but at least one can say that a tryout conducted without them is more likely to reflect the everyday circumstances in which the material will ultimately have to justify itself.

One very important category of information for authors can come directly from the tryout books. It concerns layout. One learns how one's text looks on a page. One sees it printed in different type sizes. One comes to see how much text can acceptably go on a page, and what one should do about such features as indentations, and horizontal and vertical spacing. It is perhaps worth mentioning here that in these matters authors have to communicate with the printers, but that printers are a group of workers whom authors never personally encounter. Each of us, however, can learn from the other. Effective communication, via the editors and the production manager, depends on the authors learning something of the technical language in which printing layout is discussed, and a good deal about what can and can not be done with a text at any given stage in production. Authors, on the other hand, can draw the printers' attention to the crucial importance of the way type is set for beginners: to the need, for instance, for adequate spacing between words and between lines, and, in our case, to the importance of not breaking lines in the middle of phrases. In a beginning reading scheme, all these features are part of the content, and therefore part of the authors' concern.

Ancillary material can be another source of tension between what seems educationally desirable and attractive and what the publishers consider on various grounds to be feasible. For instance, the material which we finally produced for sentence composing was not what we had originally intended. Our original plan envisaged something on the lines of *Lego*: words printed on plastic blocks which would lock together in some way. But this was considered to be too expensive to produce and the scheme was abandoned in favour of the use of limp plastic labels adhering to a laminated background. Again, a compromise; but one which proved to have in the end certain benefits, because the sentences composed in this material bore a closer physical resemblance to printed text than the more solid alternative would have produced.

Although in all this discussion the consumers – the child and the teacher – have not figured very much, they were in the forefront of our minds all the time we were working. We found ourselves always envisaging a teacher and her group of children and asking questions like: 'How is our five-year-old learner going to find his way through the first difficult stages to the point where he can read something which is in some sense "a story"?'; 'How is the teacher going to use this particular piece of material to teach him?' We faced the fact that we were, in providing what we called a 'programme', laying down a path. But I think it is important that any such path should be neither too narrow nor too rigidly walled in. There must be room for some variety and for creative extrapolation.

However, the more one lays down some kind of path, the more importance attaches to communication with the teacher. The main vehicle of this communication, apart from the material itself, is of course the teacher's manual. Manuals vary a great deal in size, in scope, in format and in objectives. Our final objective was to produce a book neither so large and detailed that teachers would not read it (it is very difficult to get teachers to read manuals in any case), nor so brief and sketchy that it was perfunctory and apparently dispensable. One essential ingredient of a reading programme which the constructors cannot supply is, of course, a good teacher; but a manual can play a very important part in helping teachers, by doing three things. Firstly, it should explain clearly why the programme has been constructed as it has been. Secondly, it should discuss ways in which the programme can be used, and indicate those ways which the authors consider most faithful to its rationale, while at the same time encouraging teachers to think of extensions and modifications for themselves. Thirdly, the manual should offer some guidance in areas of special difficulty. In our case, the three areas selected for discussion were the early stages, the stage of transition to the phraseology and the registers of literature and textbooks, and the difficulties encountered by children with specific reading and writing disabilities of some kind.

Among the smaller decisions connected with the manual was that of the placing of the word counts for the reading books. Sometimes these are put at the end of the children's books, but we decided not to do this but to put them as an appendix to the manual. This was done partly so that the children's books would not look as if they each ended with a test, and partly to encourage teachers to keep the manual by them. It provides another example of resisting a fairly common tradition because of a strongly held conviction.

It is interesting to look at some of the other schemes which have appeared recently and to see how emphases vary, how different answers have been sought to problems, and how different aspects have seemed important to different authors. There are, for instance, very big differences between schemes in the degree to which they control and grade their vocabulary. By 'control and grade' I mean pay attention to the kind of word introduced at any point, to the speed at which new words are introduced, to the number of times a word is repeated, and to the number of 'throw-away' words – words used perhaps only once in some particular story context. Some recent schemes do have regard to these features. But others are based more on the belief that books should be ancillary to a language experience approach rather than form a central teaching medium. If authors believe this, then their views on vocabulary reinforcement and grading will be different, and emphasis on the 'story' element in the early content will be likely to increase. There are of course implications for teaching strategies: you cannot use books with ungraded vocabulary in the same ways as you would use the books in a scheme where the vocabulary is mostly cumulative and set in some kind of sequence. If authors believe, on the other hand, that books should be mainly demonstrations of the spelling patterns of the written language, the principles of vocabulary control will be different again, the need for grading will reappear, and the appropriate teaching strategies will also change.

I have come to believe that one has to try to take more than one criterion into account and in particular that decisions about vocabulary cannot be divorced from decisions about sentence structure. It also seems to me that a scheme or programme which employs careful control and grading – on whatever grounds – assumes a heavier responsibility as a teaching medium than one which does not.

I want now to make a few brief final points. When you have published something, there is a sense of completion. But this must not turn into a sense of finality, a feeling that you have found all the answers and can now stop probing and puzzling. On the other hand, there are very real practical problems if you want to make emendations to your published material. In the case of, say, a textbook, this often happens, and students have to be directed to the appropriate edition. With a reading scheme the problems are somewhat different, and there is a danger that small but significant improvements may never be made in case they constitute a source of confusion in use.

And finally, authors must always be prepared for the fact that they will not appeal to everyone, and be aware that not everyone will see in a piece of work what the creators have sought to put in. I remember a five-year-old child whose painting I admired:

'What lovely trees', I said. 'Everybody says that', he replied rather sadly, 'but I meant it to be daffodils.'

References

BORMUTH, J. (1966) Readability: a new approach *Reading Research Quarterly* 1, 79–132

CHOMSKY, C. (1970) *The Acquisition of Syntax in Children from Five to Ten* Boston: MIT Press

CLAY, M. M. (1969) Reading errors and self-correction behaviour *British Journal of Educational Psychology* 39, 47–56

DOWNING, J. (1970) Children's concepts of language in learning to read *Educational Research* 12, 106–12

GOODMAN, K. (1967) Reading: a psycholinguistic guessing game *Journal of the Reading Specialist* 4, 112–35

HARDY, M. (1973) 'The development of beginning reading skills: recent findings' in M. Clark and A. Milne (Eds) *Reading and Related Skills* Ward Lock Educational

JOVANOVITCH, W. (1965) *Now, Barabbas* Longman

MENYUK, P. (1969) *Sentences Children Use* Boston: MIT Press

MERRITT, J. (1969) 'The intermediate skills' in K. Gardner (Ed) *Reading Skills, Theory and Practice* Ward Lock Educational

O'DONNELL, R. C. *et al* (1967) *The Language of Elementary School Children: A Transformational Analysis* Champaign, Illinois: NCTE Research Report No. 8

REID, J. F. (1966) Learning to think about reading *Educational Research* 9, 156–62

REID, J. F. (1970) Sentence structure in reading primers *Research in Education* 3, 23–37

REID, J. F. (1972) *Children's Comprehension of Syntactic Structures Found in some Extension Readers* (Occasional Paper No. 3) Centre for Research in Educational Sciences, University of Edinburgh

REID, J. F. (1974) *Breakthrough in Action: An Independent Evaluation of 'Breakthrough to Literacy'* Longman

REID, J. F. and LOW, J. M. (1973) *Link-Up. An Infant Reading Programme* Holmes McDougall

REID, J. F. and LOW, J. M. (1973) *The Written Word. The Teacher's Manual for 'Link-Up'* Holmes McDougall

SOUTHGATE, V. (1965) Approaching i.t.a. results with caution *Educational Research* 7, 83–96

STRICKLAND, R. G. (1962) The language of elementary school children *Bulletin of the School of Education, Indiana University* 38, 4

WEBER, R. M. (1970) A linguistic analysis of first-grade reading errors *Reading Research Quarterly* 5, 427–51

5 Educational publishing – criteria and constraints

Michael Raggett

I hope in this paper to give some insights into the publishing process, with particular reference to books published specifically for educational use – Julia MacRae's paper is concerned with the more general field of children's books. Many of these have educational applications but are not published primarily for educational use nor with educational purchasers envisaged as more than a part, albeit substantial, of the market. From my own experience and from discussions with publishing colleagues I hope to outline how the publisher selects titles for publication and how he decides on format, style of production and so on and how the two – the criteria for accepting an idea for publication and the constraints affecting the manner and type of publication – are interrelated.

The publisher's chief raw material is ideas, usually expressed in the form of a manuscript, proposal, synopsis or outline, or some artwork or other illustrative material. Increasingly often in my experience, the raw material arrives, not in a concrete form, but more frequently in conversational form – an expressed interest, a felt need, a pet theory, a bright idea. Such raw material clearly needs refinement, discussion, research and development before being expressed in the form of synopsis and sample chapter, which is the earliest written stage in the life of most publications.

Proposals for publication in one form or another are acquired by publishers in two main ways. Simply by his being in business and listed in yellow pages etc. a seemingly unstemmable flood of manuscripts and outlines will arrive on the publisher's desk. Few of these will be suitable for publication in any form and the majority will be returned with an explanatory letter, or a rejection slip. Of the remainder, most will need reworking to some extent before the publisher accepts them. Out of more than 200 titles I have published over the last seven years only six have resulted from unsolicited manuscripts published in substantially the form in which they arrived on my desk. Unsolicited manuscripts arrive by every post in most publishers' offices, from authors' friends and colleagues with recommendations and from literary agents who act as a preliminary filter before directing projects to the most likely publisher. A close working relationship between publishers' editors and literary agents ensures that each is aware of the other's strengths and weaknesses – areas for expansion and absolutely taboo subjects – and the chances of mismatch between title and publisher solely on the grounds of unsuitability for a particular publisher's list is more easily avoided. Many publishers look only for a limited amount of new material each year, relying on established backlist titles, basal schemes in various subject areas and other perennially popular series to form the core of their publishing programme. Extensions to existing series, reuse of existing material in other forms and at other levels will need writers to perform specific tasks but will be essentially publisher-controlled and therefore largely a closed market for the aspiring author wishing to see his own ideas in print.

The second form of acquisition of raw material takes the form of an active search. The publisher goes looking for ideas in schools, colleges, teachers' centres, universities and other establishments; he attends conferences and seminars in the hope of meeting people able to produce the kind of publication he feels appropriate to his list. He tries to maintain an awareness of current trends and future developments in the curriculum in the hope of matching his materials to real classroom needs at the time when they occur. Many publishers organize advisory meetings with groups of educationists on a regular or an *ad hoc* basis to keep them in constant touch with curriculum innovations and classroom practice and most have some degree of feedback from the teaching situation on the effectiveness of their publications. Many publishers retain advisers to keep a lookout for new ideas. Much of the raw material acquired in this way has probably been embryonic in its authors for some time; a chance remark from a publisher acts as the catalyst for further growth and development. This catalytic effect is often achieved also by the juxtaposition of people with similar ideas which they have expressed severally to the publisher, in ways that might not otherwise have happened.

The interplay between the editor and his advisers is critical to the selection process. How the editor chooses his advisers will obviously reflect his own educational and political beliefs, but few advisers are selected as tame 'yes men' to agree with all the bright ideas and support all the preconceived notions of the editor. There are many ways of selecting advisers and most of them have an element of chance; but all successful editor/adviser relationships are based on mutual respect and trust.

Preliminary assessment of projects

When a publishing project, in one of the several forms already discussed, arrives in the publisher's office it will be 'logged' as having been received and then passed, with luck, to an appropriate editor. Actual procedure differs here enormously, depending on the size and organization of the particular publisher; but eventually the manuscript, outline or letter of intent arrives on an editor's desk. The editor's first impression is obviously of very great importance and for an idea to proceed further it must satisfy the editor that it contains something worthy of further time and expense right at the outset.

Who, then, is the editor? He/she may be straight from school or college and learn his trade in service with a publisher. He may be a teacher who has decided to go into publishing. Whatever the background, the editor is sensitive to educational developments both theoretical and practical, probably has some literary leanings and a desire to communicate. The editor's role is very much that of an interpreter in a musical sense, seeing a clear overall pattern and the component details and, hopefully, orchestrating them into a successful whole.

Whoever he is, the editor has great power. Teachers certainly choose the materials they will use with their pupils, but the range of choice is controlled by the publishers' editors. The editor then is curriculum developer, keeper of standards, controller of content and facilitator of innovation on a large scale – a complex and powerful role not always adequately fulfilled.

Given, then, that the editor is initially disposed favourably towards a new project, he will obtain further impressions of it from colleagues within the house or from external advisers. Such advisers form an important part of any editor's contacts and will be organized and reimbursed for their work in a variety of ways. What is common to them all is the importance placed on their opinion of a project. While the project is being assessed by an adviser, the editor will be likely to carry out some bibliographical and market research at very elementary levels.

This may be no more than a glance through *British Books in Print* and a browse through other publishers' catalogues to see what the competition is, and a phone call to his sales manager to gauge his reaction to the idea, or something much more sophisticated and elaborate. Editors tend to specialize quite highly and are therefore usually well able to assess the originality, contribution and potential of a project; but before taking the decision to proceed with publication they will want to canvass opinion on as broad a base as is practicable. The editor will also, either while awaiting a report or soon after receiving a favourable one, begin to consult with design and production colleagues to clarify his ideas about format, presentation and price. Then further market research will be undertaken in order to arrive at some idea of the potential of the project in different guises and at different prices, before the editor takes the formal step of putting a proposal for publication before his board of directors or publications committee or his own conscience, whichever of these agencies gives the final sanction for the commitment of capital expenditure. The time between receipt of the original idea and the putting up of a proposal to publish will vary from weeks to years and will often involve discussion between the editor and the author, modification of the project and much internal discussion and preparation. Whatever the preamble, the stage of formal commitment to publication must be reached and agreed within the company and in order to reach this stage the project must satisfy the editor's basic criteria.

Criteria for publication

The first criterion might be covered by the phrase 'horses for courses'. I said earlier that editors tended to specialize; so do publishing companies, and one of the first criteria for accepting a project for publication must be its suitability for the publisher's list. This criterion is subject to a number of constraints concerning the publisher's sales force, reputation in the field, competition from within the publisher's own list compared with the advantages of a presence in the subject area, the problems of launching projects in an entirely new area, and so on.

The editor must be convinced that the project makes an original and significant contribution to the educational process either in terms of content or teaching methodology or preferably both. He must then be convinced – and in my view in educational publishing this is the criterion least well satisfied – that it is well written and constructed, appropriate in style and register for the intended market and capable of production in such a format that will make it accessible to the user, bearing in mind the two-fold readership of the majority of educational publications: preliminary assessment by the teacher and eventual use by the pupil.

Can the project meet the foregoing criteria and be produced at a price which is deemed appropriate to the intended market? Publishing educationally sound books at prices the market cannot afford leads to overstocked warehouses and bankrupt publishers. Can the project make a profit in a reasonably short space of time (two to five years for most publishers), or at least not sustain such losses that they cannot be offset against profit from other areas of the list? On this last criterion, individual editors are usually financially accountable for the success and failure of their own selection of titles and may well decide to go ahead with projects which sustain small losses if they can balance the overall profit figure required from their section of the list by way of more profitable titles, from their backlist for example. Obviously too much altruistic non-profit-making publishing leads to an eventual reduction in the choice of titles available and the number of publishers still in business!

Given all these paragons of virtue, criteria to the fore, patrolling the educational scene, how does so much rubbish get published? I use the term rubbish to reflect the extremely personal nature of such an opinion and the extremely personal nature of an editor's standards and views. The responsibility for much of what I (and you) would term rubbish lies with teachers, in that they still buy vast quantities of it and cause publishers to tie up capital keeping it in print, which might be spent on more innovative and valuable projects. It becomes too easy for the publisher to satisfy his profit requirements on such material and his desire to experiment and take risks can become dulled, and he will too readily suspend his critical faculties when taking on new projects especially in times of economic difficulty.

Then there is the bandwagon problem, which affects both the style and the content of publications: 'the book is dead, let's all have multimedia packages', or 'kids need working-class realism in their readers' – and we've all seen how little the kids like those. The publisher, however, having backed his false judgment to the tune of several thousand copies, has a deeply vested interest in perpetuating, at least as long as his stock, such discredited or superceded notions. The editor is again the final arbiter on matters such as these and however well advised will make mistakes; what is sad is that his mistakes may stay around for a very long time.

Without doubt then, the perpetration and proliferation of retrogressive projects of doubtful educational value is the publisher's fault. But the teachers who continue to buy and sometimes even use such material must share the blame.

Publishing constraints

Many of the constraints upon the editor have already shown themselves inextricably interrelated with the criteria he tries to work by. They fall largely into three sections – financial, facilities and timing:

Financial constraints pose questions such as: Can we afford to invest the amount required for the period required? With the mounting interest rates of recent years, publishers' accountants have been looking for a swifter return on capital investment, to avoid all profit being swallowed up in interest charges. Shall we have cash available at the time it is required, without borrowing? Cash flow has been the major problem in many industries lately and few people can have avoided the experience of a cash flow crisis at personal or professional level. For the publisher, certain months of the year tend to produce much more income than others and the editor must increasingly try to gear his production schedules so that bills can be paid from cash-in-hand rather than with borrowed capital.

The *constraints of facilities* involve such considerations as the availability of editorial and design studio time, of artistes who may be required for tape recordings or filmstrips. Warehousing and distribution arrangements of the company as a whole may often pose problems for individual units. Some of the newer multimedia projects may cause physical difficulties of storage and packaging which must be solved within a system whose major function remains the efficient processing of solid cuboids of a smallish range of sizes. Multifaceted projects may also cause problems for stock control and automatic accounting machinery.

Timing constraints have been seen already in relation to both finance and facilities, but can also relate to the importance of producing a project ahead of competition, for launching at a particular conference or exhibition, as well as the usual constraints of the timing of the school year and the requisition periods of those authorities that still have very specific periods for ordering books.

All these questions will have been raised, at least implicitly, in a publisher's particular system of commitment to publication, before such a commitment is made and a legally binding contract to publish is drawn up between the author and publisher. Then the writer writes, the printer prints and eventually, usually something like a year after delivery of the manuscript, the project is published and costs too much!

Costs

It is often difficult for the customer to understand why a product should cost the price which they see marked on it. This is true of educational books and materials as with other products, and in a time of economic stringency such as we are now experiencing, it is important that the customer appreciates the problems of the producers to at least some extent. Most teachers readily appreciate the increase in the cost of paper since they purchase it themselves but are not necessarily aware of the breakdown of costs on a typical publication.

Plant costs

There are certain basis costs which will not go away and do not depend on any variable factor once it has been agreed to produce a project in a certain format. These are called plant, or nonrecurring, costs and include the costs of typesetting, artwork, reproduction, copyright fees and sometimes block or platemaking.

Whatever form it takes, the manuscript must be typeset to achieve a suitable image for printing. This may be hot metal, filmsetting or IBM or other cold type equivalent and is related obviously to the number of words to be set, the complexity of setting – tables, mathematical, foreign and so on cost more – and the size and style of type selected.

Artwork and artistic work are costs which occur in most projects as a result of the inclusion of illustrations which must be drawn in a way suitable for photographic reproduction. These often need professional research and execution and this category also includes fees for recording and photographic studio facilities, fees to performers etc. In the event of published material being quoted in a project, or illustrations being used which are the copyright property of someone else, fees must be negotiated and paid to cover the intended use in all or certain countries of the world. These fees sometimes vary with the number of copies printed, but are a definitive plant item at the outset.

Reproduction costs are involved in turning artwork or photographs into printing film or letterpress printing blocks, for producing master slides for filmstrips and slide sets of master tapes for recorded materials; and in the most common form of printing for educational projects, offset lithography, for turning pasted-up typesetting into printing film.

The next stage in litho printing is to prepare printing plates, some of which are stored and reused and can therefore be considered a nonrecurring plant cost. Others, depending on type of publication and length of print run, are remade each time and are therefore a recurring print cost and are included below.

Recurring costs

However many copies of a publication are produced, and over however many successive reprints, there are certain costs which are directly geared to the physical production of each copy, rather than to the more general and abstract concept of format, style and content.

Paper must be purchased at the time of each printing at prevailing costs. In the last two years paper has more than doubled in price and while some savings can be made by bulk buying the problem and expense of storage have often proved them to be false economies.

Printing an image onto the blank sheets of paper is again obviously geared to the number of copies produced and is usually charged by the printer direct to the publisher as a total price to include the supply of plates, ink, time and labour. Economies can be achieved through larger print runs, since the time taken to prepare plates and adjust machines for a perfect image takes a proportionally higher part of the time required in a short print run than in a longer one. The printer's rates will also allow for his overheads and profit margin. Even where publisher and printer are part of the same firm, the printer's services will be charged at competitive rates and the printing company will be separately accountable.

Binding the publication, whether in book form, in spiral bindings or whatever, is a service that must be bought in and paid for on each occasion that a project is produced. Here again the binder's charge will include cost of materials and labour and his profit margin.

The other recurring cost is for royalties, which form an important part of the production cost of a project and are still the most common form of payment to the author; although in many instances the publisher will purchase the copyright from the author by means of an outright fee, which will then be a nonrecurring or plant cost on the project.

Incidental costs

I call the next category incidental costs because they exist as a result of the publisher being in business as a publisher, whether he publishes any projects or not. They are his overheads: the costs of salaries to his staff, his rent, rates, heating and lighting bills, his interest and depreciation charges, his bad debts, his distribution costs – postage, packaging materials, machinery, all the usual costs of any business.

Added to these are the costs of publicity and sales efforts which are usually not costed separately for each project, but form a central budget administered by specialist sales and publicity departments in close consultation with the editors. Finally the publication carries costs in the form of discounts to wholesalers and retailers which vary between 16 and 35 per cent in relation to the recommended retail price.

The cost factors of an educational, or any other, publication are obviously complex. I have greatly oversimplified and I have omitted any mention of profit for the publisher. Fortunately, many publishers do succeed in making profits in their educational lists, usually in the order of 10 to 15 per cent before tax.

The future

The last few years have been very difficult for publishers generally and have seen the collapse of Penguin Education and Dent's educational list as the dramatic outward signs of the internal problems faced by all. Many educational publishers have been hit by changes in teaching methodology, which have called for more localized provision of learning resources in many cases. Institutional publishers such as the BBC, the Open University and the Schools Council have all had an impact in siphoning increasingly restricted financial resources away from commercial publishers and many LEAs spend lamentably small amounts on learning resource materials as a proportion of their overall budgets.

I have discussed at some length the costing structures and problems of national commercial publishers. Many schools, teachers' centres, and LEA resources centres are now looking at ways of producing materials for school use at lower prices than commercial products. My own Authority is one of the leaders in the field and is as yet beset by a fairly uncritical attitude to real costs of materials. In my opinion, localized production of materials is here to stay, is a good thing and to be encouraged provided that it satisfies the same sort of criteria that the commercial editor employs. If immediacy and local interest can be satisfied, then by all means produce materials in a way that the national publisher cannot. But far too often I have seen in various areas of the country virtually identical semi-textbooks or collections of assignment sheets, poorly presented with typography and design unsuited to the age range envisaged and almost all reproduced from the same major sources – all unacknowledged and copyright fees unpaid! Children must not be given too great a part of their reading diet in unevenly printed, sketchily illustrated form, or the difficulty of processing and the unattractiveness of the presentation may well prove a deterrent to reading at all. Perhaps I overstate the case a little, but the wastage of scant resources in this kind of uncoordinated, unresearched, really unnecessary production is particularly offensive at the present time when all resources must be used to their utmost effectiveness.

The current round of setbacks and the necessary retrenchments will, I believe, operate in the long term to good effect in ensuring that publishers, both commercial and LEA, will apply more rigorously the criteria I outlined earlier and that the uncritical, needlessly competitive overproduction which has been so wasteful of resources, will be greatly lessened to the benefit of the child. I hope that cooperation between LEA production centres and commercial publishers, such as we are beginning to achieve in the ILEA, will become more common, so that expertise in the editing, design and production of materials can be readily accessed by LEAs and so that good locally-developed projects with a broader potential can be more widely disseminated.

Publishers of course have their own role to play, independently of any such cooperative schemes. Through the contribution of publishers a wide variety of materials has been made available in a wide range of curriculum areas in the last ten to twenty years and I am sure will continue to be, to the eventual benefit of the child.

6 The publisher, the writer and the child

Julia MacRae

The president's letter which introduced the printed programme for this conference stated that the theme was *The content of reading*, and went on to say:

> It calls for a fundamental questioning, not just of how we teach reading, but of what we offer children to read. This involves value judgments on writing for children and an exploration of how it is conceived, published, disseminated and used.

This statement struck me with particular force, because to some extent a publisher is in the hot seat, as much of the discussion about the content of reading is surely academic unless it relates to what is actually available *to* read and that is what first the author and then the publisher provides. Peter Dickinson, a most distinguished writer, has given his views from the writer's perspective, and Michael Raggett has analysed the situation in educational publishing. My paper is from the vantage point of a *trade* publisher, which suggests that the books we publish at Hamish Hamilton are mainly supplied to the reading public through the book trade in the form of bookshops. In fact, about 80 per cent of our books are bought by libraries and schools, which means that we cater for the same market as the educational publisher but in the form of *recreational* rather than *educational* reading. In other words, the novels and picture books which make up the greater part of our publishing programme are not curriculum-related, and are intended to be read by the child for his own private pleasure and enjoyment. They may educate, in the sense that something in their content helps a child's understanding, but it is rather by a process of osmosis, in that the child first and foremost enjoys the story and almost unconsciously takes from it the deeper levels of meaning which may stay with him for life. As an Australian, I grew up with a splendid book called *Seven Little Australians*, which I enjoyed because it was what in those days was always called 'a rattling good yarn'. Only later did I realize that from that book I had absorbed a very positive and reassuring idea about death, just as from my all-time favourite *The Wind in the Willows* I took somewhere deep into my innermost recesses an attitude about the security of a home one loves. These books 'educated' me, indeed, but that was not their primary function. In Victorian times it would have been, since children's books of the 1900s were didactic in intent and morally doom-laden in tone. Some of them actually managed to tell a good story as well, but it was often hard to find in the dense verbiage which surrounded it. One of the aspects of modern children's book publishing which I find faintly alarming is what seems to be a return to didacticism – suspicion that a book must have a message to be acceptable. This is more prevalent in such countries as Sweden and the United States, but it is beginning to be felt over here too, and I find myself depressed by the number of manuscripts which we receive which 'tell it like it is' to young readers, without humour and without much hope.

In thinking about this paper I read through many speeches I have given during the past ten or so years, and discovered that I was once young and idealistic. I used invariably to preface my remarks with a quotation from Lillian Smith's *The Unreluctant Years* which says:

> We should put into the hands of children only the books worthy of them, the books of honesty, integrity and vision, the books on which they can grow. Reading which does not stretch their minds not only wastes their time, but will not hold them permanently.

I would not now preface a discussion on publishing for children with these remarks. Something has happened to me in the intervening years. It is not that I have lost my faith, or that I do not believe what Lillian Smith says to be true. It is simply that I have become increasingly and horrifyingly aware of the fact that there really are children – and adults – who *cannot read,* thousands of them, and thousands more to whom reading is a difficult, frustrating, unrewarding experience, which opens no doors at all for them. To put in front of such people the kind of books Lillian Smith writes about would be to court disaster, because they would be entirely out of reach. You will think it naive of me to make such an obvious remark, since this is not news to you, but therein lies one of the dilemmas facing the children's book editor. I have no children. I have a highly literate staff and I deal with highly literate, talented authors and artists. We are all presumably adult. In addition to that I am the managing director of my company, and I therefore owe it to that company and all the people involved with it to run its affairs in a business-like way and to show a profit at the end of the year. We have been lucky, because of the calibre of the writers who work for us and the quality of our staff, and the imprint, Hamish Hamilton Children's Books Limited, has flourished.

But what is it we are actually doing? How do we relate our activities to the needs of children? I cannot answer that briefly. I can say that I see myself as having two responsibilities: to the writer and to the reader. I owe the writer the chance to develop his talent, to follow the right direction for his own creative satisfaction. I cannot shove or push him into the direction *I* want him to go. It follows therefore that if a writer produces a book which will by its nature and style have a limited readership because it is intellectually demanding, then I must accept this fact if I choose to publish the book. One part of me *must* accept that a good many of our publications will only reach the reading child, the committed child who already has sophisticated reading skills and can appreciate subtlety of style and nuance of meaning. Fine. That writer and child have their needs, and for a publisher the production of a book of literary excellence is a special privilege, because we surely would not be doing the job at all if we didn't respond with delight to the way in which a truly gifted writer can make words suddenly sparkle with new life. But what about all those other children – the ones who have not highly developed reading skills? They are the ones who haunt me.

A couple of years ago I called all our staff into my office and spread out our publications for that year. 'Tell me which of these books you are actually going to give to a real live child for Christmas', I said. Silence fell. As a result of the discussion which followed we decided to broaden the scope of our list, adding many more books which really *did* seem closer to children. These included such books as Eric Carle's *The Very Hungry Caterpillar*, Beverly Cleary's *Ramona the Pest*, the picture books of Michael Foreman, the novels of Honor Arundel, Joan Lingard, John Christopher and Nicholas Fisk, Raymond Brigg's *Father Christmas* – a favourite all over the world, incidentally. We added also other titles where the principal ingredient is a kind of robust enjoyment, still achieved with a high standard of creative skill, but more readily accessible than the purely literary book, which tends on the whole to be more intro-spective in appeal.

It proved a salutary lesson for all of us concerned with this list to sit down and really think that we were publishing for children, not for critics or teachers or librarians, but that we were producing books primarily for children. We began to be much, much more aware of the child whom the book was for than we had been before. But we are still all too sadly aware of the huge gulf between the child with reading problems and the child who can sit down and have his point of view transformed for life by reading a writer with the imagination of William Mayne. How we reach the other children is something that we just have to continue to think about.

I think the list now is better balanced, but I recognize that we still reach only the tip of the reading iceberg. No publisher can be all things to all men. It would be a mistake for us to attempt mass market publishing on a large scale because that is not our house style, and we would do it badly. I am proud of what we do publish, but I know we can't afford to be complacent, and that we must keep on remembering that the world of the child is not just the world of the child lucky enough to come from a stable home with good educational opportunities, but it is also the world of *Johnny-Come-Home*, the vagrant child, the illiterate child, the Bay City Rollers child – if only we could reach all these children with books which really do touch their lives. It does seem like an impossible dream, but at least one can keep trying and the cross-fertilization of ideas resulting from conferences like this is always valuable.

How shall I sum up? The current week's edition of the trade magazine, *The Bookseller*, has included two startling and paradoxical statements: one, that the first six months of 1975 showed an increase of 13 per cent over 1974's output in the same period – there had been so far 1,288 *new* children's books, which means that by the end of the year there would probably be a total of at least 2,750 new books, this in addition to the thousands of backlist titles already in print. In a period such as this, when we are all supposedly controlling our outputs to keep pace with cash and inflation problems, it seems incredible that the number of titles has actually *risen*. It is a lot of books. Are they the right books? On another page in the same issue of *The Bookseller* a leading county librarian was quoted as saying that Government instructions to reduce spending would very likely mean that current fiction and modern children's books would be either rare or nonexistent in public lending libraries for at least a decade. 'Mark my words', he says, 'the rot will set in this year.'

It is a dire prediction, and its implications are terribly serious for all of us who care about books, be it from the standpoint of the writer, the reader, or the publisher. We have survived dire predictions before, but it would be unrealistic not to accept that 1976 will be a very critical one indeed. Perhaps it will be no bad thing for publishers to be forced to look very hard at what they are doing, but it would be a sad day indeed if stringent economic conditions denied the writer and the publisher their opportunity to take risks, to be adventurous, to try to do something a little different.

In the hand of creative writers and artists, with vision and integrity, words and pictures can still be among the most potent and powerful influences in a child's life. If we are forced to play safe, to publish only that which will sell quickly and without financial risk, it will, ultimately, be the reader who will suffer – for the content of reading will cease to be the life force that it is now.

7 Learning to read, then reading

Helen Huus

Introduction

This topic has a double-barrelled theme – the knowing how and the doing. Much of the attention of teachers of young children is still focused on helping them acquire the basic skills necessary to deal with printed materials. *Which* skills depends upon the definition accepted for 'reading'. If reading is merely returning printed symbols to speech, the skills taught will be restricted to decoding, or those for word attack. If reading is acquiring and assimilating the author's meaning, then skills for doing so will be included in the teaching of how to read. If, in addition, reading is also evaluating and reacting to the material read, then skills of critical and creative reading are requisite.

Learning to read

Teachers

The importance of the teacher in the actual day-by-day teaching of reading has been reiterated in the literature, recently as a major conclusion in the Cooperative First Grade Reading Studies (Bond and Dykstra 1967). But thus far, what the teacher does to make the difference has not yet been isolated by research. My conjecture is that the better teachers (1) have specifically identified objectives, (2) know the activities and materials that help various individuals reach these objectives, (3) can organize the activities and materials into a sequence for teaching the skills (or at least enough of a sequence to know the next few steps), and (4) can tell when individual pupils have reached each goal. This implies a level of professional competency that allows a teacher to deal with individuals (perhaps within small groups) by using a continuing diagnostic approach.

Materials

In some ways, teaching how to read is easier than to keep readers reading, for experts and publishers are constantly preparing well-developed programmes, packaged in attractive form, to help a teacher guide pupils through the process of learning to read. For word attack or decoding skills, some special materials are devised for methods that begin with sight words, and others for a linguistic or phonetic analysis approach. (The very design of such material requires consummate skill – even Dr Seuss could not do much with fifty words; his popular *Cat in the Hat* has 223.)

For comprehension skills, a variety of material can be utilized, though some selections work better than others for teaching certain skills; for example, the evaluation of accuracy is more adapted to factual material than to fairy tales.

An example of specially prepared materials for adults is the series developed by the UNESCO Literacy Unit in Iran, which has designed separate booklets for men who work in the steel mills, workers in textile factories, farmers, mechanics and civil employees; for women, there are booklets on health, family planning, sewing and tailoring. Built into these materials is the known vocabulary that provides context clues for pronunciation, and a gradual progression of one lesson built upon the previous one. A newspaper for new literates is also published so that skills learned can be applied immediately.

While specific materials used for teaching how to read ought to be of interest, this does not necessarily mean, for children, using standard literary works. Some reading series have been criticized because of the poor literary quality of their content. Since some of the critics have had no practical experience in teaching reading, they fail to realize the sheer joy of recognizing familiar words or being able to figure out others and understand them, even when the selections are not wildly exciting or beautifully stated.

Furthermore, material for teaching how to read should be selected or devised to be adaptable to the task at hand. One does not hitch an American thoroughbred horse to a plough or run a Clydesdale or Percheron in the Kentucky Derby or at Epsom Downs! Neither does one usually weed a garden in an evening gown, though I must admit that sometimes today, blue jeans do go to a party. The same is true of reading materials – fitness for the purpose is important. Hence, I am not overly concerned when great literary works are omitted from books for teaching the skills of reading. And heaven forbid tampering with the author's version to force his artistic endeavour into a Procrustean bed of controlled vocabulary! Better to construct 'from scratch' interesting, catchy materials according to a specified formula, then later have pupils apply ideas learned to the literary material.

Method: reading versus literature
This raises, then, the question of how teaching reading is distinguished from teaching literature. Tiedt (1970) makes the following distinction:

> *The teaching of reading will focus on skills,* the teaching of the phoneme-grapheme relationships. It will move into the study of morphology or word forms as children learn to read these forms which are also presented in grammar instruction. *The teaching of literature, on the other hand, remains focused on ideas and the application of the writer's performance with words.*

However, the real distinction is not quite so clear-cut as first may seem. Actually, in her definition of teaching literature, Tiedt includes aspects that would be encompassed by some in a definition of reading comprehension, and the application of basic reading skills thus defined to literary materials would include interpretation, evaluation, and assimilation. The crux of the problem in using standard literary works for teaching how to read is the unstated assumption of a two-pronged purpose with material that may best be suited to one.

What reading literature will do for reading, without much direct teaching, is to increase the reader's exposure to a wide vocabulary that he may meet nowhere else. Where would most preschoolers learn *fetch*, except for Jack and Jill's fetching? Or what ten year old is likely to know about *cards* for carding wool, except through tales of pioneer days? And then there are the adults who thought the book entitled *Pride of Lions* was about proud animals! Literature also extends the experiences of a reader in time, in space, in depth of concept and in developing new concepts, and in stimulating him to rearrange his previous knowledge.

In addition, he is exposed to a variety of styles of writing, to characters that reflect human traits and foibles, and to exciting action and adventure. Literature helps him see himself in focus against a backdrop of other peoples and cultures, thus helping him come to terms with himself and consequently with others, to the enrichment of his living.

Lasser (1969) emphasizes the reader's reaction this way:

. . . nonetheless, soon after he is reading rather than learning to read, he can discover that recognition of the aptness of a word or an image or a figure of speech provides a more profound delight than merely the unconscious enjoyment of the entire work and contributes substantially to a conscious enjoyment of that work. The trained, sensitive reader responds with delight, knows why he does so, makes discriminating choices most of the time, and is increasingly willing to rely on his own judgment.

My plea, therefore, is for parallel strands of reading and literature classes in the school programme. Schools in the United States for children from five to twelve tend not to have a separate literature period, except for the daily reading aloud of a chapter from a book by the teacher, but this is not literature teaching. Schools for adolescents tend to separate the two, but the difference in purpose needs to be recognized more widely than it currently is, and the teaching adjusted accordingly.

– then reading

Goals
An ultimate goal of reading is its contribution to the quality of life of an individual and a society. Reading is important in a culture that requires an informed citizenry, that has a highly developed technology, that faces increased leisure time, and that has a rich heritage of accumulated wisdom. Reading also contributes to the individual's self-esteem, his enjoyment, his knowledge and his appreciation of a writer's skill. If reading is to do this, just learning how is not enough; the reader must continue reading throughout his lifetime. He must become so self-motivated that he continues to read after he leaves the classroom and the school.

What makes some become readers and others not? In an attempt to find out, Hansen (1969) developed a questionnaire and obtained information from forty-eight fourth graders who had differing attitudes towards reading. He found that home literary environment made:

. . . the only significant contribution to independent reading. Father's occupation and education as well as the child's test IQ showed no significant relation.

Factors he studied in the home literary environment included

'(1) availability of literary materials in the home, (2) amount of reading done with the child, (3) reading guidance and encouragement, and (4) parents as model reading examples'. He hypothesized that the most important factor was what parents did in and with the environment. In a subsequent analysis (Hansen 1973) his hypothesis held. He found:

> The one factor that stands out from all the others is the role of the parent in being involved with his child's reading activities. Working with homework; encouraging, helping select, and discussing his reading; reading to him; assistance in looking things up in dictionaries and encyclopedias; and setting reading goals were more important than the mere provision of materials.

Ranked low were parents as models and the availability of literary materials in the home. One parent, who scored high, began systematically to use the public library as soon as the child was born. Hansen then recommended that schools capitalize on these same factors to provide an easy transition. This would include: '. . . more reading aloud to groups, the provision of a wide variety and range of materials, a high individual expectation of each child with appropriate recognition of his success, and individual follow-up discussions (not stock book reports) of his recreational reading . . .'.

Sources

If teachers are to foster the reading of good books, then they need to know which these are. Fortunately, the children's sections of the national library associations, the Children's Book Council in the United States and the National Book League in England, the reading associations, and lists prepared by individuals like Nancy Larrick and Elaine Moss provide help for busy teachers. Journals like *The Horn Book* (585 Boylston Street, Boston, Massachusetts, 02116, USA), *Children's Literature in Education* (APS Publications Inc., 150 Fifth Avenue, New York, NY 10011, USA and CLE, 3 Elsynge Road, London SW18, England), and the new *Phaedrus: A Journal of Children's Literature Research* (Fairleigh Dickinson University, Madison, NJ, NJ 07940, USA) give background on authors and works and cite bibliographical references for further study. Granted, keeping up with books requires time and effort, but someone – either teacher, librarian, parent, or tutor – must know books well enough to recommend good ones to pupils, then compare reactions with them once the books are read.

Once a teacher knows the books, the next steps are to make them available, to bring books and pupils together, and to provide time to read and to share.

Availability

Fader's popular *Hooked on Books* (1968) reported that just making paperbacks available to juvenile delinquents was influential in getting them to read and to upgrade the quality of their reading. Availability is also the point in the 'Book Flood' project conducted by the New Zealand Council for Educational Research in two Auckland primary (elementary) schools, where the children are predominantly Polynesian-Maoris, Samoans and children from Niui and Cooke Islands. From 350 to 500 well-selected books are placed in each classroom, and the project attempts to find out the effect of this 'book flood' on the reading achievement of the children and on the attitude towards books and school by the children and their parents. After only six months a change in the attitude of the parents was noted, but no significant change in children's reading achievement. Since the project will continue for two years, additional reports will be forthcoming.

Starting personal libraries is the purpose of a 'Book Bank' developed by members of the New Haven (Connecticut) PTA Council. They received donations of reading materials which were sorted and renewed by volunteers, then given to disadvantaged children to keep for their own. Similarly, a Red Cross Bookmobile in Kansas City, Missouri, distributes to disadvantaged children paperback books for them to keep. Books are donated and occasionally publishers' oversupplies are purchased or received. When necessary, books are repaired by volunteers, and a retired children's librarian selects the books to go in the Bookmobile and thence to certain areas of the city on a regular schedule.

The RIF (Reading Is Fundamental) programme is now part of the US Right to Read Effort developed by the private sector under the direction of Margaret (Mrs Robert) McNamara. Its purpose is to motivate children to read by allowing them to choose and keep paperback books of interest. According to a recent report (McNamara 1975), 'RIF has distributed one and a half million books to about 275,000 children' since 1966, when this volunteer programme began. Young children are especially responsive, but all children guard their books carefully. For many who previously had few or no books in their homes, books are now becoming a part of their lives. One Pittsburgh teacher said school library circulation had doubled in the first few months after RIF began.

Interest can also be engendered by a 'paperback book swap', where children or adults trade paperbacks they no longer need, thus expanding the number of books available at no additional cost.

All these activities aim to make a variety of good books available to readers and to promote book ownership. These are not meant to supplant the libraries, both school and public, but to supplement them and to encourage their use.

Impact
Once books are available, bringing books and readers together is the next step. Reading to students (even in college) is a sure way to pique curiosity and capture interest. Notice the dead silence that accompanies a teacher's reading aloud or when the family has a read-aloud story time.

Enlisting the cooperation of parents and siblings is one way to encourage family reading. One nursery school in Palmerston North, New Zealand, sends home a story book with each child each afternoon along with the child's own notebook in which his reactions to the book are written by whoever reads the story to him. The teacher noted that some of the best reports were written by the eight-year-old sister of one of the children. These notebooks provide a daily link with the home and also serve as a ready record of stories each child has heard.

Helping students learn to choose their own books from among the many in a library entails more than just their knowing Dewey classifications. How to use the dust jacket information and to scan for reading difficulty are but two possibilities. One librarian tells the students to read a page, and if it contains more than three words he does not know (except for proper names), the book is probably too difficult for him. Students also can learn to use recommended lists and usually do so gratefully when they find these books are fun to read.

Library listening posts, where as many as six children can don earphones and listen to a taped story or poem, provide another means to connect pupils with books.

Roeder and Less (1973) list twenty-five 'techniques teachers have found to be most effective in encouraging students to read for their own enjoyment'. Included are book clubs, bulletin boards, library corners, reading to younger children, reading to the class, bringing

73

books from home, having a topic-of-the-month, pretending to sell or auction a book, reading a series or several books by one author, taping book sections for later identification, and 'above all' exuding enthusiasm. Another idea is building reading 'ladders', starting where the children are.

All these ideas call attention to specific books supposedly of interest to the intended audience. Such preselection accompanied by enthusiastic endorsement by one who has read the book does provide good bait; but unfortunately, even then, some get away.

Time

Once the book and the reader meet, what is then needed is time – time to read and time to share. Petre (1971) reports that in the State of Maryland, more than fifty elementary, middle and secondary schools have instituted a 'reading break', an uninterrupted thirty-five minutes when the school shuts down and everyone reads material he has selected for himself – students, teachers, the principal and the secretaries. Though the janitor was not mentioned, it is assumed that he, too, reads. Paperback books were placed throughout the schools, and bookswapping became 'epidemic'. One middle school principal reported a 50 per cent drop in discipline cases after the school began the programme, and in another, students complained their schedules were too tight to allow enough time to go to the library. A coach reported his students introduced him to some good sports books, and another teacher said she had seven books on her nightstand that students wanted her to read so that they could discuss them.

The desire to share books, whether through discussion or other means, is a natural outcome of interested readers. Role playing, dramatics, pictures, posters, murals, mobiles and collage are all creative alternatives to the book report. Often the resistance to a regular report is due to the fact that students have never received adequate help in learning to write an acceptable report. One teacher of eight year olds started by having pupils write the author and title, then 'Why I liked or did not like this book'. Later, other aspects like character development were added.

In my literature classes, students write a summary and an evaluation of books they read. Some write at a difficulty level appropriate for the pupils they teach or expect to teach, then place their files in the classroom. Pupils use the files when selecting their books, then add their comments and recommendations when they have finished a book. And what is this but a book report? Asking searching questions that require a synthesis and evaluation of ideas or making comparisons between books on similar topics are also ways of sharing that require a sure knowledge of the book's contents by teacher and pupil alike.

Availability, impact and time – these are the requisites for developing a life-long interest in reading.

Conclusion

Hallowell Bowser (1969), one-time general editor of *Saturday Review*, once wrote an editorial entitled, 'Books are not expendable'. If this be true, then the school's job, along with that of the home and other agencies in society, is to help students learn to read quickly and easily, while at the same time books of quality are being read to them at a level higher than they can read for themselves. Then, as they gain in reading skill and versatility, they can read ever more difficult books for themselves, thus making possible the lasting enjoyment and benefit that comes from contact with the best minds of this or any generation. And who knows what a 'Reading Society' could accomplish? It would be gratifying to have the chance to find out!

References

BOND, G. and DYKSTRA, R. (1967) The cooperative research program in first grade reading instruction *Reading Research Quarterly* 2, 5–142

BOWSER, H. (1969) Books are not expendable *Saturday Review* 7 June 22

CRISCUOLO, N. P. (1970) Involvement: key to successful reading programs *Elementary English* 47, 392–3

FADER, D. N. and McNEIL, E. B. (1968) *Hooked on Books* Pergamon

HANSEN, H. S. (1969) The impact of the home literary environment on reading attitude *Elementary English* 46, 17–24

HANSEN, H. S. (1973) The home literary environment – a follow-up report *Elementary English* 50, 97–8, 122

LASSER, M. L. (1969) Literature in the elementary school: a view from above *Elementary English* 46, 639–44

McNAMARA, M. (1975) 'Reading is fundamental' in J. S. Nemeth (Ed) *Reading RX: Better Teachers, Better Supervisors, Better Programs* Newark, Delaware: International Reading Association

PETRE, R. M. (1971) Reading breaks make it in Maryland *Journal of Reading* 15, 191–4

ROEDER, H. E. and LESS, N. (1973) Twenty-five teacher-tested ways to encourage voluntary reading *The Reading Teacher* 27, 48–50

TIEDT, I. M. (1970) Planning an elementary school literature program *Elementary English* 47, 193–208

8   Books in schools – hopes and realities

Nicholas Tucker

My subject is books in schools – hopes and realities. I will not say too much about the hopes because I expect people are fairly familiar with all the many claims that have been made about literature in the past. The Plowden Report (DES 1967) said, 'As children listen to stories they may be choosing their future and the values that will dominate it', and that claim is fairly mild compared with other claims I have seen made for literature. Frank Whitehead, in his book *The Disappearing Dais*, somehow equates reading books with good physical health in childhood. I, personally, find all these claims rather inflated; I think books can have an enormous effect upon children and they can also have absolutely no effect at all, and I slightly distrust the new evangelism that makes books religious texts and visiting the library rather like going to Church on Sunday! But if those are the hopes, I suppose I should say a little about the reality.

First of all, it would not be at all hard for me to describe how badly provided many schools are with books. There is always a temptation in this country to think that once an old-fashioned practice has been exposed in education it automatically disappears; in fact, it doesn't. It disappears in the progressive schools, but it lingers on in the others, and I expect if you visited a cross-section of schools today you would find a complete conspectus of teaching methods going back to the latter part of the nineteenth century. Thus, there are some schools I know where Readers are still given out as literature, or where books are read around the class paragraph by paragraph, and there are many more such horror stories. This is not just the routine teacher-bashing that one gets at every educational conference – it is absolutely true and it has been regretted in every single Government report that mentions reading from Plowden to Bullock, all stressing the need to increase the amount and range of children's voluntary reading. But I expect this is common knowledge.

So what I would rather do is take a situation where a school has taken some of this to heart and become more progressive, and see what has happened. When I say 'progressive', I mean it has actually invested in new books and cast out its *Travels with a Donkey*, *The Last of the Mohicans*, *Lorna Doone* and so many others of those ponderous nineteenth-century books that go under the name of 'classics'. One book recommended as a class reader in this school was *The Owl Service* by Alan Garner. Well, *The Owl Service* must be one of the most renowned books written for children since the war; it won the Guardian and the Carnegie Awards, and it is almost synonymous, I would have thought, with the new breakthrough in children's literature. It deals with adolescence, love and betrayal, all in one brilliantly conceived pattern. It is recommended by Aidan Chambers in his book *The Reluctant Reader* where *The Owl Service* comes under the heading of 'Five-Star Books'. This must be a fairly serious recommendation because Aidan Chambers includes some of his own books under this category!

I had a mature student who was teaching at this school ask children what they thought of *The Owl Service*. These were thirteen year olds in a comprehensive school in a fairly all-right social area in Sussex. Nevertheless, when she came back with some of the reports from her class on *The Owl Service*, they were extremely discouraging. She asked various questions such as, 'What do you like about the book?' The answer – 'The cover.' 'What do you dislike about the book?' — 'Reading it.' And so on; you would not have thought they were referring to a book that had had such critical acclaim. So I thought perhaps thirteen was a bit young for the book, regardless of the fact that children of this age were already reading things like *Skinhead* and *Chopper*. So I recommended another book with an age range of nine-fourteen: *Children on the Oregon Trail* by the Dutch author A. Rutgers van der Loeff. I would just say a little about the book: it is set in America in the last century, about a pioneer family going West with their caravan. The parents die, and the oldest boy takes on the appalling responsibility of going on independently with his brother and sister. They get separated from the main caravan trail, go through frightful privation, starvation, flood, are raided by Indians and literally arrive at their destination more dead than alive – and this is based on a true story. I read it and found it an exciting and sometimes a painful experience. But here are some of a young audience's responses to it. 'What do you like about this book?' — 'The end.' 'It was boring and not exciting enough.' 'Nothing was really happening.' (And this of a book literally packed with incidents.) 'How could you have improved this book?' — 'They could have had a gun fight with Indians.' 'It would have been better if he'd made it more up to date.' 'I didn't really like most of the bits in the book because it was nothing about people falling in love, etc.' 'I can't stand books that go on and on about nothing. This book was really like that, but otherwise it was very good.' Another comment – 'It should be about a modern family, not about something that happened a hundred years ago.'

Now you must take my word for it that I am not just selecting the bad and funny answers – these answers were completely typical. I will agree that this was a student-teacher, but she was a good student. A more experienced English teacher may have done things differently, but we have got to find books that work with all sorts of teachers, not the very gifted ones who can get anything through to their pupils. The basic point that came out to me was that this school was ill-advised to give these particular books to the children. Many of the best books that are written for children are in fact written for a tiny minority, so all those slogans such as 'A must for every nine year old' are often total nonsense. This year a children's book in America won three of the big awards. It is called *M. C. Higgins The Great*. It has now been published over here and I read it the other day. I will bet my bottom dollar, or any other hard currency, that it is totally unreadable for 99 per cent of children. Now, I would absolutely defend Carnegie and Newbery's right to give it the award: it probably is the *best* children's book put on the market this year. It is a very interesting and good achievement, but the trouble is that that sort of book is recommended to us to try out on all children, with very little idea that it is really written for a minority of very bookish children. It is almost as if the *Daily Mirror* had a holiday reading section in August that said 'Why not try Proust on your beach holiday this year?' or 'Dip into James Joyce and have a bit of a giggle.' Now as far as adult reading is concerned, I think we recognize that there are very different levels of achievement that we can expect from fluent readers. As far as children's reading is concerned, we do not, and therefore I think there is this vast confusion and people like my student can take two very good books that have been very well reviewed and are in the right age bracket and yet come a cropper.

What is the way out of this? Well, I think it is to be a little bit more realistic. I think immature readers will sometimes go for literature which reflects this immaturity – books sometimes referred to as of 'high interest and low vocabulary'. Another possibility is to provide more bookshops in schools; there are now two thousand school bookshops and this gives children and, of course, their parents and the staff, a chance to go and root among the paperbacks to find something to read for themselves which they have chosen for themselves. But I do not want you to think that I am now saying that the clever bookish children can read the best books and we should look for 'good rubbish' for the other sort of children. I am not saying anything of the sort.

Here is another comment: we asked these children 'What sort of books do you like reading?' Well, some of them put things like *Slade* in *Flame* and other books about current pop singers. But three of them mentioned one modern classic; as one wrote 'I like to read horror stories like a book we read in the middle school – it was about some children who had a plane crash and were stranded on an island without any grown ups.' Of course, this is William Golding's *Lord of the Flies*. Now that is obviously a classic novel, and yet it is a book that can get through to children of all sorts. Another book mentioned was *Charlotte's Web*, 'because it isn't serious like the Oregon Trail. And you know Charlotte will save Wilbur's life. It is seeing how she does it that makes it so interesting.' *Charlotte's Web*, by E. B. White, is a very good book and about something serious. So you see what I am arguing for is as follows. There are some books that are good but hard and will never be popular with a majority of children. There are some books that are extremely good and have a pretty good chance of interesting lots of children. And the question, I think, for teachers is how do we find out which books these are.

Of course, one can never be sure, but there are certain steps one can take towards making better choices. For example, we can learn from other practitioners who pass on relevant information. This has been done in magazines like *The Use of English* and *Children's Literature in Education*, where there are always lists of books suggested by practising teachers that might have a chance of going down well. One can also, of course, talk to other colleagues. You can also read books on children's literature such as Aidan Chambers' *The Reluctant Reader* for some good advice. But if you really want to take this seriously and get books that have a good chance of interesting your children, I personally think this is best done at a local level. That is the trouble with reading articles about what your class should read: it could be that each area has local tastes. And also you have to be very up to date, because if there's a paperback out next week or a television programme or film based on a book, there might be a case of instant popularity that will catch any preconceived book lists rather on the hop. I would also have suggested you convene a course on current children's literature at your local teachers' centre, but of course teachers' centres are being cut back at the minute and courses will not be quite so numerous as they used to be. I wonder what you think of the idea of teachers at the local level, perhaps through their LEA, having some kind of bush telegraph service? Perhaps every term heads of departments could send round lists, mentioning titles of books they have found to be fairly successful, and this list could be changed every term to be kept up to date.

If you do not do this, then I think you are really up against quite a difficult problem because, like some of you, I review children's books and it really is very difficult as a reviewer to fulfil your responsibilities to the book, and at the same time try to guess how many children will like it. If you really take reading seriously, once you have taught children to read, they must have something they really enjoy and I am afraid it is just not good enough reading *The Times Literary Supplement* or any book about children's literature and then going out and buying a handful and ending up with *The Owl Service* and *Children on the Oregon Trail*. If you want to do better than that then I think there is absolutely no substitute for local information on current literary taste. And if we have that sort of thing it would be very interesting to see, for example, if Manchester children like books that are, in some ways, different from those preferred by London children.

Reference

DES (1967) *Children and their Primary Schools* (Plowden Report) HMSO

9 Books in schools – curriculum problems

Ronald W. Johnson

I intend to tackle my brief by following on from Nicholas Tucker's paper, extending the discussion on fiction, and finally spending a little time on the use of non-fiction books.

There are three particular ingredients which I hope to be able to indentify:

1 The contribution which reading can make towards personal development; and this will arise out of the consideration of fiction.
2 Reading development as part of a total language arts programme; and this I hope to illustrate when dealing with non-fiction.
3 I shall be keeping an eye on the problems of the teacher.

In considering fiction, we are, I think, as far as the teacher is concerned, in an area of great uncertainty. This uncertainty is reflected in:

1 The haphazard collections to be found in many schools. Not only is the quality inadequate for the school, but the state and the quality often leaves much to be desired. Frequently the provision varies even within the school, from class to class. The variety of themes within the collections is often limited and there are similar deficiencies in the range of interest ages and the range of readability levels. Rarely are the book collections supplemented by extracts, short stories, or printed versions of the children's own writing.
2 The lack of an explicit corporate policy for the organization, deployment and exploitation of the available resources: central collections, class-based collections, use of fiction in school and policy on out-of-school use, links with other specialist agencies such as branch libraries and contact with qualified children's librarians.

3 The total time allocated to this kind of reading and the kind of time. I see the teacher as being, amongst other things, a provider, not only of resources but also of time and opportunity. By relegating the activity to odd moments the effect is to undervalue it. Worse still, to transmit an attitude that it is an activity reserved only for those occasions when the real work is done and it is not worth starting something else, is to devalue the activity in the eyes of the children.

4 The lack of knowledge on the part of the teacher of what is available, apart from the well-known children's classics. When I am working with much smaller and much less sophisticated groups than today's audience I often at this stage put things to the test by allowing a couple of minutes to jot down a selection of, say, ten modern stories for children – and their authors!

These kinds of shortcomings are so prevalent at individual ages and stages that there is almost no hope of finding schools which have a continuous developmental programme for fiction in education. This suggests that we are unsure of the gains to be had from significantly, if not substantially, including this kind of reading in the total reading curriculum.

I do not want to go exhaustively into all the reasons for this state of affairs. But I do want to concentrate on one, and that one may serve to bring other reasons to a level of conscious awareness. And in making my point, I am, of course, making my plea.

The aspect I want to concentrate on is the historical view of the school curriculum, which is that it should be functional, utilitarian, and concerned with performance; the kind of performance that is measurable. Everything, even stories, must serve a greater purpose.

I have a children's book at home called *Favourite Stories for the Young*. It was published before the turn of the century and presented to a favoured child at a school which still very much exists in my county. The first story is entitled *Upwards and Downwards* and beneath the title is a quotation from Proverbs XIII, 4:

The soul of the sluggard desireth, and hath nothing; but the soul of the diligent shall be made fat.

And then the story begins:

'Good-bye, Ellie dear – bless you!' cried Willie Deane, with a choking voice, as he embraced his little blind sister again and again at the gloomy door of the poor-house.

I had better not go on because I see that many of you are already becoming distressed!

The deep roots of the system are to be located in the productivity deal which Robert Lowe made with the House of Commons in 1862. Introducing the Revised Code which laid the foundations of Payment by Results (cash in return for performance) he said:

I cannot promise the House that this system will be an economical one, and I cannot promise that it will be an efficient one, but I can promise that it shall be either one or the other. If it is not cheap, it shall be efficient; if it is not efficient, it shall be cheap.

Value for money is, of course, quite an acceptable idea. It is just a question of deciding what is valuable.

You will remember that H. G. Wells's Mr Polly went to such a school. He went to the National School at six and finally emerged from 'the shadow of the valley of education' at fourteen. By that time 'vast regions had been devastated by the school curriculum' but at thirteen he suddenly discovered reading and its joys. One suspects that through his imagination and his fantasies he kept his sanity. As Peter Dickinson said, 'myth' is necessary to our sanity – we cannot live by reason alone. But returning to Mr Polly:

He would read tales about hunters and explorers, and imagine himself riding mustangs as fleet as the wind across the prairies of Western America, or coming as a conquering and adored white man into the swarming villages of Central Africa. He shot bears with a revolver – a cigarette in the other hand – and made a necklace of their teeth and claws for the chief's beautiful young daughter. Also, he killed a lion with a pointed stake, stabbing through the beast's heart as it stood over him.

He thought it would be splendid to be a diver and go down into the dark green mysteries of the sea.

He led stormers against wellnigh impregnable forts, and died on the ramparts at the moment of victory (his grave was watered by a nation's tears).

He rammed and torpedoed ships, one against ten.

He was beloved by queens in barbaric lands, and reconciled

whole nations to the Christian faith.

He was martyred, and took it very calmly and beautifully – but only once or twice after the Revivalist week. It did not become a habit with him.

He explored the Amazon, and found, newly exposed by the fall of a great tree, a rock of gold.

Engaged in these pursuits he would neglect the work immediately in hand, sitting somewhere slackly on the form and projecting himself in a manner tempting to a schoolmaster with a cane . . . And twice he had books confiscated.

But in spite of his schooling, deep in the darkness, deep in his being, there crawled a persuasion that there was somewhere – a delight, magically inaccessible perhaps, but somewhere, there were pure and easy and joyous states of body and mind. Poor Polly junior! As far as his teacher was concerned reading was not for that kind of purpose; it was about *performance*, not product.

There is a story from about this period (which I cannot vouch for) about a frightened child who was called before the government inspector to read. She began, but in a state of terror she dropped the book – but still read on to the end of the page.

Because I think we worry incessantly about visible productivity, I liked a remark I heard in a radio interview with Clive Jenkins. He said: 'I find the notion that no one could be said to be working hard unless the sweat is dropping from his brow – inelegant.' And again, in preparing an Open University radio programme about children and their fiction, Helen Cresswell said that it was a pity that we did not have some kind of apparatus to fit on to the heads of children who are reading story books, so that a bulb lights up to reassure us that *activity* is taking place.

It is a pity that we need this kind of reassurance: it is partly due to other curriculum pressures and partly to the historical legacy which from time to time reactivates our primitive instincts. Just as the children in *Lord of the Flies* demonstrated how thin is the veneer of civilization, so I suspect we are prone to slip back to the primeval stages of education when, from time to time, we are astounded, perhaps a little bewildered and sometimes quite frightened at the distance we have travelled from the original swamp.

My justification for including this kind of reading in the reading curriculum would not be in the form of a list of objectives – although I have seen such lists and they can be helpful to those who are uncertain – rather it would be in an attempt to describe the reading activity. It is creative reading, the products of which are unique to the individual, and it calls for a personal response. It is the opportunity for reflective thinking of an exploratory nature, which is self-generated rather than imposed. It does, naturally, for us what we often spend a lot of time on trying to contrive and engineer.

The role of the knowledgeable reading teacher may be described as that of a sensitive entrepreneur. The analogy which comes to mind is that of the expert grower, the gardener who knows the seasons and the structure of his soil, who knows the likes, the dislikes, the weaknesses, the strengths, the habits of his plants. And when we look at the product – the full bloom – we sense not only the knowledge, the skill, but some of the commitment and some of the affection which has gone into its creation.

I am saying the obvious:

that the teacher must provide materials, time, opportunity
that the teacher must know the child
that the teacher must be ready to match them both when required
that the teacher must be alert for growth points
that the teacher must infect the child with his own enthusiasm.

This is teaching with sensitivity, with elegance, at a level of excellence – and when you see it, it is a joyful experience.

My final section concerns books of non-fiction – books for information (as if there were in fiction no information!). The distinction is unfortunate if it implies that one category is for *enjoyment* and the other for *labour*. Children are great collectors – and there seems no reason why the collection of information should not be a satisfying experience. In general, however, it seems to me that if we are only at the foothills of fiction, we have probably got stuck on a plateau with regard to non-fiction.

Our collections are more or less adequate (by comparison). The range, the quantity, the quality – in some cases the organization and deployment – have all made strides in recent years. But we ought to remind ourselves of the part of the Presidential Address which mentions bias, often unintentional, and misrepresentation – and there is therefore work to be done on the content. It occurs to me that there is scope for comparative reading. Older children might survey and evaluate some of the texts for younger children.

But accepting for the moment what we have got, I want to suggest that we often lack the finesse, the expertise in using non-fiction books, and that the children's work is consequently threadbare and purposeless. Nowhere is this more evident than in the use of books as resources for 'topic', 'thematic', 'centre of interest', 'integrated study' approaches in the middle years.

Go back to the historical legacy we once had of 'the talking teacher and the listening child'; we quite often now have an expectation based upon 'the reading child and the writing child'. In the first, the teacher is all too evident; in the second she is nowhere in evidence; in both situations there is often no communication.

In talking about fiction I have suggested that teacher intervention should be cautious and sensitively opportunist, for it could be an intrusion. I am now suggesting that teacher intervention should be more planned and more positive. I can illustrate my point by suggesting an improved approach to topic or thematic work:

Stage 1 Task definition – much of the work founders at this earliest stage. More often than not, the task is so ill defined, so broad (and incidentally purposeless), that it is still-born. What is needed at this stage is much discussion between teacher/ child or teacher/child groups to define the task, so that it is manageable and purposes are identified.

Stage 2 Identification of resource material – books will play an unimportant part in comparison with other forms of print, tape, slides and human beings. At this point, the range of possible print will need to be surveyed and selection made in the light of defined purpose, informed judgments, bringing appropriate skills into play.

Stage 3 Discussion on the final product – handwritten book or booklet, wall display, illustration, diagrams, charts. What is the target audience – this group, this class, this school, some other audience? Planning the production.

Stage 4 Research and record.

Stage 5 Polished production and evaluation; published perfection.

Perhaps, in that rather sketchy account you may see how all the language arts are *essentially* brought into play.

Finally, our aim is to create readers – we shall do this by helping our 'apprentices' to become *confident* with print – therefore the need to be skilful is important; and to become *comfortable* with print –

therefore the quality of the experience is important. And as they grow in skill and experience they will, hopefully, become increasingly discriminating in their choice of reading material.

Part 2
Beginning reading

10 Oral language and the development of reading

Gordon Wells and Bridie Raban

Reading, like listening, is a form of language behaviour; discussion of how children should be taught to read should therefore be conducted, we believe, against a background of understanding of the form of language and of how it is used in interpersonal communication. Work on linguistic form – phonology/graphology, syntax and semantics – has already had its impact on the initial teaching of reading, but much less attention has so far been paid to the communicative function of language. Whether spoken or written, language is essentially a code for communicating meanings between individuals who share certain beliefs and values about the social and physical world in which they live. It will be helpful, therefore, to start with a consideration of the way in which interpersonal linguistic communication typically occurs.

As the accompanying diagram (Figure 1 on page 92) shows, communication takes place in a situation which contains a sender, a receiver and a third element which forms the content of the communication. Although the objects and events that surround the participants may be referred to in the utterances that occur, the third element of the situation is just as likely to be found in a different time or place or in the abstract world of hypothetical or imaginary events. What is important about the situation, therefore, is that it is actually brought into being by the act of communication, and that its nature is defined by the meanings that are exchanged within it. In speech, this process of definition is usually negotiated as a conversation proceeds. In written language the process is more one-sided, though, as we shall see, the receiver's contribution is not insignificant, even in the written form.

In the following discussion, we shall consider only the sending and receiving of a single utterance. But this can be taken as representative, as long as it is remembered that the person who is the

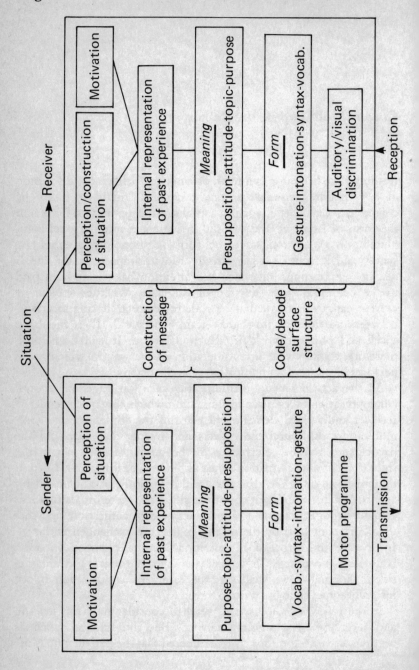

Figure 1   A model of the communication situation

receiver will subsequently have the opportunity to be the sender of a further utterance, and that the way in which the processes to be described apply in the case of a specific utterance will depend, in part, on the place of that utterance within the larger conversational context.

An utterance originates in the current state of motivation of the sender, which requires him to interact with another person in order to achieve whatever purpose he has in mind. This purpose is, of course, related to the situation as he perceives it, and both purpose and perception of the situation are dependent on the internalized model of the world that the sender has gradually built up on the basis of his past experience. Drawing upon what is relevant of this past experience, the sender formulates a 'meaning intention' which he wishes to be understood by the receiver. This meaning intention has three major components: a *purpose* that he wishes his communication to achieve in relation to the receiver; a *topic* to which his communication refers; and his *attitudes* both to the receiver and to the topic. The sender also *presupposes* knowledge and attitudes in his receiver which he can take for granted, both as a result of what he knows about him and in the light of any preceding conversation. As a result, the message that he codes is formulated to provide that information which he judges will most help the receiver to arrive at his meaning intention at this particular point in time. If the message is to be communicated linguistically, it is then coded by the sender selecting, from the resources available to him, those lexical items, syntactic structures and intonation patterns that are most appropriate for the message. The resulting plan for an utterance is finally transmitted by the appropriate motor acts of speaking.

This schematic account of the production of an utterance corresponds to a top-to-bottom progress through the label *Sender* in the diagram. It might therefore be expected that the reception of an utterance would merely require the receiver to reverse this progress and to proceed in a bottom-to-top direction in order to achieve comprehension. Although this is how comprehension has often been viewed in the past, the truth of the matter is very different, as recent research has shown (Bruner 1974; Bransford and McCarrell 1974; Wells 1976). Being the receiver of an utterance is, in fact, quite like being the sender, for the aim of the receiver is also to construct a message – the message that he judges the sender to intend.

In doing this he draws upon a number of sources of information. Firstly, his own past experience and current motivation lead him to perceive the situation in a certain way, thus predisposing him to expect messages with certain purposes and topics rather than others. Secondly, nonverbal information from the situation and shared information, built up during preceding conversation, may also be available, providing further expectations about the message to be received. Finally, the utterance itself has its own internal structure which allows quite precise expectations to be set up and verified in terms of the sequence of linguistic elements of which it is made up. These various sources of information have then to be compared until a match is achieved and understanding is reached.

The essential point to be made, therefore, is that comprehension of an utterance is an active process of 'meaning construction', which involves an interaction between the linguistic cues provided by the sender and the expectations that the receiver can derive from various sources and bring to bear in making sense of those cues. The balance between linguistic cues and the expectations that the receiver brings may vary, but both are always necessary.

This discussion of linguistic communication has been about speaking and listening, but it applies just as much to writing and reading. There are, of course, differences in the sensory modalities most concerned and in the typical contexts, content and form of the messages communicated through written language. But in reading, as in listening, the task of the receiver is to utilize all the available information in predicting and matching linguistic cues with these predictions, in order to construct the message he judges to have been intended by the sender. The same knowledge of the world and of the semantic and syntactic organization of language are drawn upon in both conditions (Goodman 1967; Kolers 1970; Smith 1971).

Given the close similarity between listening and reading, it would be expected that skill in the former would be related to skill in the latter. This is, indeed, the expectation on which the 'language experience' approach is based. However, although this expectation has proved correct for children aged nine and upwards, a number of studies have failed to find a correlation with somewhat younger children (five to eight years) either in England (Francis 1974) or in the United States (Strickland 1962). Ignoring the possibility that this may have resulted from the selection of unsatisfactory measures to assess the two receptive skills, two explanations might be advanced for this initially unexpected finding. Firstly, there may have been a mismatch, for the children concerned, between their oral language and the written language of the early reading texts and materials. This problem is gradually becoming less serious as there is now a much greater concern on the part of both teachers and publishers to ensure that the books and other material presented to children in the early stages of learning to read are developed from, or conform to, the language that the children habitually speak and listen to.

The second possible explanation, which is of greater theoretical and practical significance, is that the usefulness of the knowledge and strategies that the children have acquired in relation to oral language may be overshadowed, in the early stages of learning to read, by the difficulties experienced in acquiring certain new skills specific to the visual representation of a text. Furthermore, these difficulties may be increased by the method of instruction employed.

Clearly, some of the orientation and skills that a child has to acquire in order to be able to reconstruct the writer's meaning from a printed text are not very closely related to the skills he already has with regard to spoken language. For example, unless the child has already had pleasurable experiences of hearing stories read aloud from books, he may have little incentive to cope with a new and little-understood activity. Learning to read is also more likely to be attended by failure and punishment than the acquisition of speech. Related to lack of motivation is a lack of understanding of what reading is about. Children from homes where literacy is valued will probably already have had experience of being read to and will know that books 'tell you what to say'. But for a large majority of children there is little understanding of what the reader has to do, or of the terminology for talking about the process of reading (Reid 1966; Downing 1969), and in many cases the teacher's explanation does little to dispel the 'cognitive confusion and lack of system' which Vernon (1957) found to be 'the fundamental and basic characteristic of reading disability'. In addition to a general understanding of what it is to read, there are also a number of specific skills to be mastered:

1 Orientation to the conventions of visual presentation of the text. This includes the left to right, top to bottom direction of reading and the more specific orientation of individual letters.
2 Visual discrimination of abstract symbols. Very few children lack the ability to make fine visual discriminations in relation to concrete objects, but the distinctive features that distinguish letters from each other (e.g. 'b', 'd', 'p') or those that are to be treated as functionally equivalent (e.g. a, *a*, A) are much more arbitrary. The development of these discriminating skills will be greatly assisted by a clear understanding of the function of the

symbols and by appropriate experience of meaningful contrasts between them (Smith 1971).

3 Matching visual and auditory information. In an alphabetic writing system like English, the written words are spatially ordered sequences of letters which bear a systematic relation to the temporal sequence of sounds in speech. As well as having to learn to discriminate both letters and sounds, the child also has to learn to match them, first at the level of word and morpheme and then at the level of phoneme-grapheme correspondence. The complex spelling patterns of English do not make this latter task an easy one.

However, although these contributory skills do present new and rather abstract tasks, where there is strong motivation and an understanding of the major purposes of reading, the general strategies that the child uses for reconstructing spoken messages should, when applied to suitably designed materials, allow him to acquire these skills without too much difficulty. The way in which the activity of reading is presented to the child by the teacher will obviously play an important part: where the emphasis throughout is on constructing a meaning, and the child is encouraged to 'guess' on the basis of context, and then check his guess against visual cues provided by the text, this will be helpful; too great a concentration on 'skills' in isolation fragments the text and isolates language into highly abtract units. Furthermore, where there is a premium on correct vocal response to the words on the page and incorrect guesses are treated only as errors and signs of failure, the child will be given little encouragement to utilize the knowledge he has as a listener in making intelligent guesses, and may develop strategies that will impede his progress towards fluent reading.

In sum, we would argue that texts and methods of instruction that aim to build upon the child's oral command of language, by pointing up the similarities in form between writing and speech, will be even more successful if they are embedded in the sort of context of 'meaning making' that characterizes spoken communication. Books contain messages from writers, who are trying to communicate. Writers play their part by offering those linguistic, and often also pictorial, cues that will help the reader to reconstruct their messages: children learning to read should be encouraged to approach their task of discovering those messages in the same active and constructive way as they have already been successfully following in their listening for several years before coming to school. How this is to be achieved is a matter for each teacher to decide for each individual child. Given the wide variation between children in motivation, ability and preferred learning styles, there is no reason to suppose that there could be any one programme of instruction that would meet the needs of all the children in any one class. What is required therefore is, within the framework outlined above, an increased understanding of the interaction between the various factors that influence the acquisition of reading skills, so that teachers will be better able to design learning programmes that are optimally suited to meeting the needs of specific individuals.

References

BRANSFORD, J. D. and McCARRELL, J. S. (1974) 'A sketch of a cognitive approach to comprehension' in W. B. Weiner and D. S. Palermo (Eds) *Cognition and the Symbolic Process* Hillsdale, New Jersey: Lawrence Erlbaum Associates

BRUNER, J. S. (1974) *Beyond the Information Given* George Allen and Unwin

DOWNING, J. (1969) How children think about reading *The Reading Teacher* 23 217–30

FRANCIS, H. (1974) Social background, speech and learning to read *British Journal of Educational Psychology* 44 290–9

GOODMAN, K. (1967) Reading: a psycholinguistic guessing game *Journal of the Reading Specialist* 4 112–35

KOLERS, P. (1970) 'Three stages of reading' in H. Levine and J. Williams (Eds) *Basic Studies in Reading* New York: Basic Books

REID, J. F. (1966) Learning to think about reading *Educational Research* 9 56–62

SMITH, F. (1971) *Understanding Reading* New York: Holt, Rinehart and Winston

STRICKLAND, R. G. (1962) The language of elementary school children *Bulletin of the School of Education, Indiana University* 38, No. 4

VERNON, M. D. (1957) *Backwardness in Reading* Cambridge University Press

WELLS, C. G. (1976) Comprehension: what it means to understand *English in Education* (in press)

D

11 The development of prereading procedures based upon the reading of rebus material

Kenneth R. Jones

The Bullock Committee (DES 1975), in its analysis of current practice in teaching the early stages of reading to six year olds, reports that 35.4 per cent of teachers in the sample made use of prereading exercises. In those classes which were deliberately vertically grouped, the prereading exercises were used by 61.2 per cent of teachers, and in classes which were not vertically grouped, by 21.2 per cent of teachers. The difference is significant at or beyond the .05 level and it is suggested that the difference can be accounted for by the fact that only the vertically grouped classes would contain reception-stage children (pages 372–5).

There is acknowledgment of the fact that it is not easy to provide a concise definition for the term 'prereading exercises' but the following definition is given: 'Exercises and activities designed to help children acquire the generalized learning sets which provide the essential bases for reading.' (page 592). Earlier in the report (page 101) there is acknowledgment of the fact that the ability to read depends upon adequate vision and that visual perception is dependent for its development on the experience the child gets in exploring, identifying and manipulating a wide variety of objects and shapes.

The evidence relating to the provision of specific training in visual perception is said to be inconclusive and to suggest on balance that such training would appear to be of value only to those children who have had a limited range of perceptual experience.

The Committee suggests that if perceptual learning is thought to be necessary, it should consist of activities which help the child to respond to form, orientation and directionality and provide practice in systematic visual tracking. The suggested activities amount to no more than drawing, tracing, copying, matching, sequencing, tessellating and constructing which are said to be the stock-in-trade of the nursery and infant school. No details of techniques, practices and sequences currently in use are provided and there is no statement of objectives which might be suggested for the nursery or reception-class teacher.

It is only possible to say that in some kind of generalized way, teachers of very young children do provide prereading experience – and it can be argued that very often this prereading experience does not relate directly to the task of reading. It is not surprising in these circumstances that children can successfully complete prereading exercises, particularly in visual perception, and yet still encounter difficulties when faced with the task of learning to read.

The particular difficulties encountered by children beginning reading surround their orientation to the task of communication. Some of the difficulties which may be listed are:

1 recognizing the function of a symbol
2 matching spoken language to printed symbols
3 matching word order to symbol order
4 conforming with the left-right, down-the-page and page-to-page conventions of reading
5 deriving feedback which is relevant to comprehension rather than utterance
6 deriving feedback which is intrinsic to the act rather than adult-dependent.

The *Peabody Rebus Reading Program* (Woodcock *et al* 1969) contains elements which suggest that some of the difficulties may be overcome before the further problem of decoding is encountered.

The programme is said to be a unique one, which introduces children to reading by first allowing them to learn a vocabulary of rebuses in the place of spelled words. A rebus is defined as being a symbol or a picture which represents an entire word in contrast to letters which represent sounds. A rebus may be pictorial, geometric, or completely abstract.

The complete *Peabody Rebus Reading Program* consists of three *Introducing Reading* workbooks and two readers. The first of the workbooks represents a complete readiness programme which is compatible with any other teaching method used at the stage of beginning reading. When the complete programme is used the child's reading vocabulary is developed to a total of 172 words, 122 of which occur in traditional orthography. Twenty-nine of the t.o. words are learned through the application of phonic principles.

By completion of the first *Introducing Reading* workbook it is claimed that the child will have developed a rebus vocabulary of thirty-five words and the following skills:

1 the normal left-to-right, down-the-page, and page-to-page conventions of reading
2 the awareness that words are the basic units of language and that sentences are combinations of words
3 the use of pictorial and textual context clues in word perception
4 the ability to read a wide variety of sentence structures
5 comprehension skills, including the awareness that the purpose of reading is to interpret and react to what is read
6 workbook and test-taking skills, including procedures for answering matching, multiple-choice, yes/no and completion-type questions
7 the ability to work independently for short periods of time without direct teacher supervision.

Each page in the programmed workbook is divided into four frames and each frame presents a reading task which requires interpretation and subsequent selection of an answer from two or three possible responses. To make a response, the child moistens the tip of a pencil eraser on a wet cloth or sponge and rubs the eraser across the response area beneath the selected answer. If the selected answer is correct, the ink in the response area turns green; if the selected answer is wrong the ink turns red. The child is taught that green means 'Go – go on to the next frame' and that red means 'Stop – do the frame again'. The precise shades used were selected following an evaluation of the shades most easy for colour-blind subjects to discriminate.

The Peabody readiness programme was used in Bristol in a controlled experiment with seventy-two preschool children who were attending local playgroups. Each child was allocated at random to one of three groups as follows:

1 Rebus group   Mean age 52.6 months
2 Language Kit group   Mean age 50.6 months
3 Control group   Mean age 52.4 months

There were equal numbers of children and of boys and girls in each group.

Playgroup leaders acted as teachers during the experimental period of six weeks and received two hours of instruction per week throughout the experiment. The children received experience appropriate to their group for three periods of twenty minutes each per week for the period of six weeks:

Group 1   using rebus materials
Group 2   using Peabody Language Development Kit (Level 'P')
Group 3   normal playgroup regime.

The preschool version of the English Picture Vocabulary Test was administered before the teaching programme began; the mean raw scores obtained were:

Group 1   Rebus   Raw Score   26 – 29   SD 9.29
Group 2   PLDK   Raw Score   25 – 27   SD 9.33
Group 3   Control   Raw Score   29 – 30   SD 6.76

During the experimental period the rate of progress of each child differed from 192 completed frames at the lower end to 768 completed frames at the upper end. There was no significant relationship between age, sex or EPVT Raw Score and completed number of frames.

A delayed, prereading post-test which was used six months after completion of the experimental period consisted of:

Test 1   A recognition test in which the child was asked to identify one of three printed words as equivalent to a spoken word. The first part of the task supported the printed word with a picture and the second part presented the same words in a different order without the picture.

Test 2   This was a test of correspondence between the serial position of a word in speech and of a location in linear space. The task for the child was to find the space that the word would occupy if it were written, having listened to a sentence.

Test 3   A test of shape and directional discrimination. The child's task was to select from four shapes, letters or words, two which were the same. In each item the four elements were arranged at the corners of a square.

Summary of differences (*Analysis of covariance*)

Significance levels in favour of Rebus group

	Test 1	Test 2	Test 3
Between Rebus group and group 2	.05	.01	.01
Between Rebus group and group 3	ns	.01	.01

It is not argued here that the significant levels of differences which were observed occurred as a result of any particular attribute of rebus itself; but rather that the organization of the programme represents something more meaningful and developmental than a heterogeneous collection of prereading exercises.

Several points can be made to support the use of rebus as pre-reading experience. John Downing (1974) has used some available evidence in support of i.t.a. and substantially the same evidence can be used to support rebus. Warburton and Southgate (1969) in their report on i.t.a. concluded: 'There is no evidence whatsoever for the belief that the best way to learn to read in traditional orthography is to learn to read in traditional orthography.' (pages 234–5). They then suggest that it would appear that learning to read in i.t.a. might be the best way to learn to read in traditional orthography. Had data from rebus studies been available to them it might have appeared to be the case that learning to read in rebus has advantages similar to those claimed for i.t.a.

Ohnmacht (1969), Johnson (1970) and Samuels (1971) are quoted by Downing as providing evidence that letter-name teaching gives the child no help whatsoever in learning to read. Meuhl (1960) submits evidence that children look at and can match letters before they can read. The evidence of the Bristol experiment suggests that the provision of rebus experience, within which no attempt is made to introduce letter forms, significantly raises the ability of the child to discriminate and match both shape and letter form.

Further work quoted by Downing is that of Elkonin (1973) who is reported as stating:

. . . the perception and discrimination of printed characters is only the external side of the process of reading, behind which lies hidden the more essential and basic behaviour, which the reader produces with the sounds of language. The speed of the movement of the eye does not define the speed of reading (i.e. the number of graphic symbols perceived simultaneously). Of considerably greater importance than the speed of eye-movements and the span of apprehension is the speed of the underlying more central processes concerned with the behaviour creating the sound forms of the word and connected with it, its comprehension.

The results of Test 2 in the Bristol experiment lend some support to the idea that the organization of the rebus programme may facilitate and accelerate the development of these central processes. In rebus the non-reader can see the words which he has heard in spoken language.

The research of Serafica and Sigel (1970) helps to direct thinking towards what may be the more important issues of the rebus approach. Their evidence indicated that disabled readers were better at visual discrimination than normal readers. An explanation for this phenomenon is provided by Kephart (in Ball 1971, page 135). Kephart uses the example of two squares, one straight-sided and one wavy-sided. For the person with mature form perception the identity of the form of the square is not altered when the sides are wavy. But the person at the level of the perception of elements is involved in a change which represents a major disruption of continuity.

Kephart then argues that the person with defective perception would be expected to show a significantly greater discrepancy in thresholds when presented with paired straight-sided squares in contrast to paired wavy-sided squares, than would the person with normal perception. Under certain conditions this may lead to keener than normal discrimination. This explanation might well account for the information provided by Robinson (see Downing 1974) that some children failed in reading because of undue concern with unimportant details which are irrelevant to the task of reading. An example provided is that of a child who was confused by the extra curl at the bottom of the letter 'L' and as a consequence could not read the word 'Leg'. The successful reader, according to Downing, is one who tries to sort unknown symbols into a category which makes sense. Thus it is the central process of categorization which is of major importance and this is the process which is required continually in the rebus programme.

John Merritt (1970) has suggested that a willingness to make mistakes is likely to be part of the learning-to-read process; and Goodman (1967) has described reading as a psycholinguistic guessing game, the model for which includes sampling, prediction, testing and confirming. The model relates well to the processing model of learning (TOTE) proposed by Miller, Galanter and Pribram (1960). The rebus programme appears to fit well with these models and also with the general views of Downing and Merritt, at least as far as the earliest stages of reading are concerned.

The final issue for discussion is that of veridicality – a concept proposed by Kephart and explored in some detail by Bruner (1974). In an account of perceptual readiness, Bruner states that perception involves an act of categorization. All perception is generic in that what is perceived is placed in, and acquires meaning from, the class of percepts with which it is grouped. When perceptual experience is free of categorial identity it is 'doomed to be a gem, serene, locked in the silence of private experience' (page 9).

Veridicality itself is defined as the representative function of perception. What is perceived is a representation of the external world. That is, the object which is seen can also be felt and smelled and there will be a match between what is seen, felt and smelled. What is seen will be proved to be the same thing if it is investigated more closely. Further the placement of an object in a category is predictive of appropriate consequences in terms of later behaviour directed towards the object perceived.

This, then, may be what goes on in a non-ordered way when children are at play in a nursery or reception class. The variety of experiences provided leads to the acquisition of attributive or sensory data from which are derived cues for inferring identification. These are the 'stock-in-trade' of the nursery and infant school which are mentioned by Bullock. The more specifically-oriented visual perceptual exercises may be occurring simultaneously, but when not in association with the input of attributive or sensory data the activities may be the 'occupiers' during the time that the teacher is involved with the small group (see Roberts 1975, page 22). Rebus goes some way towards making ordered use of attributive and sensory data and as a consequence the learning experience is likely to be more veridical than non-structured experience.

It does appear from the very limited evidence available that rebus could be a useful, effective prereading experience when used within the multi-sensory regime of the nursery and infant school, and that its strength lies not least in its structuring and sequencing of experience. The rebus programme is also sufficiently flexible to accommodate various teaching approaches or methods; for example, rebus flash cards could be used in the traditional way, or more productively perhaps in a language experience or *Breakthrough to Literacy* approach. The teacher can demonstrate that symbols can be manipulated to relate form to meaning. The child is enabled to see the nature of the function of symbols and can begin to learn through participation.

The work with rebus is continuing at Redland College, Bristol, and has included the pilot testing of sixty new rebuses and a restyling of a programmed text. Rebuses have been used with nursery school children, adolescent non-readers and children in the ESN(M) and ESN(S) categories. Each of the new rebuses used has been selected on the basis of known previous experience of the children concerned. The work will be further developed during the next two years towards the production of a rebus programme based entirely on English cultural experience.

References

BALL, T. S. (1971) *Itard, Séguin and Kephart, Sensory Education – A Learning Interpretation* Columbus, Ohio: Merrill

BRIMER, M. A. and DUNN, L. (1962) *English Picture Vocabulary Test* (Preschool Version) Bristol: Educational Evaluation Enterprises

BRUNER, J. S. (1974) *Beyond the Information Given* Allen and Unwin

DES (1975) *A Language for Life* (Bullock Report) HMSO

DOWNING, J. (1974) Some curious paradoxes in reading research *Reading* 8, 3, 2–10

ELKONIN, D. B. (1973) USSR in J. Downing (Ed) *Comparative Reading* New York: Macmillan

GOODMAN, K. (1967) Reading: a psycholinguistic guessing game *Journal of the Reading Specialist* 4, 126–35

JOHNSON, R. J. (1970) The effect of training on letter names on success in beginning reading for children of differing abilities. Paper presented to the *American Educational Research Association*

MERRITT, J. (1970) Teaching reading in junior and secondary schools *Teaching Reading* (ACE Forum 4) Ginn

MEUHL, S. (1960) The effects of visual discrimination pretraining on learning to read a vocabulary list in kindergarten children *Journal of Educational Psychology* 51 217–21

MILLER, G. A., GALANTER, E. and PRIBRAM, K. (1960) *Plans and the Structure of Behavior* New York: Holt, Rinehart and Winston

OHNMACHT, D. (1969) The effects of letter knowledge on achievement in reading in the first grade. Paper presented to the *American Educational Research Association*

ROBERTS, G. (1975) Early reading *Reading* 9, 2, 14–23

SAMUELS, S. J. (1971) Letter-name versus letter-sound knowledge in learning to read *The Reading Teacher* 24 604–8

SERAFICA, F. C. and SIGEL, I. E. (1970) Styles of categorization and reading disability *Journal of Reading Behaviour* 2 105–15

WARBURTON, F. W. and SOUTHGATE, V. (1969) *i.t.a.: An Independent Evaluation* John Murray and W. and R. Chambers

WOODCOCK, R. W. *et al* (1969) *Teacher's Guide: The Peabody Rebus Reading Program* Minnesota: American Guidance Service

Part 3
Children reading and writing

12   Style and substance in the reading programme: contrasting American and British children's literature

Sam L. Sebesta

There is an old paradox that states, 'All generalizations are false, including this one.' To generalize about the children's literature of two productive countries, the United States and England, may be misleading and false. Each of these countries produces from two to three thousand new titles each year. Somewhere among these titles you can find an exception to almost every generalization, almost every trend or comparison. Yet, as one samples the output of the two places, comparing them with the past and with each other, certain observations do seem warranted. Perhaps, after all, such generalizations can be of help to authors, to students of children's literature, and above all to those of us who guide children in the selection and use of this vast treasure.

Although I cannot hope to cite the entire field, I shall attempt to touch the bases of adolescent fiction, of books geared for intermediate ages and of picture books. My emphasis will be on matters of content and style that have special relevance for the teacher and hence for the audience for whom the books are intended – children and adolescents.

The most striking difference between the literary fare of the two nations seems to be at the pre-adolescent and adolescent level. American young people in recent years have been deluged with novels about the problems of growing up. Emphasis is on the *problems*. Very often these problems, as presented by their numerous authors, are portrayed as beyond solution, and the novels are grim. *Go Ask Alice*, one of the most popular in America, is the diary of a girl who dies of an overdose of drugs. The number of stories about pre-adolescents and adolescents who run away from home is almost legion. They are dark picaresques about innocents who escape from a hypocritical society into a subculture in which only their own kind can be tolerated. In their language and incidents nearly all the old taboos are broken. The only sin left, according to them, seems to be exuberance.

What are the real themes of these grim problem novels about American young people who run away? What, in other words, is the significance of their actions? One theory is that more and more American adolescents *are* running away, or want to. These books, as they say, 'tell it like it is'. A different possibility is that, for many of their readers, the running-away motif is more escapist than confrontive, more metaphoric than realistic. Huck Finn in a different generation escaped to the metaphor of river, Holden Caulfield to the faceless city, Claudia and her brother in *From the Mixed-Up Files of Mrs Basil E. Frankweiler* to New York's Metropolitan Art Museum. Perhaps today's grim stories about running away serve up a metaphor that explores the age-old option of escape.

If we look at these adolescent novels in the light of tradition, another explanation appears. It is the one most often reflected in interviews with modern taboo-breaking authors. The tradition they most frequently mention is a genteel one in children's literature: the 1930s and 1940s, two different decades in American history, two decades that began with domestic crisis and continued into international conflict. Yet the children's literature of those two decades is tranquil. It is genteel. The economic depression appears as a backdrop, it is never central. Hunger and despair, disheartened or embittered parents, and neglected or abandoned children are left to folklore. You will seldom find them in so-called realistic stories of the 1930s. The wartime years in America are also softened. What has been called the Golden Age in children's literature was really, in America, a genteel age.

Under the guise of realism, many modern novels for the adolescent are reactions to that genteel age, when writers and educators idealized childhood, shielding it from sociological turmoil. Their plain style, their frequent use of language and situations once considered taboo, are assertions of uniqueness. They are a kind of literary protest.

British stories for this age group – those available to the American reader – do not contain the same kind of protest. K. M. Peyton's *Pennington* series presents a taboo-breaking hero, it is true, and the realistic stories of John Rowe Townsend are often set against a grim background of poverty and uncertain home life. But the majority of British fiction about growing up seems to me to present the rite of passage in a surprising manner. Major authors such as William Mayne, Alan Garner and Penelope Farmer give us mystical stories. In their works, growing up is to encounter strange history-derived forces – unfriendly ones that threaten to engulf the modern hero or heroine. In William Mayne's *Earthfasts*, for example, giants come walking out of the past; the past subjugates one of the adolescents, body and soul, until the book's climax. In *The Owl Service* by Alan Garner, the modern heroine is possessed by the parallel figures of a legend. In John Rowe Townsend's latest work, published this year in America, the hero must come of age by confronting a mystical tiger straight from William Blake. In contrast to American problem stories for adolescents, these British books say that the transition to adulthood is fraught with mysterious danger, a choice between good and evil where the cards are held by the past.

The typical styles of writing of the two nations also differ markedly. American authors seek closeness to their readers by assuming the chief character's point of view, often using the first person. The style is conversational and plain. The protagonist tells the story as one would describe experiences extemporaneousyl. British authors more often adopt an omniscient point of view, with balanced, periodic syntax. Sometimes the British style causes difficulty for American readers, who have often been taught that writing consists of speech written down. The British books – for example, the upper-grade works of Rosemary Sutcliff, Peter Dickinson and Cynthia Harnett – need to be read aloud in America to aid familiarity with style.

In spite of the great quantity of children's books published each year, there appears to be a shortage of good new titles for middle childhood. This is unfortunate, for the eight-to-eleven group comprises some of our most avid readers. One well-known American author expresses the view that middle childhood is being squeezed out in our culture. Many American children are expected to move immediately from primary age into the sophistication of adolescence. To offset this neglect, a few well-known American writers attempt to produce fiction on an easier scale. These include Lloyd Alexander, Andre Norton, Robert Burch and the very popular Judy Blume. The wonderful British writer Joan Aiken also produces stories written at an easier level than her longer major works. But not all of these writers feel at home with middle childhood. This age level needs a new champion in America. In the meantime, it embraces Beverly Cleary, the American writer most comfortable at the intermediate level, and the ever popular Laura Ingalls Wilder.

In Britain, a new award has been established for distinguished middle childhood writing. I think America should follow suit, since our Newbery Award is now most frequently given to upper-grade fiction. In both countries it is heartening to find a great increase in middle-grade non-fiction. With the publication of Margery Fisher's *Matters of Fact*, a marvellous review and critique of juvenile non-fiction, we should expect to see an overall improvement in the quality of informational materials.

The picture book for younger readers has been a special delight for nearly a century. It is a universal medium, bridging nations and generations. In great picture books such as those of Maurice Sendak, Pat Hutchins and John Burningham, pictures do more than complement text: they are a complete language in themselves. Recently, artists in both America and England have turned to folklore for their inspiration. America's Caldecott Award in the past few years has gone almost exclusively to illustrations for folk tales. To balance this trend, however, we have in both nations a new wealth in wordless books – wonderful ones by John S. Goodall, Mercer Mayer and Pat Hutchins' *Changes Changes*.

Children in both nations are deluged with pictures. Some have learned to tune out the visual barrage just as we have all learned to tune out extraneous noise. For this reason, it is important to teach children to 'read' high quality pictures in high quality picture books, not just the content or representation of a picture but its artistry as well, its elements of design and composition. Visual literacy augments reading. Here is one area of response to literature that has been neglected.

These have been a few comments, a few generalizations, about the state of the art of children's literature today. I shall combine these with observations made along the way as my colleagues and I travelled across England and Scotland visiting sites associated with our literary heritage. Using both of these experiences, I would offer a few ideas for enhancing the reading programme through rich literary content.

First, the wealth of *modern* titles does not necessarily provide young readers with a variety of literary style, tone and content. Good literature at all levels should present options for problem-solving, information and enjoyment. To limit reading material to modern works only, as some American reading programmes have done, is to ignore some of these options. One can argue that authors of the past write with a style and content unfamiliar to modern youth, but such a judgment is superficial. It fails to recognize the universality of good literature. Hence the fantasy of Edith Nesbit, the 'pruned' style of Beatrix Potter, the rich balanced language of Kenneth Grahame and Walter de la Mare are relevant so long as there remains a reason for reading. It is true that they ask for sustained attention, but all art asks for sustained attention. It is also true that for some readers they will not be independent, voluntary choices; but this argues for skilled teaching, not for exclusion. There is a great need for the kind of inspired teaching that builds readiness for style and setting; above all, for the fine oral reader who can thaw literature from its frozen print.

Which leads me to a second suggestion, this time in regard to teacher preparation. Teachers in America take courses in *how* to teach reading. If they are fortunate, they also take a course in children's literature or literature for the adolescent, although such a course is required in only about half the states. But a most difficult type of training to come by is a *synthesis* of 'how' and 'what' – the skills needed to present good literature effectively within the reading programme. Lacking such skills, lacking this synthesis of content and process, we become overly dependent on packaged materials – the graded reading-and-literature textbook series that tries to be teacher-proof. Yet it is the person, not the package, that best mediates literary response, showing children that learning to read is worth the effort. The growing affiliation between literature specialists and reading specialists, such as there has been in this conference, is the most heartening development in reading instruction. Its effects will be a boon to teacher training.

Finally, the continuing need to select literature wisely is best met by good literary critics. Thus the critic is in a central role to influence the quality of reading programmes. In this regard, England is most fortunate. The perceptive and intensive evaluation of children's literature by Margery Fisher, John Rowe Townsend, Elaine Moss and others is invaluable. These people take their work very seriously, and they add to our insight and appreciation. Every teacher should read them. American commentary on the state of the art inclines more to survey, with briefer concentration on individual works; but we do see some effort at more extensive evaluation, notably Zena Sutherland's *Bulletin of the Center for Children's Books*, published at the University of Chicago, and Eleanor Cameron's *The Green and Growing Tree*. The author-critic Natalie Babbitt recently commented that we worry more about our selection of baby food than about our children's literary diet. Critics in Britain and America will help us right that balance!

Touring England and Scotland in search of literary background, as my colleagues and I have just done, is the experience of a lifetime. The evidence gained from our tour and this conference is reason enough to proclaim a new Golden Age for children's literature. This, more than any other influence, will mean a Golden Age for reading instruction.

13   Structuring a literature programme

Michael R. Molloy

This paper examines the problem of planning and implementing a literature programme in the curriculum of the primary school. The programme concentrates on fiction, and is structured in such a way that children are exposed to a balanced range of fiction, and encounter a variety of learning experiences in their interaction with literature.

There is no simple classification of fiction, into which all stories can be categorized. Assuming that some structuring of different genres of story is possible, there arises the question of the relative weighting that should be given to these at different stages of child development. This calls for some degree of knowledge and understanding of the content and range of children's literature, and of the pattern of child development. The second problem is curricular in nature and demands some understanding and competency in organizing learning experiences for different purposes.

The aims of a literature programme in the curriculum have been examined by various authors, notably Arbuthnot (1964), Huus (1973), Jones and Buttrey (1970) and Peel (1962). However, it is interesting to look at the views of someone not directly concerned with the curriculum but who passionately advocates the teaching of literature in all schools. Alexander Solzhenitsyn (in Stauffer 1973) views literature as:

. . . having a miracle within its power. It can instill in us the grief and joy of faraway others. It can overcome the liability of learning only from one's experience. The only substitutes we have for experience are the arts and literature. Literature is one of the most delicate and responsive instruments of human existence.

This inspiring and challenging conception of literature is

reflected in Peel's (1962) view that stories extend children's experience into regions that are fascinating and exciting and, above all, personal and important to them. Stories, she claims, are not something a child grows out of but something he grows through.

What categories?

A number of writers on children's literature deplore the use of categories, arguing (Peel 1962) that it is 'false and harmful to make children think in categories, for there are as many kinds of stories as there are kinds of people, settings and ways of life'. While it may be false to attempt to put stories into watertight compartments, it is difficult to imagine how it can be harmful. One could argue that only by categorizing stories in some way can the teacher ensure she is

Figure 1   Categories of children's literature

Whitehead (1968)
Adventure
Animal tales
Biography
Fable, folk, fairy tale
Humour
Informational
Myths
Nursery rhymes
Other regions, lands
   and people
Poetry

Nebraska (1966)
Folk tale
Fanciful tale
Animal story
Adventure
Myth
Fable
Other lands and people
Historical fiction
Biography

Jones and Buttrey (1970)
Stories of the familiar
Folk tales
Myths and legends
Real life situations

Arbuthnot (1964)
Picture stories
Folk tales
Family life
Historical fiction
Biography
Animal stories
Fantasy

Puffin books
Myths and legends
Fantasy and magic
Family adventure
Animal stories
Humour
Adventure, mystery and travel
Science fiction

giving her children a balanced diet of different kinds of stories. When children move from one teacher to another, it is surely valuable for the second teacher to know what literature these children have experienced beforehand. To remove the haphazard nature of literature teaching in the school as a whole, categories are useful planning instruments in the hands of a team of cooperating teachers.

Yet one can have considerable sympathy for Peel's rejection of categories: there is no agreed category system. Five different systems are shown in Figure 1 (page 116). The most extensive programme is that of Whitehead (1968). Obviously a list confined to fiction would exclude informational books, but would it exclude biography and poetry? The Nebraska (1966) guide excludes poetry but includes biography, on the grounds that there should be a separate poetry programme, and that biography, if written as a story, is sometimes stranger than fiction. In contrast to these systems with a large number of categories, is that of Jones and Buttrey (1970) with only four categories, two of which (stories of the familiar and real life situations) are not even clearly distinguishable from each other. Puffin books are organized into seven categories, with an additional special section for picture stories. The introduction of the picture characteristic as a distinguishing feature involves the use of a format rather than a content criterion. This policy is also adopted by Arbuthnot (1964), the most renowned American writer on children's literature.

The following list of categories of fiction has been derived from the previous lists. Biography has been included and poetry excluded for the reasons stated:

picture stories	family life
fable	adventure and mystery
folk and fairy tale	historical fiction
myths and legends	science fiction
animal tales	biography
fantasy	

This list may be used by teachers or pupils to plan and record the books they read. Teachers could make charts, listing the books available (and including indications of reading and interest ages) to ensure all of these categories are represented. Pupils could also make a chart of their own, writing in the title and/or category-type of each book read.

What categories for what children?

It seems impossible to arrive at a simple set of criteria for matching books and children. A recent study in *The Reading Teacher* (Beta Upsilon Chapter, 1974) showed that the majority of children from seven to nine preferred animal stories and funny stories, while those of ten and eleven liked mystery stories best. Does this mean we need only animal stories, funny stories and mystery stories in our literature programme? Field (1968) has tried to relate children's reading interests to their psychological development and concludes that the preferences of children from six to eleven lie on a continuum from fantasy stories to naturalistic adventure stories. Peel (1962) points to the differences between boys, who seem to prefer fighting and suspense stories, and girls, who seem to prefer stories which give them opportunities for feeling and emotional reaction. However, she also argues that both boys and girls demand action in their stories, even if it is of a different kind. The action of a story should 'involve some quest, journey or adventure that carries them far away from the here and now, lets them take part in some testing experience and brings them back invigorated at the end'. This is the pattern of Allison Uttley's Tim Rabbit (in *The Adventures of No Ordinary Rabbit*, Faber and Faber) who leaves the security of home to encounter the rain, wind, thunder and dog, returning petrified to his mother's arms for 'a curly yellow pancake with sugar on top' which he sits and munches, his troubles forgotten. For older children, the pattern remains the same, but the quest is much further away and the terrain and events more naturalistic as in, for example, *Flight of the Doves* (W. Macken, Pan Books) or *The Cave* (R. Church, Penguin Books), the first being a story about escaping from a cruel uncle, the second being a group adventure underground.

In the absence of clear guidelines, teachers will have to decide for themselves both the titles of the books they give to their pupils and the weighting that will be given to each category at various age and reading levels. Some teachers may wish to leave out certain categories for certain pupils, such as picture stories for ten year olds, or science fiction for six year olds. If some children seem to be restricting themselves to relatively few categories, the teacher might wish to influence them to spread their reading wings by reading aloud extracts from unpopular categories.

Readability

The application of the most reliable reading formula to a large number of books is an operation for a computer, which has only just begun (see Harrison 1974). Meanwhile, the matching of pupils of different reading abilities with books of varying difficulty will continue to be done subjectively and intuitively by teachers knowing their children and knowing the books. To help them in this formidable task, teachers, in addition to the recommendations of other teachers or librarians, can make use of two simple but reasonably reliable instruments. The first is a codification devised by the Children's Book Group of the Publishers Association which gives each book a reading ability age and an interest age. Unfortunately this is not used by all publishers. The second instrument is a readability formula which attempts to give each book a precise reading age level. The most reliable of these, the Dale-Chall Formula (Dale and Chall 1948), is too time-consuming for use by individual teachers. However, reasonably reliable assessments can be obtained using the Fog Index (Gunning 1952) and the SMOG formula. The latter is the quickest and simplest to use (see Livingstone 1973).

With the aid of categories of stories classified by content, and the measure of readability provided by the coding system and the readability formula, the teacher is in a stronger position to structure the selection and organization of the books, match children and books in a systematic way, and keep track of what individual children read. Books could be marked to indicate content category and reading level.

The structure of books and stories

In this section we will consider two aspects of the book – its content and its format. In fiction, the content is organized as a story. The story is presented in a format which is peculiar to books. Both story and format have characteristic structures.

The structure of a story (story parts) is taken to refer to the way in which the story is put together by the author. The most important characteristics of a story from the point of view of its content are its characters, setting, 'things' and events.

Every story has a set of characters. These may be people, or animals, or objects given life for the purposes of the story. The reader must identify these characters, work out the relationships, interrelationships, or lack of relationships between them, and determine the influence each is having on the development of the story. Similarities and differences, changes in behaviour and attitudes can be observed, inferred and reacted to by the reader.

Every story has a setting or number of settings in which the characters operate. The reader has to recognize the characteristics of each setting, naturalistic or fantastic, through which the action of a story moves, and note the changes caused by various characters or events. One of the most important things the reader must do is translate the descriptive words used by the author into images and pictures, which create in his mind the experience and feeling of being there with the characters, as they interact with each other and with the various settings. These words describe settings for the reader but also help to create in his mind a sense of mood, atmosphere and excitement.

Associated with the places in which a story develops are the many 'things' used by the characters – swords and helmets, magic sticks and carpets, bundles, vehicles, machines and instruments of all kinds – real or imaginary, useful or dangerous. The reader will have to determine their characteristics and purposes, and recognize what effect they have on the characters and settings in the unfolding of the story.

All these – characters, places and things – interact in the action or events of the story. The action is made up of what the characters do or say to each other, or what they do to or with the things or settings around them. While some actions will be predictable, others will be accidental or unexpected, with mysterious twists and surprises, which will be fully understood only as the story unfolds.

Finally, valuable clues to the content and development of the story can be gained from book parts other than the text. A survey or detailed analysis of a book's title, table of contents, illustrations or maps will provide the reader with insights into its characters, settings, things and events.

Levels of response in reading literature

The aspect of reading to which response is most closely related is comprehension. This is the process by which ideas are grasped, interpreted, reflected upon and reacted to by the reader. Barrett (in Clymer 1968) has suggested that this activity involves the reader in several levels of thinking, which lie on a continuum from purely literal grasping of the author's ideas to uniquely subjective and personal reactions to these ideas. The literal level involves recognizing such things as the details and main ideas of a story, the sequence of events, or character traits, comparisons and other relationships. At the second level (reorganization) the reader puts these ideas into some kind of structure, such as an outline or summary. The next level (inferential) involves the reader in making inferences, partly from what the author has said and partly from his own experiences and intuition. In the fourth level (critical) the reader judges the quality of the story, evaluating such things as descriptions of reality, fantasy, characters or settings. The highest level of response is the appreciative, which is the reader's affective reaction in emotion and feeling to the content of the story, its characters or events, its mood and atmosphere, or its language and tone.

While each of these levels is important in reading literature, the emphasis should be on the development of appreciation, the underlying levels being employed as stepping stones to this goal.

The dynamic interrelationships between the three structures considered so far in this section – story parts, book parts and levels of response – may be evident when presented in a model as suggested in Figure 2 below. This model can be used as a guide in setting purposes for reading, and designing questions or other activities which will deepen children's involvement in their experience of literature.

Figure 2 Model showing interrelationships between story parts and levels of response to stories

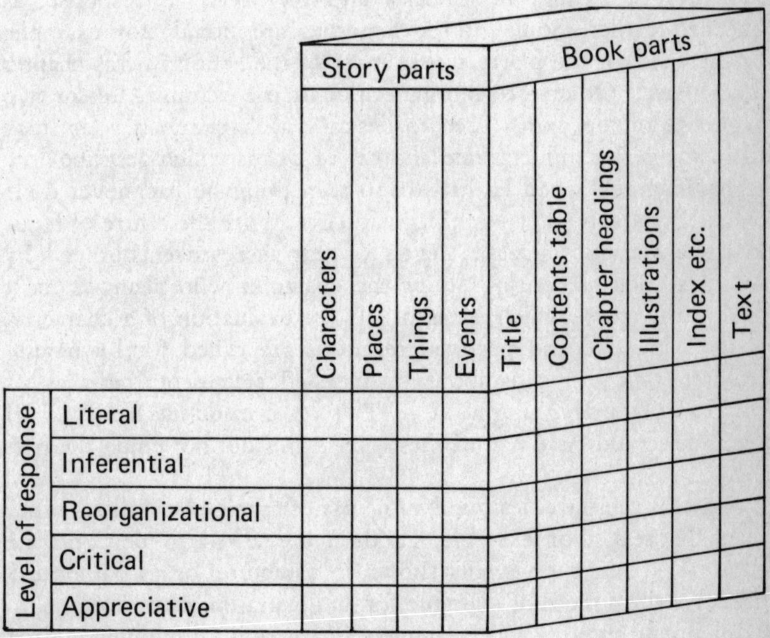

Level of response		Characters	Places	Things	Events	Title	Contents table	Chapter headings	Illustrations	Index etc.	Text
	Literal										
	Inferential										
	Reorganizational										
	Critical										
	Appreciative										

(Column groups: Story parts — Characters, Places, Things, Events; Book parts — Title, Contents table, Chapter headings, Illustrations, Index etc., Text)

Interaction with literature

It is not difficult for any teacher to obtain detailed descriptions of approaches to the presentation of literature in the classroom. Perhaps the most stimulating and helpful are those of Whitehead (1968), Peel (1962), Jones and Buttrey (1970) and Marshall (1966), the latter being associated with a television programme. One approach will be considered here, one which has been used in a variety of classrooms in primary schools with the cooperation of teachers who took part in an inservice reading course, where the basic ideas underlying the approach were described.

The approach is based on the concept of individualized reading as described by Hunt (1966), Molloy (1972) and West (1964). A large number of books is made available to pupils covering the range of categories suggested earlier and a range of reading levels. Children choose freely from this selection, do the reading independently, and meet with the teacher for a regular conference. The books are supported by reading guides which suggest a range of independent or group activities from which children may choose. Small groups meet to share their reactions to what they have read or to carry out a group assignment.

The activities presented in the reading guides are based on the structure of stories, book parts and the levels of response, as outlined earlier. Some of the activities are literal; for example, 'Make a list of the places where most of the action in this chapter takes place.' Others are reorganizational; for example, 'Make two lists, one of the words used to describe a character in your story who was very confident, and another of words which describe how a character felt when he had to do something he had never done before.' Characters, places, things and events are the centre of focus in these activities. Deeper levels of response are encouraged by activites such as writing about the character who changed most during the story, which is essentially the evaluation of a character. More subjective and personal reactions are called for by having children talk or write about open-ended statements such as, 'I could not stop laughing at . . .', 'This place made me feel . . .', 'If everyone could have one of these . . .' or, 'I did not enjoy the part that . . .'.

Some of the activities involve the use of specific book parts other than the text. For example, children are asked to describe the characters, things or events shown in a picture, or to compose a title or write a piece of dialogue for an illustration map or diagram. To maintain interest and excitement, the activities involve children in producing a variety of end-products, using different media. The following is a sample from the activities suggested for independent work:

1 Make a picture dictionary for the things mentioned in this story.
2 Prepare a comic strip presentation of part of the story, putting conversation into bubbles.
3 Make a large poster to advertise your favourite book on the classroom noticeboard.
4 Make models, or puppets, or dioramas, or action pictures of some of the characters, places or things in the story.
5 Write the script and make a series of illustrations for a 'strip' or 'slide' presentation of your story.

In addition to this independent work, children can share with each other something of their story (important incidents, fascinating characters, mysterious places) and something of their personal reactions to their story. Sharing sessions require advance planning by the teacher and the children. Those whose turn it is to share must put a lot of thought and practice into what they are going to do and say: selecting and practising extracts to read aloud; deciding what characters to mime and dramatize; preparing illustrations, models, puppets, photographs; rereading the text to check features of landscape, points about characters, the order of events or details of conversation. As for independent work, the activities should be the product of each child's personality, imagination and skill. The following is a sample of such activities:

1 Mime or dramatize two or three contrasting characters in a story. Illustrate by reading short descriptive extracts from the book.
2 Tell or read part of the story to a background of suitable sound effects or music.
3 A small group collects extracts from their various stories which illustrate themes such as fear, battles, storms, love, hate, being lost, escape, feeling lonely, moving house etc.
4 Have a group or class pantomime in which each pupil, dressed up as a character from a book, takes part in a market, party or carnival.

About one hundred cards have been prepared of activities like these, more than half of them being independent in nature. One quarter of them deal with characters, one quarter focus on events, the remainder being spread equally on book parts, things and places.

In the classroom it has been found that these suggestions prove a most valuable resource for the teacher. During a conference, the teacher can match each pupil with an activity which is appropriate to his level of development and to the part of the story he is reading. The activities are not used for every chapter of every book. However the resource cards provide pupils with interesting, worthwhile and enjoyable purposes for reading, and opportunities for reacting to the story. The cards prove extremely flexible in that they are not book-specific. Pupils, with the help and guidance of the teacher, have to interpret each activity in relation to their current books. As the activities provide a range of response levels and a variety of end-products, there is considerable physical, intellectual and emotional involvement in children's interaction with their stories.

One important advantage of devising activities which are not book-specific is that it is possible to launch a literature scheme without the teacher having to read all the books in advance, as suggested by Livingstone (1973). Teachers were able to read as many books as possible along with the children.

In implementing these proposals, it is necessary to keep a check on the balance of time spent on the activities and on actual reading. Clearly, reading time should have priority. The activities increase the appetite for reading of those who have not previously been very interested in books. Gradually the thirst for another story makes it possible to reduce the time spent on follow-up activities, though the group sharing experiences continue to be popular.

Evaluating the children's response

Hunt (1967) has suggested an approach to the evaluation of children's reading of literature which can be carried out by any teacher 'armed with the right questions and oriented to appropriate observations'. He considers the evaluation of a child's reading a matter of observing how much the book matters to the child and the depth and breadth of response the child makes to the ideas in his book. The teacher-pupil conference is ideal for this purpose. Evaluation, therefore, is formative, ongoing, part of the interaction between child, book and teacher. The teacher can use insights gained from evaluation questions and techniques to guide each child towards an appropriate book, or independent or group activity. The resource bank of activity cards can be adjusted to the personal needs or wishes of each child or group of children.

The following aspects of pupil interaction with books can be evaluated from the record cards suggested:

1 the quantity and range of stories and books read
2 the range of independent and group activities in which each child becomes involved.

Obviously the quality and depth of commitment to, involvement in and response to literature cannot be judged only by quantitative measures. Hunt (1967) has suggested that there are three important categories of questions which the teacher can use in an individual conference to evaluate each child's strength as a reader. These categories, with examples of relevant questions, are as follows:

1 Appropriateness of the book for a particular child.
   (a) Why was this a good book for you to read?
   (b) Were there places where you got mixed up and did not understand?
   (c) Did you want to keep on reading, or did you have to force yourself to finish the book?

2 Appreciation of the book.
   (a) What was it about this book that made you like it or dislike it?
   (b) Where would you place this book in comparison to other books you have read recently?
   (c) Would you like to read other books of this type or would you prefer to read a different type next?

3 Values gained from the book.
   (a) Did anything happen in this book which you would like to have happened to you?
   (b) What were the high points of the book for you?
   (c) Did you learn something new from this book?

In the classroom, teachers have also found it possible to evaluate children's levels of response, understanding and enjoyment by discussing their independent work during the pupil-teacher conference. Similarly, judgments can be made of children's contribution to group work and sharing sessions. The end-products from the activity cards provide discussion points for evaluation. If teachers wished to employ more detailed instruments in evaluation, informal reading inventories could be constructed for a sample of books in the literature programme at various levels of difficulty.

The record forms suggested could all be enclosed in one notebook and retained by each child as a kind of passport, as recommended by the International Institute for Children's Literature and Reading Research (1974).

Evaluation of the programme

It has not been possible to implement all of these structures in any one classroom. The elements of these proposals most extensively attempted in cooperation with several teachers have been the pupil-teacher conference, the use of activity cards and the system of recording books read and activities completed. Some teachers preferred to adapt the cards to the specific books in their classroom, only allowing a book into the programme when they had read it and prepared a supporting activity card. Gradually, as more books were made available more children were brought into the programme. There were also teachers who preferred a completely free literature programme, where pupils were given time to read what they wished. No attempt has been made to monitor or evaluate children's response. Generally those who like reading enjoy this freedom but the others move haphazardly from book to book without really becoming involved in the experience of literature.

The most striking effect of the structured programme has been the quantity of reading actually done by the children. Some children were reading more books in one week during this programme than they would normally have read in one term. The children become really excited about books, read them at odd moments during the school day or at break times, demand to be allowed to take books home, join and use the local library, and discuss informally among themselves the 'great' books they have read. Often the themes of the stories sparked off interests which were followed up in topic work. For example, the key role of the spider in E. B. White's *Charlotte's Web* has led many children to the study of spiders and other insects. However, the most satisfactory outcome of these attempts to structure the literature programme has been the sight of children eagerly committed to books and enjoying the excitement of reading.

References

ARBUTHNOT, M. H. (1964) *Children and Books* (Third edition) Chicago: Scott, Foresman
BETA UPSILON CHAPTER, PI LAMBDA THETA (1974) Children's

reading interests classified by age level *The Reading Teacher* 27 694–700

CLYMER, T. (1968) 'What is reading? Some current concepts' in H. M. Robinson (Ed) *Innovation and Change in Reading Instruction* Chicago: University of Chicago Press

DALE, E. and CHALL, J. S. (1948) A formula for predicting readability *Educational Research Bulletin* 27 11–20

FIELD, C. (1968) Reading and child development in the junior years *The School Librarian* 16 145–50

GUNNING, R. (1952) *The Techniques of Clear Writing* New York: McGraw-Hill

HARRISON, C. (1974) Readability and school. Paper presented to the *Fifth IRA World Congress on Reading* Vienna

HUNT, L. C. (1966) 'The individualized reading programme: a perspective' in L. C. Hunt (Ed) *The Individualized Reading Program* Newark, Delaware: International Reading Association

HUNT, L. C. (1967) 'Evaluation through teacher-pupil conferences' in T. C. Barrett (Ed) *The Evaluation of Children's Reading Achievement* Newark, Delaware: International Reading Association

HUUS, H. (1973) Teaching literature at the elementary school level *The Reading Teacher* 26 795–801

INTERNATIONAL INSTITUTE FOR CHILDREN'S LITERATURE AND READING RESEARCH (1974) *Reader's Passport to Fourth Grade* Vienna: IICLRR

JONES, A. and BUTTREY, J. (1970) *Children and Stories* Basil Blackwell

LIVINGSTONE, G. (1973) A reading programme based on children's literature *Reading* 7, 3, 25–30

MARSHALL, S. (1966 and annually) *Picture Box* (Teacher's handbook) Manchester: Granada Television

MOLLOY, M. R. (1972) *An Individualized Reading Programme* Queen's University, Belfast: Unpublished dissertation

NEBRASKA CURRICULUM DEVELOPMENT CENTRE (1966) *A Curriculum for English* Nebraska: University of Nebraska Press

PEEL, M. (1962) *Seeing to the Heart* Chatto and Windus

STAUFFER, R. G. (1973) Will beauty save the world? *The Reading Teacher* 26 774–5

WEST, R. (1964) *Individualized Reading Instruction* New York: Kennikat Press

WHITEHEAD, R. (1968) *Children's Literature: Strategies in Teaching* New York: Prentice-Hall

14 Motivating children's writing and reading through college/school relationships: a Young Writers' Conference

Lenore D. Parker

The idea of sponsoring a Young Writers' Conference grew out of a desire to influence how children see themselves as writers, and out of a commitment to college-elementary school cooperative efforts in teacher training. Conferences, traditionally, are adult functions where people with similar interests gather to share their knowledge and concerns about their profession. For children to gather, in a similar manner, to think together, talk together, read together and write together, seemed an ideal way to attach relevance and importance to their roles as writers. At the same time, college graduate students, faculty and elementary school teachers could interact throughout the months spent working together, implementing the total experience.

And so, the first Young Writers' Conference was held at the Lesley College Graduate School of Education on Friday, 17 January, 1975. Elementary school principals in the Greater Boston area were invited to send teachers and children from Grades 1–6 to the all-day event, where children were to share their original writing and teachers could attend a language arts workshop.

The pre-conference planning
A children's conference of this kind, to our knowledge, had never been held before, so that all the preparation for the day was based on what was known about adult experiences. These were considered in relation to the needs and interests of more than 110 elementary school children, who could be accommodated in the available building. The Washington Hill campus of Lesley College consists of a large mansion built in 1887, and a carriage house. Both buildings have been converted into offices and classrooms, but the charm and

original beauty of this historic site have been carefully preserved. The mansion was selected as an ideal environment for housing the young writers: the teachers' workshop was located in the carriage house.

Preliminary planning for the conference involved a series of meetings of faculty members, student volunteers and graduate students who had enrolled in a two-credit course, *Creative Writing for Young Children: The Young Writers' Conference*. Earning two credits was possible by assuming responsibility for pre-planning, for conducting sessions on the day of the conference, and for participating in the final evaluation of the experience.

Ultimately, the programme for the day evolved out of the preplanning meetings. Together we 'brainstormed' ideas, searching for experiences that would appeal to children. We wanted to highlight the role of the writer in the creation of print materials and in writing for the media. The final decision was to have a different topic for each session. The sessions would include both oral reading of the writing children had brought with them, and the writing of new material. Some time during the day would also be devoted to just 'rapping' about writing, if children seemed responsive to that idea. Throughout the day, children could also decide, at any time, to visit the art workshop or see the *Weston Woods* films of children's books.

The final programme consisted of thirty sessions, scheduled so that for almost all of the time-slots a choice could be made between two offerings. The opportunity for children to make such choices was an important consideration in the development of the programme. There was no desire to impose writing experiences on children. Rather, the goal was to be able to offer relevant and meaningful sessions, so that each child would find his or her interests represented. In addition, the option of the art workshop or films provided yet additional alternatives.

Children were assigned by grades within the sessions. Grades 1 and 2 were grouped together, as were Grades 3 and 4, and Grades 5 and 6. At the levels from Grades 1–4 each of the sessions was planned for a half-hour, while the upper grade children were allotted an hour or more. The wide variety of experiences planned for the day included the writing of autobiographies, plays, fiction, puppet shows, poetry, newspaper articles and advertisements, traditional literature forms and radio and TV scripts. Many of the sessions were organized to include the use of media, and to stress oral reading of the children's own writing, followed by discussion.

129

F

Graduate students wrote detailed plans for each session and collected any materials that were to be used.

Developing strategies for the sessions was only one part of the pre-conference planning. We were also anxious to assist and support the cooperating schools in their preparation for the experience. This was accomplished in two ways. The programme for the day was distributed well in advance of 17 January, so that children who were to attend could select their sessions and return their choices to us early enough to be properly assigned. For teachers, a booklet of ideas for the teaching of creative writing was distributed at the same time. Since children were expected to bring appropriate samples of their writing to the sessions they had selected, the 'creative writing idea book' was provided to offer supplementary teaching strategies that might be useful in generating the writing being prepared for the conference. The booklet, compiled by graduate students, contains ideas gleaned from many sources and from the creativity of the graduate students themselves. It also contains an extensive bibliography of publications offering additional ideas for encouraging children's writing.

Two teachers from each participating school were expected to attend the conference, to escort the children and to participate in a language arts workshop. Arrangements were made for Albert Cullum, author of *Push Back the Desks*, *Shake Hands with Shakespeare* and other works, to conduct the three-hour workshop. Teachers were to be completely free to participate in their own conference experience.

Final pre-planning activities revolved around organization of art supplies, ordering of films, assignment of graduate students to specific sessions and duties, and the myriad details of name tags, lunch distribution and registration procedures.

The Young Writers' Conference
On the day of the conference, the careful advance planning paid off. As children arrived with their teachers, they were greeted by the graduate students, appropriately tagged, and ushered to the first session of their choice. That location served as home base for the day, with children returning to that room for lunch and for their coats at the end of the day.

In their first session, the children were welcomed by the graduate students, and were told how the day would proceed. They were reassured that their teachers were close by, were told about the availability of the art room and the films, and were assured that the ushers in the corridors would help them in any way. The teachers also received a sheet explaining the organization of the day and the arrangements for leaving with the children.

For the young writers, thirty different sessions throughout the day focused on reading, writing, and speaking and listening skills, and incorporated the use of a variety of media, such as tape recorders, record players, musical instruments, art materials, filmstrips, cameras and slides.

For the first and second graders, many of the sessions involved the use of manipulative materials and stressed listening and speaking activities. In one session children created *Blobbo Bug* by dropping blobs of paint on paper, folding it, and spreading the paint. They opened the paper, chose from an assortment of crayons and pens and added their art work to the image to make it conform to their conceptualizations of *Blobbo Bug*. Then the children wrote stories telling about the habits of this rare creature.

In another session for first and second graders, children wrote comic strips and cartoons. They were given copies of comic strip characters with blank balloons. After writing in the words for the characters, they shared their results with the total group.

Sessions for third and fourth graders ranged from developing skills for interviewing to writing of poetry, short stories, practical writing forms and diaries. In a session on interviewing, children considered what questions should be asked in order to find out about one another and what techniques would be needed for writing up the interview. Working in pairs, they interviewed one another, wrote up the information, and discussed the procedure. In a poetry session, children began by sharing the poems they had brought with them. The discussion that followed focused on such questions as: How do you begin to write a poem? What poets do you read and why? What is your favorite image? The remainder of the time was devoted to the writing of an original poem by the group. In order to inspire the writing, children closed their eyes and extended their arms to feel three mobiles which brushed past them, carried by three volunteers. One mobile was wooden, one metallic and one woollen. The mobiles were removed, children opened their eyes and wrote their impressions of the feeling experience. Then the mobiles were returned to the room and as children gave their spontaneous impressions of the experience, their ideas were recorded on the blackboard. Using these ideas and those they had jotted down on paper, the group wrote an original poem about the universe.

A recording of space and rocket sounds was used in a session of fiction writing for fifth and sixth graders. The session began with the sharing of the fiction contributions children had brought with them, followed by a discussion of attributes of writing that identify it as a piece of fiction. As they moved into the writing phase of the session, children were first asked to close their eyes for a moment, project themselves in time and imagine what was happening. The record of space and rocket sounds played, as they imagined life in the future. They then wrote fiction selections inspired by the music and their thinking.

A short time later, the same children attended a session on writing autobiographies. Again they transposed themselves in time, imagining life about twenty years hence, and contemplating what their lives would be like at that future time.

One child (Alexandra Briggs, Grade 5 (eleven year olds), Peabody School, Cambridge, Massachusetts) wrote:

Grown-Up Me
In the years to come I would like to go to Harvard College and have two major studies these two would be, Philosophy and creative writing (I have no idea of any other major study's they might have there.) I would take organ lessons with a private teacher. I would also like to be a grand opera singer and sing at the Metropolitan theater. Art is one of the wonderful things I would love to be. My feet are always moving and are very graceful. I do different things I've never seen before and I'm sure nobody else has either. Writing is one of the loveliest things. I always find myself writing something. I would like to explore it more thoroughly.

Throughout the day children wrote, shared their writing with one another and generated a sense of excitement about what was happening. Many of them visited the art workshop, some to illustrate something they had written, others to draw and paint their ideas. The art workshop served as a change of pace from the more structured activities of the sessions. Children were heard planning their time so that they could work in the art room and leave on time for their next scheduled session. The same was true for the films, which were being shown throughout the day.

The final outcome of the conference, the *Creative Writing Journal*, contains selections of writing of most of the children who attended. Some of the material was written at the conference, some was brought or sent in. The illustrations were also the work of the children, some submitted with their writing, others drawn specifically for the publication. The journal reflects the variety of literary forms and the uniqueness of conceptualizations that characterize the writing of youngsters when they express their own thoughts, feelings and ideas in written form.

Teachers and principals who attended the conference spent the morning hours with Mr Cullum, trying out a variety of techniques that could be implemented in their own classrooms. Basic to his approach is an emphasis on developing an atmosphere where people feel at home with themselves and others and are free to express themselves. Teachers shared their fantasies, talked about the affective aspects of writing, had fun with words and acted out Cullum's version of Aesop's fables. A film showing Mr Cullum interacting with children pictured a scene in a school playground with a huge strip of paper running down the length of the playground. Children simulated swimming the Mississippi River and then wrote about it.

In the afternoon, some teachers met informally with Mr Cullum to rap about writing and the teaching of creative writing in elementary classrooms: others watched the film *Born Free* with their pupils.

Assessing the outcome

Judging from the attitudes of teachers, children and graduate students, and from the reams of creative writing that had been collected, the general impression, at the end of the day, was that the Young Writers' Conference had been a success. A final assessment was conducted several weeks later, when graduate students interviewed the children and teachers who had participated.

Interviewing of the children focused on determining their reactions to the total experience. They were asked questions to find out if they had enjoyed the day, what they felt were the most valuable aspects of the experience, what they thought ought to be changed, and if they had continued to write after the conference. For the 113 children attending the conference, seventy-three interviews were returned. In each school represented in the returns several children had been interviewed individually, others were seen in groups.

The responses showed that almost every child interviewed had positive attitudes about the total experience, would like to return next year, had come to the conference prepared to share his or her own writing with others, and had written new material during and following the conference. These responses tend to support the conclusion that children who were involved in the Young Writers' Conference may well have gained an increased sense of pride in authorship and a sense of importance as writers. At the time of the interviews the *Creative Writing Journal* had not yet been published, so that the effects of the outcome of the conference, that of seeing their own work in print, could not be assessed. It seems reasonable to assume that the journal will contribute to even more positive attitudes towards writing and reading.

The interviewing of the children also focused on their perceptions of weaknesses of the day's format, so that planning for the following year could be more effective. They were quite clear on what they saw as weaknesses, and gave a variety of suggestions for change. Suggestions were extremely varied, with individual children identifying specific unsatisfactory aspects of one session or another. The only consistent comment dealt with the length of the sessions. It points up the need to have longer sessions, even for the younger children, so that they can have ample time to finish what they have started to write and additional time to interact with their new friends.

Teacher interviews provided insights about their sessions, and about the effectiveness of the children's participation. Teachers felt the conference was a valuable use of children's time in many ways. They reported that children had gained a sense of importance about what they were doing, had stimulated other children to want to participate, had been excited and talkative about their experiences on the drive home, were inspired by such an event, and had benefited from being involved with children from other schools. Additional comments stressed the value of being exposed to writers from other schools, and to differing writing approaches. One teacher pointed out that it was valuable for children to discover that there was some place for writing outside of school.

Teachers also reported that they had used the creative writing idea booklet distributed prior to the conference. In those cases where it had been received, all teachers tried some of the suggestions in their classrooms. In some cases other teachers in the school made use of it, and in a few instances copies were made for every staff member. The interviews also revealed that in a number of schools the teachers had not received the booklet. A more effective means of distribution of materials in advance of any future conference is clearly needed.

In suggesting some alteration of conference procedures, the only consistent suggestion made by teachers was that it would have been nice to see what the children were doing in their sessions. Most teachers found the morning session with Albert Cullum extremely valuable and later used the ideas he had presented in their own classrooms.

Conclusions
The overall impression gained from the many months of involvement in the Young Writers' Conference was that events of this kind benefit teacher-training programmes in several ways. As a cooperative venture of the college and local schools, it increases the interaction between teachers, college faculty and graduate students, and provides for greater understanding and learning. For the children, the results of the interviews indicate that it was a valuable experience. Impressions of those who conducted the sessions and the responses of the children and teachers very strongly supports the conclusion that, as a result of their participation, children did gain a sense of pride in authorship and an increasingly positive view of the importance of writing. It is best summed up in the words of a fourth grader who wrote, 'Happiness is to get a letter from a friend even if you can't read.'

Part 4

The adult reader

15   The adult literacy curriculum: the content must be the goal

Tom MacFarlane

> A book is a loaded gun in the house next door. Burn it. Take the shot from the weapon. Breach man's mind. Who knows who might be the target of the well-read man? Me? I won't stomach them for a minute. (Bradbury 1954)

Ray Bradbury's fireman, living in a utopian fireproof world, now has the job of burning books '. . . as custodian of our peace of mind . . .' because, as he explains to a woman caught in possession: 'None of those books agree with each other.'

Bruner (1967) has argued convincingly that the goals of instruction should be oriented to 'process' and not 'product'. He claims that product-oriented curricula ignore '. . . the major difficulty . . . that while a body of knowledge is given life and direction by the conjectures and dilemmas that brought it into being and sustained its growth, pupils who are being taught often do not have a corresponding sense of conjectures and dilemmas'.

Russell Stauffer (1968) has linked this view of the curriculum to the field of reading, arguing that the skills of learning to read only have relevance in the wider context of 'productive reading thinking'.

Stauffer's outline of methodology (which is eminently practical) deserves to be better known, whether we are teaching reading to the six year old or the fifty-six year old. That it is of urgent relevance to adult literacy curricula has been convincingly argued by Donald Mocker (1975) who takes the view that the problem with the traditional approach to reading (using reading schemes etc.) is threefold: (a) it fails in ' . . . not recognizing the experience and knowledge which each student brings to the class', (b) it fails in not ' . . . placing responsibility for learning on the student, thus not helping the adult to become more independent' and (c) it encourages the pupil to see the teacher as the person 'with all the answers' rather than as a 'co-learner'.

There are two intertwined reasons for the difficulty I have always experienced on training courses for tutors in arguing for the process view of the teaching of reading (leaving aside the problem of time).

Firstly, most of us are in varying degrees handicapped by our product-selection oriented system of education. As Popper (1945) pointed out, such a system encourages students 'to acquire only such knowledge as is serviceable in getting (them) over the hurdles which they must clear for the sake of advancement . . . instead of encouraging . . . a real love for (the) subject and for inquiry'.

It is a logical concomitant of a system that values facts-regurgitated rather than facts-transformed that we have all learned (teachers and pupils) to see the teacher's role as that of curricular (as well as behavioural) authority. Bruner's call for the teacher to be a 'catalyst of events' goes unheeded despite the existence of detailed curricular models such as MACOS (Hanley *et al* 1969).

Secondly, and related very strongly to this first issue, is the tutor's own view of the reading process. The question for our training courses may well have to shift from, 'How do we produce good reading tutors?' to, 'How do we approach the problem that we ourselves are very often uncritical and ineffective readers, are frequently the passive victims of slick advertising, fraudulent political arguments and obscurely written "explanatory notes"?' – to name but a few of the manipulations of the printed media to which we can be subjected.

Chapman (1973) concluded his research with this claim: 'It would seem, then, that not only must the college of education student be taught to teach reading, but in many cases he must be taught to read.'

Can I rewrite that claim in an adult literacy context? It would seem, then, that not only must tutors be taught to teach reading, they must also be shown that reading is a thinking, responsive, process with all the massive personal and curricular implications that are attendant upon such a change of objectives.

Ray Bradbury's fireman remains locked away in his novel, but we ought to ask ourselves if his attitudes have not been with us for centuries. In analysing Plato's effect on education, Popper (1945) would claim that this has been the case – it may well be that the teacher of critical responsive reading is a menace to the '. . . custodians of our peace of mind'. One thing seems to me to be true, even if all this speculation is dismissed: unless we are prepared to set our sights higher than the mastery of narrow word attack skills we are likely merely to exchange adult illiteracy for adult ex-literacy.

Finally, may I offer some suggested headings towards adult literacy tutor-training:

1 Tutors should consider their own reading. Responses to controversial reading material. Simulated reading-thinking activities.
2 Reading breakdown. Tutors should consider under what circumstances and for what reasons their own reading breaks down.
3 The comprehension process. Simulation activities to demonstrate to tutors that 'words are not the units of meaning'.
4 The effective reader. Tutors to build a picture of the effective reader and the skills he uses.
5 Develop working models of integrated levels of reading for use at the beginning stages.
6 Attitudes towards, and beliefs about, pupils. If numbers 1–5 are one pillar, this is the other and equally vital support in building a relevant curriculum. For personal as well as technical reasons tutors need to be persuaded against the 'authority' view of the teacher-curriculum, and towards the 'co-learner' concept.

References

BRADBURY, R. (1954) *Fahrenheit 451* Corgi Books

BRUNER, J. S. (1967) *Toward a Theory of Instruction* Harvard: Belknap Press

CHAPMAN, L. J. (1973) Reading comprehension in a college of education *Reading* 7, 1, 24–31

HANLEY, J. P. *et al* (1969) *Man – A Course of Study – An Evaluation* Cambridge, Massachusetts: Educational Development Center

MOCKER, D. (1975) Cooperative learning process: shared learning experience in teaching adults to read *Journal of Reading* 18 440–4

POPPER, K. R. (1945) *The Open Society and its Enemies* vol. I *Plato* Routledge and Kegan Paul

STAUFFER, R. (1968) 'Productive reading thinking at the first grade level' in M. Dawson (Ed) *Developing Critical Reading* Newark, Delaware: International Reading Association

16   Effective reading in higher education

Anthony K. Pugh

Introduction

In this country, although the reading difficulties of students have sometimes been recognized (Beard 1972; Latham 1975; Reid 1973), their needs have not been well met. Whereas in Canada and in the United States many students at colleges and universities receive help in learning to read efficiently for study purposes (Hayward 1971; Shaw 1961), only two British universities (Brunel and Leeds) have devoted resources to helping their students read more effectively. Another university (Sussex) has been aware of the problem and has allowed a commercial concern to offer a version of the Dynamic Reading Institute's speed reading course (Watts 1972). It is doubtful, however, whether speed reading has much relevance to students in view of the various different kinds of reading they undertake (Pugh 1972a; 1975).

One unfortunate effect of this lack of concern with students' reading in higher education is the scarcity of suitable British tests for assessing students' reading abilities and diagnosing their weaknesses. The only test readily available is by Black (1954). This has been used recently for assessing the reading standards of college of education students (Chapman 1973), but it is outdated and, even when new, had little value as a predictor of students' success in other areas. There is also a sentence-completion test (Warden 1956) which has been used in colleges and was found, with a group of overseas undergraduates, to be a good predictor of examination performance (Heaton and Pugh 1975). However, it has been found to correlate poorly with native students' performance in other tasks (Pugh 1974) and it seems likely that native English-speaking sixth formers and undergraduates are too near the ceiling of the test for it to discriminate well.

The lack of tests not only makes for difficulties in deciding which students need help; it also makes it difficult to evaluate the effective-

142

ness of the help they receive. This paper is concerned with the design and evaluation of a course entitled *Techniques for Effective Reading* (Pugh 1972b) which, between 1971 and 1974, was attended by over 600 students and staff at the University of Leeds. The purpose of the paper is to clarify some of the problems involved in teaching and testing reading in higher education, and to put forward some solutions.

The 'Techniques for Effective Reading' course
From 1965 until 1974 the University of Leeds offered, free of charge, courses in reading efficiency to any students or members of staff who wished to enrol. The courses were initiated as a result of a visit to the United States by the then Professor of Law, who took a speed reading course and was impressed by it. Early courses at Leeds were mainly concerned with speed of reading, although gradually it came to be realized that this concern was too narrow. In 1971, the present writer was appointed to continue to teach the courses, redesigning them as necessary, and to provide a full evaluation of them.

Objectives of the course
The main objective of the course was to enable students to read more efficiently. Efficiency was defined as a ratio between effort expended and useful work done, although the difficulties of measuring both effort and work in this context were recognized. Also, since a person's efficiency may only be judged in relation to what he is trying to do (or, perhaps, what he should be doing), it is clear that not only skill but also purpose must be taken into account. Consequently, some more specific objectives were:

1   to enable students to use a variety of reading skills, styles and strategies;
2   to enable students to clarify as specifically as possible their own reading purposes when they encounter a text;
3   to help students adopt the appropriate skills and strategies for achieving their purposes.

Also, in view of the effects of physical conditions on reading (see Carmichael and Dearborn 1948; Tinker 1965) it was necessary to add a further objective:

4   to enable students to recognize physical conditions which affect efficiency.

Brief description of the course

A typical course consisted of eight weekly meetings of one and a quarter hours. Meetings comprised exercises, an informal lecture and group discussion. The main purpose of the group discussion was to relate what was dealt with in the meeting to the students' own study reading.

At the beginning of a course, students were given tests (which had been field-tested with other groups) of two types of reading. For one of the tests the purpose was to find an answer to a question as quickly as possible. There were, in all, five questions and five passages in this test. For the other test the student's purpose was to read a passage as he would if he were to discuss it fairly soon afterwards in a tutorial or seminar. He was told to follow the author's argument, to remember his main points but not to attempt to remember detail. These two quite different reading strategies (designated 'search reading' and 'receptive reading') were chosen partly because they lent themselves to testing, but also to illustrate the importance of purpose in deciding how to approach a text. At the end of the course, equivalent forms of these tests were given to assess changes in performance during the course.

During the course, exercises were given which involved search reading and receptive reading, but practice was also given in skimming. Skimming is often described as a skill for obtaining the gist of a passage, but it seemed important to emphasize that it is often used as a processing strategy; that is, a reader may skim to decide whether to read a text and/or how to read a text. Thus, he may use skimming in order to clarify, in the light of some knowledge of what the writer has to offer, his own purpose in reading.

A full list of the strategies discussed in the course is given elsewhere (Pugh 1975), with fuller information on them. It must be noted, however, that the importance of purpose in reading was stressed by giving practice in reading tasks where different strategies were needed to achieve different purposes. Unfortunately, difficulties arose over testing skimming, in view of the subjectivity involved in assessing what was achieved from skimming a text.

The importance of transfer to realistic reading tasks and normal study situations was emphasized throughout the course and for this reason each of the following topics had most of a lecture devoted to them: conditions for reading; memory and note-taking; using a book for study. Although there was some practical work on these topics, it seems likely that the exercises and tests which students do themselves will have the greatest impression on them. Much more work needs to be done on devising exercises which give students reasonably accurate feedback on their performance.

The inaccuracy of feedback during a course was partly overcome by admitting frankly to students that the exercises had serious limitations and that they must also make their own assessments of their success (or otherwise). However, in the early part of the course, weaknesses in tests of the speed reading type were put to good effect, for by using such tests most students were able to read about twice as quickly in a passage of the order of 1000 words, when their purpose was to read receptively. This practice was certainly motivational, and was a useful preparation for skimming. It may also have helped some students to settle down quickly to their study reading tasks.

Evaluation of the course

Evaluation of performance was limited, because of the problems of testing already noted. However, it was found that (taking group mean time) students worked significantly more quickly at the end of a course than at the beginning, when compared on comparable tests of search reading and receptive reading. Also, they tended to be slightly more accurate. These effects could, however, be explained by familiarity with the type of task rather than taken as evidence of any real improvement.

Just over 50 per cent of those who enrolled completed a course. Questionnaires and interviews suggested that most of these students considered that they had benefited. Also, most students were able, in their questionnaires, to instance situations or tasks where what they had learned in the course proved useful. Skimming was considered to be the most useful strategy learned.

A controlled study was carried out with twenty-one first-year students in an experimental group and a similar number in a matched control group to determine the effect of the course on tasks involving the use of books for locating information. It was found that the experimental subjects were no faster than the control group, but that they tended to be more accurate.

Conclusions

The design and evaluation of the course brought to light considerable difficulties in the testing of reading at this level. There is no overwhelming evidence that the course was entirely successful in achieving its objectives, although there is fairly convincing evidence that students who completed the course felt that it had done them good. Also, it seems likely that in a broad sense it is useful for students in higher education to be given some stimulus and opportunity to think about and discuss their approaches to reading.

The course described here provides a basis for further work in this field. The fact that about one fifth of all new students at Leeds considered it worth their while to enquire about the course suggests that there is a demand, perhaps even a need, among the most literate school leavers for help in learning to read efficiently for study in higher education.

References

BEARD, R. (1972) *Teaching and Learning in Higher Education* (second edition) Penguin

BLACK, E. L. (1954) *Comprehension Test for College of Education Students* NFER

CARMICHAEL, L. and DEARBORN, W. F. (1948) *Reading and Visual Fatigue* Harrap

CHAPMAN, L. J. (1973) Reading comprehension in a college of education *Reading* 7, 1, 24–31

HAYWARD, F. M. (1971) Reading and study instruction in Canadian universities and colleges *Journal of Reading* 15 27–9

HEATON, J. B. and PUGH, A. K. (1975) The relationship between overseas students' English test scores and their academic achievement *The Times Higher Educational Supplement* 14 March, 10

LATHAM, W. (1975) 'The teaching of reading – a crisis?' in W. Latham (Ed) *The Road to Effective Reading* Ward Lock Educational

PUGH, A. K. (1972a) Adult reading: theory and practice *Reading* 6, 3, 23–9

PUGH, A. K. (1972b) *Techniques for Effective Reading* (student booklet; tutor notes; test and practice materials) The University of Leeds Reading Efficiency Unit

PUGH, A. K. (1974) *The Design and Evaluation of Reading Efficiency Courses* unpublished M.Phil. thesis: The University of Leeds

PUGH, A. K. (1975) 'The development of silent reading' in W. Latham (Ed) *The Road to Effective Reading* Ward Lock Educational

REID, J. F. (1973) Students who cannot study *University of Edinburgh Bulletin* 9, 11, 1–2

SHAW, P. (1961) 'Reading in college' in N. B. Henry (Ed) *Development In and Through Reading* Chicago: University of Chicago Press

TINKER, M. A. (1965) *Bases for Effective Reading* Minneapolis: University of Minnesota Press

WARDEN, V. B. (1956) *Construction and Standardization of a Reading Comprehension Test* unpublished M.A. thesis: University of London

WATTS, W. J. (1972) *A Critical Investigation of Advanced Learning Methods as Taught by the College of Advanced Reading* University of Sussex Centre for Educational Technology

Part 5

Research and assessment

Eric A. Lunzer

The project described in this paper has been under way for the best part of two years, having commenced in September 1973. It has a further year to run before completion. I propose to outline the project as a whole, what its aims are and how we have sought to implement them. I will briefly cover the work we have done so far, and then concentrate on two studies which we have recently completed. I will also mention the work we plan to do next year, to honour our commitment to the Schools Council. But because most of our work bears on the problems of reading comprehension in general, I want to devote part of the paper to discussing this. Naturally, I cannot hope to do justice to any of these themes and hope that this will be forgiven.

I will begin by setting out the aims of the project. They are:

1   to investigate what reading demands are made of pupils by teachers
2   to investigate what teachers expect children to gain from their reading
3   to investigate what the children in fact gain from their reading
4   if there are significant differences between 2 and 3 to establish what reasons might be suggested and how these might be evaluated
5   to make suggestions for the improvement of reading for learning in the secondary school.

I should perhaps add that, although we do not intend to leave literary reading out altogether, we have concentrated most of our attention on reading for learning. In consequence, our work must lose a great deal of its charm, but I hope it will still retain considerable interest.

My next task is to tell you who are the members of our team. They are:

Keith Gardner (co-director)
Colin Harrison
John Cole
Terry Dolan
Roy Fawcett
Maurice Waite.

Not all of these are employed directly by the Schools Council. But all have worked very hard on the project, contributing both ideas, knowhow and the sheer hard grind that is an inseparable part of all research. The work that I am reporting is the work of the team in which I play a very minor part. I am, as it were, the front man – and that is all.

Now let me present some idea of the various jobs we have been doing to try to implement our aims. To find out what children are reading we concerned ourselves first of all with observing lessons in the last year of the junior school and in the first and fourth year of the secondary school and recording our observations on carefully prepared schedules. We noted what the teacher did and what was done by one chosen child, and we recorded over a hundred such sessions. As a result we have accumulated a detailed and not un-representative account of the sort of thing that actually goes on in lessons of all kinds right across the curriculum and the part that reading plays therein. Perhaps the most important conclusion that we reached from these observations related to the span of 'reading episodes'. Whereas something like 16 per cent of the time spent in lessons is spent in reading of some sort (it varied of course from one subject to another, and sometimes from one year to another), most of the reading done in the classroom is of fairly short tracts. The average reading episode lasts considerably less than a minute, and this will be followed by doing something else, perhaps writing, but not always. The kind of reading that extends to two or three pages or more plays a relatively small part in actual lesson time.

Next year we are going on to find how much of this more extended reading is done in homework time. We have already mounted a pilot enquiry along these lines. A number of teachers have suggested to us that, when you are faced with mixed-ability groups, it does not necessarily make sense to use reading to introduce new subject matter, or to rely on reading as the main instrument of instruction.

Their argument is surely not unreasonable. It may be that extended reading is more often required in homework than it is in school time. But are teachers giving enough encouragement to pupils to make use of reading as a means of learning and do they give them sufficient help? We found that in some of the classes we visited the answer was yes. But they are a minority. We have also augmented our observations in local schools with many visits to schools all over the country, schools that were selected for us by LEAS because they were doing interesting things in reading. These visits were very instructive to us and we hope we will be able to pass on some of what struck us as significant instances of good practice in our report. There are many schools up and down the country which do concentrate on reading across the curriculum. We found science teachers and mathematics teachers as well as several English teachers who were very interested in how reading can be used in the curriculum and how it can be taught. The observations of these teachers will be included in our report and will, I am sure, prove a focus of interest for other teachers.

But we have not relied solely on the reports of others. In addition, we have ourselves been conducting study groups in the course of which we have tried to explore a number of different ways of helping pupils to gain in their comprehension of what they read. Among the activities with which we have been mainly concerned I should mention group prediction and group cloze. In group prediction the text to be discussed is first broken up into smaller chunks, usually of paragraph length, and these are exposed successively with a discussion break between one chunk and the next. During these intervals the group will discuss what has been said and what is likely to follow and why. We found it useful to ask members of the group to act as discussion leaders instead of the teacher. The procedure for group cloze is very similar. As in the individualized cloze comprehension passages, a number of words are deleted from the text which is shown to the group, and the object of the exercise is to establish what are the missing words and why. We have also been experimenting with cutting up texts and then requiring pupils, again acting as a group, to restore the correct order. All these are exercises which are designed to encourage children, not simply to read, but to reflect on what they are reading. The idea of reflecting on what is being read is central in this presentation and I will come back to it towards the end.

Next I would mention our study of the readability of texts used in the course of secondary education. To find out something about the relative difficulty of the reading matter used in the various subjects of the curriculum, we began by making a collection of all the books and other material used during a single week by first and fourth year secondary pupils in all the secondary schools in one area of Nottingham, eleven schools in all. We are now carrying out a readability study of these. First of all, we are applying a large number of different formulae to find out how they agree with one another. We are testing the formulae against pupil comprehension as measured by cloze procedure and we are also testing them against pupil estimate of difficulty and teacher estimate of difficulty. As a result of these procedures we should be in a position to give some guidance to teachers about the problems that exist in selecting the most appropriate material for reading within their subjects and how to overcome them.

With the exception of the observations of lessons, none of the studies I have described is yet complete. Nor are we satisfied that we have cast our net sufficiently widely in our attempt to resolve the questions with which we set out. For instance, during the coming year, we would like to clarify our ideas about just what goes on in the course of reading for learning, perhaps by running a few simple laboratory-type experiments designed to elucidate the process involved in skimming a text, or in scanning it for a word or a concept. We also hope to run a brief experiment to test the effectiveness of such methods as group prediction and group cloze. But I am sure you would prefer to read more about what we have accomplished so far than about our plans for the future.

So I would like to provide a brief account of two studies that have been completed. The first is a very ambitious study carried out by Roy Fawcett on the effectiveness of SRA. Such an enquiry was needed, as the number of studies carried out in this country is relatively small and the controls have been relatively limited, although there have been numerous studies in the context of the United States and some in Australia. Roy Fawcett carried out this particular study in three groups of schools, each comprising three age groups, that is fourth year juniors, first year secondary and fourth year secondary. All of the pupils concerned went through the complete SRA programme – a crash course given over a period of one term – after the manner prescribed by Parker. Considerable guidance was given by Roy himself to all the teachers concerned. Altogether the experiment involved 630 experimental pupils; that is to say, pupils who worked through the SRA material. There were 570 control pupils who carried on with their normal English lessons, and I should add that all these schools were willing to give up a very considerable proportion of their English timetable in order to carry out this experiment and for this we are greatly in their debt.

Now the results of this enquiry were completely unequivocal. Significant gains were made by the experimental pupils as compared with the controls on all the measures that were used. These gains were noted in the first place between September and January, which is the period during which the experiment was carried out. But further improvement was found for the following six months; that is, January to June. The principal measure used in this enquiry was the Gates MacGinitie battery (forms E and D), which yields separate scores for speed, accuracy, vocabulary and comprehension. We found the taught groups gained in every one of the measures at each of the three age levels, and in the vast majority of cases these gains were significant. Similar findings were obtained using the NFER battery and our own test, which I will be describing below. Since the gains continued during the six-month period after the SRA teaching had ceased, one must infer that the pupils concerned had learned something about how to read, something which continued to help them after the crash course had ceased. Of course it may well be true that if you took these measures again in a year's time, those differences might cease to exist. But it would surely be unrealistic to expect a single crash course to have a continued effect on a pupil throughout his school life.

I would add that this experiment was mounted as a test of the potential usefulness of structured material as a whole. Nevertheless it is interesting to note that there was a significant advantage to the SRA material as compared with that of Ward Lock Educational. This was established by Roy Fawcett in the course of a subsidiary experiment involving three classes of third year juniors. He believes that this is probably due to two things. First, there is the importance attached in SRA to the actual way in which children attack their reading. Heavy emphasis is laid on the SQ3R method: survey, question, read, recite, review. It is far from a perfect recipe. Rather it is a drill. But a drill is something to start off with and it seems to pay off. A second reason may perhaps lie in the attention given to motivation in the instructions for the SRA as compared with some other materials.

Next, I want to turn to a quite extensive study that we have conducted on reading comprehension. We set out to construct a test which would be more realistic than the ordinary comprehension test. Such a test would present the pupil with a reading situation which was similar to that which he might encounter in the classroom or at home. The passage should be of a certain length and the questions should be reasonably demanding. Basing ourselves on the various lists of reading skills that have been put out, we deliberately constructed questions to discriminate between them, if possible. There were eight groups of questions, as follows:

1 word meaning
2 word meaning as indicated by context
3 literal comprehension of phrases
4 inferences drawn from one part of the passage
5 inferences drawn from several parts taken together
6 interpretation of metaphors
7 picking out salient points
8 evaluating in relation to the previous knowledge of the reader.

We envisaged these as constituting a hierarchy of comprehension skills. Several questions were framed in each area for each of the passages that we used, and we retained only those questions that were found to be most discriminating and most valid. We constructed four such tests, each based on a separate passage. Most of the work was done by Maurice Waite, ably assisted by Terry Dolan.

Our results were in some ways unexpected. First, we were able to construct tests which had very considerable appeal both to pupils and to teachers, with questions that were indeed as demanding as we had hoped for. The teachers who saw these tests were agreed that they were such as to encourage pupils to reflect on their reading. So the actual experience of doing the tests could be regarded as a valuable learning experience and not a waste of time. We are rather pleased with these tests and hope to publish them in due course. Second – and this is the important point – we did not find any statistical techniques that were successful in separating out the separate skills we had tried to build into the tests. The distribution of scores of items and subskills all point to a single factor which may be termed comprehension. We found exactly the same when we used the Edinburgh Reading Test. This has five different sections, reading for facts, comprehension of sequences, retention of main ideas, comprehension of points of view and vocabulary. We found the correlations between these various subtests and our own tests were uniformly high, ranging from 0.7 to 0.9. The Edinburgh tests are less easy than ours to administer, but like our tests they measure reading comprehension reasonably well. But here again there was no suggestion, or very little suggestion, that the different subscales were measuring distinct skills.

As a final resort we carried out a cluster analysis on our 300 subjects: that is, we grouped together those pupils who had obtained similar patterns of scores on the different subtests. We found it useful to look at three clusters. The first consisted of pupils who had obtained high scores on all measures, while the third group had obtained low scores on all measures. But we were particularly interested in the intermediate group. This was because their raw scores suggested that perhaps they had been more successful in the more elementary tasks of word meaning, literal comprehension and inference from specific parts of the text, than in the remainder of the tasks. If this was indeed the case, it could be argued that there is a hierarchy of comprehension skills, and that our tests are tapping this hierarchy at two levels. Accordingly we converted all the raw scores to ipsative measures. More precisely, we calculated the regression of scores for the more demanding tasks on those obtained in the three tasks just mentioned. We then expressed each individual's score in these tasks as a deviation from his expected score. We predicted that both the high scoring group and the low scoring group should get deviation scores of near zero, suggesting a flat profile: good all round or poor all round. The intermediate group should obtain predominantly negative scores, reflecting their relative weakness at the predicted tasks. Our findings were quite different: the high scorers were even better at the predicted tasks, the intermediate group were indeed weaker, but the lowest group was the weakest of all. In other words, the five tests spread the pupils a little more than did the three, and that is all.

This finding did not in any way support the idea of there being a number of different comprehension skills, rather that comprehension was something unitary.

At this point we were led to re-examine our thinking. Our failure to identify a number of subskills in reading is not an isolated one, and the majority of American studies in this area have yielded results that are essentially similar. Many of those that do report more than one comprehension factor are open to objections of various kinds. The suggestion I would like to make is that comprehension is not a composite of many skills. It is not a skill at all. Rather it is an aptitude which relies on a skill – the skill of reading, together with an attitude of mind; the willingness to reflect on what one is reading or has just read.

This conclusion is based on a more rigorous examination of the term 'skill' in its technical sense, as used by psychologists. Those who make most use of the term are those who study the development of athletic abilities and of abilities in other areas of complex goal-directed behaviour such as musical performance. Now we find that there are a number of features that are common to all such skills, over and above the observation that they allow of a more or less flexible organization of goal-directed activity:

1 Skilled performance implies the integration of several different component organizations of behaviour by means of a hierarchy of controls.
2 Decisions are often required in one system at the same time as other decisions within another.
3 Decisions arrived at in one part of the system are apt to affect decisions in other parts.
4 Any new refinements that are acquired cannot simply be added to the behaviour; they must be integrated within the control system at several points.
5 It is usually possible to describe a number of subskills within the skill as a whole.

Each of those features is illustrated in Table 1 (page 159) with reference to four very different skills: playing the game of tennis, playing the violin, talking and reading. Perhaps the most salient of them is the high degree of complexity in skilled behaviour, as manifested by the number of mutually interacting decisions that need to be made within a limited time scope. It is this which gives rise to the importance of automatization of subroutines in skilled performance, to plateaux in learning, to the importance of timing and so on.

Despite this, it would be foolish to ignore the usefulness of the analogy between the requirements of skilled performance in physical skills on the one hand and in scholastic tasks on the other. For instance, in the relatively simple skill of driving a car, one knows that the novice who needs to think about just how to change gear is liable to find either that his steering goes awry for lack of feedback at the proper moment, or that he simply has not the time left to take a turn smoothly. In much the same way, a pupil faced with the solution of a problem in calculus is seriously handicapped if he doesn't dispose of a ready armoury of algebraic techniques, together with a knowledge of when they are appropriate. If he

Table 1 Critical features of true skills

	Tennis	Playing the violin	Speech	Reading
Hierarchy of control systems	1 Winning the point 2 Choice of shot 3 Positioning and follow through	1 Rendering 2 Bowing and fingering 3 Pressure and vibrato	1 Communication 2 Selection of lexical and grammatical options 3 Selection of phonological options	1 Finding meaning 2 Use of semantic and syntactic cues 3 Use of orthographic cues
Near simultaneity of decisions	Type of shot and placement	Change in volume and tempo	Options in lexis, grammar and in intonation	Interpretation of cues from several sources Interpretation of lexical and grammatical meanings
Interaction of component systems	Visual feedback determines body movements as well as eye movements (keeping eye on ball)	Alternative fingerings affect bowing	Rearrangement of syntax affects total utterance as in 'It is unfortunate that...' and similar transformations	As above
Refinements to be integrated	How to handle spin	Vibrato, more difficult keys	Acquisition of negative and interrogative	Skimming, speed-reading, scanning and use of dictionary
Subskills	Variety of shots e.g. backhand service	Pluck, bowing	Intimate, polite and formal registers	Use of phonic rules

has to make a selection out of a relatively large number of these instead of homing in on the most appropriate fairly automatically, and if any or all of those he considers must be regenerated from first principles, then the load on his attention capacity may well become excessive, with the result that he may forget why he did the conversion in the first place in the context of the problem as a whole. Automatization of routines, both in terms of their execution and of the indications for their execution, is clearly an important common factor in the two situations. The constraints in the one case are time constraints arising out of changes in the external field, while in the other they are load constraints depending on the pupil's capacity for handling a complex informational programme (which is presumably in part a problem of short-term memory).

Nevertheless, the very aptness of the analogy suggests something about the specificity of the 'skill' element in intellectual performance. It is a specificity which arises from the content of the given domain rather than the nature of the thinking operation. The competent mathematician is not always equally competent as a literary critic and neither may he shine at bridge, even if he knows the rules of the game.

Such considerations lead us to question whether there is anything that might be called a general skill of comprehension, and even more to question whether the so-called subskills we tried to find are skills in any sense of the term. I prefer to think of comprehension as a unitary aptitude which consists in the ability and the willingness to reflect on the matter that one is reading. Reflection itself is a matter of extracting meanings and finding other meanings, both in the text as a whole and in the long-term memory store of the reader, and in reconciling these meanings by disambiguation and inference. This process of reflection is required in any demanding task, which is why one finds such high correlations between different 'comprehension skills', correlations that are as high as the reliability of the supposed improvements.

On the other hand, I do believe that there are a number of ways in which one can help pupils to tackle the problem of learning from written material. It does seem to be legitimate to regard such modifications of the reading process as skimming, scanning and rapid reading as being subskills which can be trained, and which are appropriate at some times and not at others. The reader can be helped to decide when they are appropriate.

The accompanying diagram (Figure 1 on page 161) may help to illustrate what I mean. The reader who has had no instruction in

Figure 1   Reading strategies

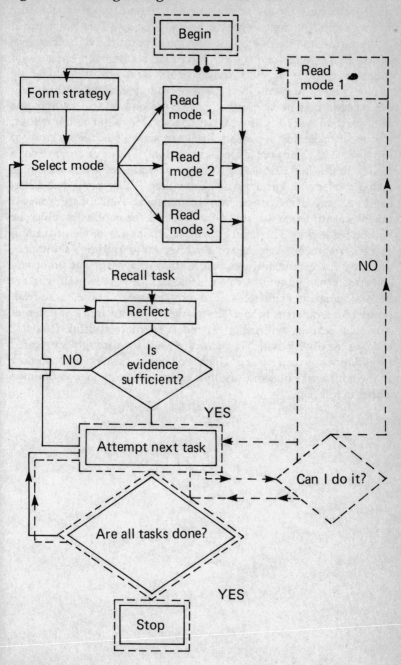

how to learn from what he reads can be expected to bring the same strategy to bear on his reading of text regardless of its difficulty and regardless of the task which he has been set. This is illustrated in the right-hand pathway. The only reading made available to him is Mode I, sometimes called receptive reading. It consists in successively decoding the passage word by word and phrase by phrase, with little variation in speed of reading, and without pausing for reflection. If he is given a task at the end of the reading, the same method is used as often as necessary. (One might add, however, that most readers at secondary level can scan a passage to look for the right 'bit' to answer a specific question.) The more sophisticated reader has at his disposal a variety of strategies from which he makes a selection. His approach to reading is illustrated in the left-hand pathway. His first step is to formulate an appropriate strategy, having regard to the nature of the text and the context in which he will be reading it. The strategy will determine the mode of reading at each stage, be it receptive reading, rapid reading, skimming, scanning for certain features, verification of a particular point and so forth. When he returns to a specific task he asks himself whether he has sufficient evidence, and if not, he may choose to re-read, perhaps in a different mode. The availability of a variety of different modes of reading will make his reflection more fruitful. It is this kind of flexibility which is achieved in part through structured programmes of reading and which we hope to develop and promote in the course of our work, using a variety of techniques as outlined earlier in this paper.

18 *Extending Beginning Reading:* an outline of the research project

Vera Southgate

The Schools Council project *Extending Beginning Reading* was originally planned as a three-year project. The excellent response from practising teachers, who worked as members of a reading research group with the project team during the first year, led to a proposal for a year's extension of the programme being granted. As a result, the project is now planned to last four years, from September 1973 to August 1977. The research team, which is based at Manchester University, consists of the director, two research associates and one secretary.

Rationale underlying the research

'Beginning reading' is a phrase imported from the USA. In this country it may perhaps be defined fairly loosely as the early stages of reading development which lead to the average level of reading attainment in children at the end of the infant school. At this stage an average child of seven and a half years has generally completed an infant reading scheme with the help of his teacher and is able to read simple books by himself, with understanding, for his own pleasure and information.

Until fairly recently in the United Kingdom, there has been a tacit belief that when a child has reached this stage of reading ability, the teacher's task consists of supplying him with sufficient books at the appropriate level, listening to him reading aloud and prompting him when he fails to read a word and, occasionally, providing him with brief periods of direct instruction. This acceptance of the minimum amount of reading tuition required by the average and above-average readers in junior and secondary classes has enabled the teachers to devote the larger proportion of their time to helping those children who fail to reach average reading standards. Certainly up to the late 1960s, few teachers had been trained to regard learning to read as a long-term process extending as far as adulthood, and thus they were not well equipped for teaching the more advanced stages of reading.

In such a climate of thought, it was inevitable that reading research had usually been concerned with either the beginning reader or the failing reader. Few reading investigations had concentrated on those normal developmental processes following the infant stage, which eventually lead children of average reading ability to become effective adult readers. Accordingly, when the proposal for the current research project was first outlined in 1969, the focus of attention was on those average readers of seven-plus who had mastered the 'beginning' reading stage.

The main aims of the project are: to discover exact details of these children's competencies and the ways in which they utilize their reading skills; to locate points at which difficulties occur and the strategies the children employ to overcome these difficulties; to note the methods their teachers employ to help them to 'extend' their proficiency during their next two years of schooling, as well as the progress the children make during this period; and to examine, in the children, habits and attitudes likely to encourage them to utilize their reading abilities fully outside school and when they finally leave school.

The rationale underlying the project was responsible for two of its most important features. First, it is essentially a detailed investigation of current practices in schools, based on the belief that a clear insight into what is currently happening in their classes will provide teachers with the most effective basis for considering whether it is possible or desirable to effect improvements and, if so, how this might best be done. The project was therefore planned as an 'intensive' rather than an 'extensive' study. In other words, rather than attempting to gain a small amount of probably superficial information about large numbers of children drawn from a nation-wide sample of schools, the proposal was to study a smaller number of schools in depth, thereby gaining a great deal of information about fewer subjects. It is for this reason that the project is based on an area within a thirty mile radius of Manchester University.

Secondly, the project is firmly school-based, all the field work being carried out in normal classroom conditions. The entire project leans very heavily on the contributions of practising teachers. The two main methods being used, teachers' reading research groups and detailed observations in schools, are complementary to each other and both are wholly dependent upon the cooperation of teachers.

Teachers' reading research groups

One side of the investigation has involved practising teachers, recruited as members of reading research groups, carrying out various reading assessments of children in their own classes and providing the project team with the results, together with other details of their own and the children's reading practices. Throughout the first two years of the project's life, the response from teachers applying to join the research groups has been overwhelming.

The first Teachers' Reading Research Group operating during 1973-74, consisted of 440 teachers, working in teams drawn from 119 schools, situated in fourteen LEAS within the area training organization of Manchester University.

The first task which the research team set themselves was to devise a scheme whereby these teachers might, by completing two questionnaires, either confirm that the project as planned would produce information of practical value to them or indicate those areas of the project's brief which they would prefer to see emphasized. The results of this 'preferred outcomes' enquiry indicated full support for the plans outlined. The teachers showed interest in a number of general questions relating to seven to nine year olds learning to read. For example, they wanted to know more about:

what needs to be learned at this stage
how children actually do learn to read
how this learning process can be eased and accelerated
how positive attitudes to reading can be developed
where the 'sticking points' occur.

They were also interested in questions of assessment, diagnosis and record-keeping and in the grading of reading books in order to match these to children's individual reading abilities. Later work in the project is being geared as far as possible to the expressed preferences of these teachers.

Teachers in the First Reading Research Group undertook various assessments in first and second year junior classes; the information being returned on some 1,800 forms. Teachers in the Second Reading Research Group of 1974-5 consisted of 258 teachers working in teams drawn from sixty-four schools. They undertook somewhat different assignments and returned a large amount of data, much of which has yet to be processed. Teachers in both these groups also attended regular meetings at the university, gave helpful comments on the assessments they had undertaken, and supported and encouraged the project team in every conceivable way. The following are among the assignments the teachers carried out.

1 They tested the reading ability of all the children (some 3,380 of them) in their classes. Even more important, before doing so they estimated the result which each child would achieve.
2 They estimated the number of errors children would make in reading a passage from a book and then tested to verify the accuracy of their estimates.
3 They prepared individual reading profiles of average children, including assessments of:
   (a) look and say words;
   (b) phonic rules;
   (c) number of errors made in reading aloud from a teacher-selected book, a story book of the child's own choice and an information book of the child's own choice.
4 Children's miscues in oral reading were examined and classified.
5 Children were tested using cloze procedure (every tenth word being deleted), to investigate how successfully they were using contextual clues in silent reading.

Classroom observations
The second main method of investigation is by means of classroom observations and assessments of children's reading development, made by members of the project team. Work in this area has gone on continuously throughout the past two years, as part of the developmental planning leading to the intensive study of the third year. Some indications of the extent of this 'intensive' work already undertaken is provided by the following figures: members of the team have worked with 750 children, in twenty different schools, drawn from five LEAs.

The immediate aim of all these observations in schools, and discussions with headteachers and their staff has been to list all those ongoing activities which could in any way be regarded as relating to children's reading. The long-term aim has been to develop instruments, in the form of questionnaires, individual interviews, logs, various measures of achievement and observation schedules, for use in the third year's intensive study in selected schools. By using such a diverse battery of probing techniques it is hoped that an accurate picture can be re-created of all those dynamic processes affecting reading progress which constantly occur in schools throughout the normal working day.

This intensive study will be taking place in some twelve schools, drawn from four LEAs, during the entire school year from September 1975 to July 1976. In this work, the three members of the project team will be helped by experienced teachers who are studying at Manchester University for diplomas and higher degrees and by college of education students in their final year of a B.Ed. course.

A few tentative pointers

During the first two years, the work of the project has been of an exploratory nature, in preparation for the intensive study of the third year. As data from the intensive study will not be available for analysis until August 1976, no firm findings from the project can be expected until after that date.

Nevertheless, certain trends are beginning to manifest themselves. At this stage they certainly cannot be regarded as more than suggestions of possible future findings, particularly as the schools involved were not selected by any sampling technique. However, as so many teachers and others have expressed great eagerness to learn something of the findings of the project, a few tentative pointers are given. It is hoped that they will be accepted as such. As these trends are based mainly on information provided by the 450 volunteer teachers who comprised the first Teachers' Reading Research Group, they cannot at this stage be regarded as firm research findings.

1   *Estimating children's reading levels*
    The majority of teachers in the first research group appeared to be fairly good at estimating the level of reading ability, as tested by Schonell's Graded Word Reading Test, of children in their own classes, in that approximately 60 per cent of them estimated the children's actual scores to within six months. These average findings, however, disguised the fact that the teachers' estimates usually varied according to the sex of the child. The girls' reading levels tended to be slightly over-estimated and the boys' levels appreciably underestimated.

2   *Key Words To Literacy*
    The teachers found that a small proportion of average readers

among eight year olds and even a few average readers among nine year olds were not sufficiently familiar with all the first 200 words of *Key Words To Literacy* (McNally and Murray 1962) to be able to pronounce them unhesitatingly on sight.

3 *Phonics*

There were indications that, among average readers in both first and second year junior classes, there was a percentage of children who were not familiar with the sounds of common digraphs and other phonic rules. For example, the results from one assessment made by the teachers suggested that about 20 per cent of their pupils had no general concept of the rule of the silent 'e' at the end of a word causing the preceding vowel to take the long sound (e.g. in 'made', 'these' and 'nice'). Furthermore, there did not appear to be any progression between the first and second years.

4 *Levels and difficulty of books*

Tentative suggestions regarding the levels of difficulty of the books which these 'average' children were reading in school, based on the number of errors made by the children when reading aloud from them, are as follows:

(a) As many as half of the children in first and second year junior classes were reading, under their teachers' direction, books which they could profitably read on their own without any assistance. In other words, the books which the teachers had selected for them appeared to be too easy for use as instructional materials.

(b) There were wide variations in the difficulty of the books selected by different teachers for children of similar reading levels. For example, the following books of strikingly different levels of difficulty, were being read by eight-year-old children of average ability:
Easy books – Happy Venture Book 2 and Happy Trio Book 2
Difficult books – Wide Range Book 6 and Ladybird Book 12a.

(c) In reading aloud from self-selected story books children averaged more errors than when reading from teacher-provided books – thus suggesting that the books were more difficult for them.

(d) The information books which the children had selected to read on their own, judged by the errors made in reading aloud, appeared even more difficult than their self-selected story books and very much more difficult than their teacher-selected reading books.

5 *Miscues*

The data supplied by teachers on their pupils' miscues in oral reading suggest the following tentative findings:

(a) Fluent oral reading was achieved by most second year junior children, whereas most first year children read word-by-word.

(b) Refusals to attempt words diminished across the age range, although children did not seem to correct themselves more in the second than the first year.

(c) Substitutions, which constituted the largest number of miscues, were made more frequently by first year than second year children.

(d) There was no significant difference between boys and girls on the number or type of miscues.

The end product

Sifting and analysing all the data collected during the first three years of the project's life and writing up the report will occupy the entire fourth year. This means that the report will not be presented to the Schools Council until towards the end of 1977 and that the publication date is likely to be during 1978.

The final form which the report will take cannot be decided until all the data has been processed. Teachers, however, may rest assured that whatever form the report or reports take, the findings will be expressed in readily understandable terms. As the members of the team are well aware of the desires of practising teachers to forward their pupils' reading progress, practical pointers towards the achievement of this end will be drawn out from the research findings.

Reference

MCNALLY, J. and MURRAY, W. (1962) *Key Words to Literacy* The Schoolmaster Publishing Company

19 'Good teaching' and reading progress: a critical review

John Gray

The importance of the teacher

The conclusions of the Bullock Report (DES 1975) reflect something of a turning point in the ongoing debates about the teaching of reading. First, the report rejects the whole series of debates which have dominated discussion about the pros and cons of various 'methods', as marginal to the central issues of teaching children to read. It concludes unequivocally that: 'There is no one method, medium, device or philosophy that holds the key to the process of learning to read.' (page 521). And second, it asserts the importance of the teacher: 'The quality of learning is fashioned in the day-to-day atmosphere of the classroom through the knowledge, intuitions and skill of individual teachers.' (page xxxii). In consequence many of its recommendations are directed entirely at the teacher.

Both conclusions will be welcomed by experienced practitioners who, retrospectively, may wonder why so much energy was expended on what was probably an unreal distinction. Teachers use methods and methods depend for their existence on the teachers who use them. The discussion of 'importance' is then a relative one. A concern for the quality of teaching embraces both. It is difficult to conceive of ways of improving teaching without ensuring more effective use of methods and vice versa.

In fact, although emphasis on the teacher has grown in recent years, it is by no means novel. Over forty years ago Gray (1931) asserted that 'the skill of the teacher and the capacity of the pupils to learn' were more important than the method. Moyle (1974) has claimed that 'there is little doubt that the teacher is rather more important than the materials or the method'. Southgate (1972) has suggested that 'reading drive' (the beliefs and attitudes of the staff about the importance of reading) and the 'teacher's competence in reading tuition' (represented by a combination of ability, beliefs, training and experience) are more crucial than media, methods, materials and procedures in influencing reading progress. Again, in the introduction to the NFER's recent study of the teaching of reading in infant schools (Cane and Smithers 1971), Wiseman argues that: 'we have further evidence of the necessity for much greater emphasis on research in this area'.

Prima facie, these conclusions derive support from the major American studies of reading conducted during the mid and late sixties. The summaries of Bond and Dykstra (1967) with respect to the 'Cooperative Research Programme in First Grade Reading' and Harris (1969) with respect to the CRAFT Project have been particularly influential. The former wrote: 'To improve reading instruction it is necessary to train better teachers of reading rather than to expect a panacea in the form of materials.'; whilst the latter suggested that: 'Recent research has amply demonstrated that differences among teachers are far more important than differences among methods and materials in influencing the reading achievement of children.'

In brief, commonsense, professional experience and the conclusions of several prominent researchers have combined to support the assertion of the teacher's importance. As a direct result, increased efforts to secure implementation of the 'best' of current teaching practices can be expected. In consequence, a general rise in reading standards and a reduction in the incidence of reading failure are anticipated. But to what extent are these expectations matched by the available research evidence to date? The present paper is concerned to seek an answer to this important question.

A more modest view of the research

Unfortunately, in practice, the research justifies a far less confident perspective on the teacher's importance. The almost exclusive concern of the research with methods has left us ill equipped to answer questions with respect to teachers. Briefly, the evidence may be summarized in the following terms: some classes of children in reading research projects have made more progress in reading than others; little or none of the variations in reading outcomes between classrooms has been explained by perceived differences in methods; hence, in consequence, it *might* have been attributable to some other source such as differences between teachers and the teaching relationships they establish in their classrooms. Nevertheless, however likely the explanation, evidence that differences in outcomes are not explained by one variable is poor proof that they are explained by some other variable. Given the overwhelming concern of researchers to date to provide methodologically sophisticated answers to questions about methods, they have usually collected only a bare minimum of potentially relevant data on teachers.

The teacher is, without doubt, an obvious explanation and certainly constitutes one of the major differences between classrooms of children, if not *the* major one. From a research perspective, however, we know remarkably little about what constitutes effective teaching of reading. In particular the idea that there is a single best type of teacher for all situations needs careful and critical examination. Hundreds of studies of methods and pupils must be contrasted with a mere handful on the teacher's contribution. What can be learned from studies of teacher effectiveness?

Research on teacher effectiveness

A large number of studies of teacher effectiveness have been conducted. They can be divided into three types. First, those that have focused on teachers without reference to their pupils' achievements – some teachers and teaching practices are 'obviously good'; second, those that have studied the influence of various background teacher characteristics such as their amount of education, intelligence or scores on a variety of personality and attitude tests, in relation to their pupils' achievement; and third, those that have attempted to relate classroom interaction between teacher and pupil (which of course encompasses many of the foregoing characteristics), to pupil achievement.

The failure of the first type of study to identify successful teaching (defined in terms of improved pupil progress) is scarcely surprising, given that the relationship was implicitly assumed rather than explicitly established. The second type, despite major efforts, has also produced little of practical use. In summarizing both types of study Getzels and Jackson (1963) comment:

> It is said . . . that good teachers are friendly, cheerful, sympathetic and morally virtuous, rather than cruel, depresssed, unsympathetic and morally depraved. But when this has been said, not much that is especially useful has been revealed. For what conceivable human interaction – and teaching implies first and foremost a human interaction – is not better if the people involved are friendly, cheerful, sympathetic and virtuous rather than the opposite?

In contrast, very few studies of the third type have been conducted. Rosenshine (1971), in a comprehensive review, could only identify some fifty in all, not all of which generated significant results and some of which employed concepts which were too vague to be replicated. Of these fifty studies, only eleven are of particular interest to those concerned with the teaching of reading. None of them, incidentally, are British (Gray 1975). Even with respect to these studies, however, the general comments of one reviewer (Averch 1972), who was in turn summarizing the opinions of other reviewers, seem appropriate: 'In spite of this large implied expenditure of time and money, little is known about what constitute desirable teacher characteristics or especially what the influence of teachers is on student performance.' In sum, there seems little prospect of building up profiles of 'effective' teaching from the studies of teacher effectiveness to date.

Practical/professional experience and teacher competence

The reader who is familiar with studies of teacher effectiveness may be forgiven for feeling, however, that the concepts which have tended to dominate this research tradition bear little relationship to the practical/professional experience upon which everyday decisions about the quality of teaching are usually based. Few, if any, practitioners analyse their classroom performances, or those of others, in terms of their 'achievement orientation', 'intellectual effectiveness', 'use of minimum reinforcement' or 'amount of non-verbal affection'. Whilst these concepts may have everyday equivalents, they are remote from the understanding of 'good' teaching which emerges from practical/professional experience. Start (1974) has described this process in the following terms:

> What are used might be termed adjunct criteria. These appear to be logical derivations from what are seen to be 'obviously good' teachers and teaching practices. In this category are professional global assessments by experienced practitioners such as headteachers, college tutors and inspectors. They know that good teaching produces good learning and 'know' they can recognize a good teaching performance when they see it.

It is to this commonsense experience and knowledge that those in training and advisory positions turn when they seek to improve the quality of teaching.

The Bullock Report echoes this view. When it refers to 'the knowledge, intuitions and skill of individual teachers' it is almost certainly drawing upon this body of practical/professional experience. Its recommendations are designed to foster an approach in which each school sets up its own model of 'good practice' in the light of its particular combination of abilities and experience. Within each school, some teachers are seen to possess the relevant skills more than others. The remainder are encouraged to copy or learn from them. The implementation of the Bullock recommendations along the lines proposed can be expected to strengthen this process of decision-making within the school.

How successful will this approach to improving reading standards or reducing reading failure be? Its success depends to a large extent on the relationship between practical/professional experience and reading progress. The pessimistic conclusions of the methods debates were largely reached because of the failure to discover a method (or methods) that was systematically related to reading progress. It would seem appropriate to judge 'effective' teaching at least partly in this light. As Harris (1969) has argued: 'growth in measured reading skill is not a complete criterion of teacher effectiveness, but it is a minimum essential'. On this criterion, then, a 'more effective' teacher would be one whose class, taking into account their abilities and background, made more than average progress in measured reading skills over the year, a 'less effective' teacher one whose class made less than average progress.

Of course, merely knowing that a teacher is effective in this narrow sense would be only part of the picture one would wish to establish of good practice. One would need to include other aspects as well and convince oneself that children's learning had not suffered in other respects before proceeding to make confident recommendations. Nevertheless it is difficult to conceive of a definition of teacher quality or competence which did not include this aspect. What does research to date suggest is the nature of the relationship between practical/professional experience and reading progress?

A first-class teacher?

A variety of descriptions of good teaching are available in the literature, but not all of them are based on classroom observation. One that is has been presented by Morris (1966), who built up her picture of an 'A' grade or 'first-class' teacher from discussion with a large number of heads and observation of an equally large number of classrooms. Claiming a high measure of agreement between herself and the heads in rating teachers, she reports (page 142) that:

. . . (they) made a great effort to improve their classroom environment, showed a keen interest in their pupils' progress, enjoyed reading themselves and were interested in research in reading and education generally. They believed that all children, unless classified as 'educationally subnormal', could achieve adequate reading standards by the end of their primary course, and, if some failed to do so, it was the result of unsatisfactory school conditions. In other words they felt that the children's initial difficulties, either in themselves or in their home circumstances, could be overcome with sympathetic understanding on the part of teachers. These 'A' teachers had an extensive knowledge of reading methods and materials. In practice their methods were appropriate for all pupils, whilst they used the books provided in the best possible way. For instance, they checked whether they had been read by orally questioning their pupils and by marking their written commentaries. Additionally, in allocating other books, they made sure that they were appropriate in difficulty and content for their recipients. They liked and understood their pupils who in turn liked and respected them. Finally their discipline was excellent in that it was apparently effortless, and their charges were not only well behaved but they worked industriously and happily.

Although Morris's picture would probably still command considerable agreement today, it is just one example of a more general process through which definitions of teacher quality or competence are established, acted upon and reinforced. It is this latter process which is of more enduring interest. Schools and teachers are constantly involved in the task of setting up models of good practice. Many and varying factors are taken into account and the relevant components probably change over time. Nevertheless, at any one stage some teachers are felt to be better than others. Few headteachers in primary schools, for example, would hesitate when asked who their best teacher of reading was. But what are the effects of these decisions on reading progress?

In stressing the importance of each school's autonomy to develop the 'knowledge, intuitions and skill of (its) individual teachers', the Bullock Report is placing heavy reliance on the expertise of professional practitioners. To what extent is the account of 'obviously good' practice, described by Start, matched by the evidence from research on reading progress? In other words, what will be the likely outcome of developing current definitions of teacher competence in terms of reading improvement?

Teacher competence: some research evidence

In examining studies for inclusion in this review I drew up the following criteria: (1) that the study should relate to the teaching of children under normal classroom conditions (studies of remedial education, for example, were excluded); (2) that the age range of the children should be one where the teaching of reading was still likely to be a major objective for the teachers (i.e. the primary years, 6–11); (3) that it should include measures of pupil *growth* in reading that could be related to particular teachers; and (4) that it should also include, amongst its measures on teachers, a variable representing teacher 'quality' or 'competence', as rated by experienced practitioners.

I have already suggested that the number of relevant studies linking teachers and reading is small. The introduction of the criteria listed above reduces these to a handful. Table 1 (on page 177) presents the evidence from these studies on the relationship between teacher quality or competence (as rated by experienced practitioners) and reading progress. The studies cover the primary years and concentrate on the earlier stages. However, their overall coverage is scarcely comprehensive.

The final column of Table 1 presents a summary measure of the relationship between the various ratings of teacher competence and reading progress. This relationship is presented in the form of a correlation coefficient. Correlation analysis measures the extent to which two or more variables vary together. The correlation coefficient (r) provides a measure of the strength of this relationship. It is expressed in values which range from +1.00 (perfect positive correlation) to −1.00 (perfect negative correlation). A value of 0.00 indicates that the two variables are independent; that is, that there is no relationship between them. In terms of the present discussion, if there were a very strong relationship between the various ratings of teacher competence and reading progress, then the values in Table 1 would approach +1.00. If there were a non-existent or weak relationship then the values would approach 0.00. The statistical significance of a correlation coefficient can also be tested.

From the correlations in Table 1 it is immediately obvious that

Table 1 **The relationship between teacher quality or competence (as rated by experienced practitioners) and reading progress**

Name of study	Country	Year of rating	No. of classes	Age group	'r' between rating and reading progress
Morris (1966)*	UK	1955–7	91	8–11	0.03
Bond & Dykstra (1967)**	USA	1964–5	159	6–7	0.14 (mdn)
Harris (1966 and 1968)**	USA	1965–6	30	6–7	0.30 (mdn)
		1965–6	28	7–8	0.13 (mdn)
		1966–7	21	7–8	0.12 (mdn)
Gray (1975)	UK	1972–3	41	6–7	0.20
		1973–4	41	6–7	0.10

(mdn) = median correlation. Where a number of reading subtests were employed the correlation in the table is the median one for the test battery.

* This correlation is based on the 'below average' children in Morris's sample. For the whole sample she reports a negative and statistically significant correlation ($r = -0.1$) but advances reasons for discounting this result. My own reanalysis of her evidence (Gray 1976) takes account of some of these problems but, in general, confirms her original results.

** These studies at the 6–7 age level do not, strictly speaking fulfil criterion (3) mentioned earlier relating to 'pupil growth in reading' since they employ a 'reading readiness' test as the initial measure, rather than a reading test. With very young children this is usually necessary, since they are unable to attempt a conventional reading test. Nevertheless, the former is a less satisfactory 'control' than the latter.

there is a weak relationship between ratings of teacher competence and reading progress. The correlations range from 0.03 to 0.30, depending on the study; none of them are statistically significant. The consequence is that we are able to explain very little of the variation in reading outcomes between classes by knowing how highly a teacher is rated. At best we can only explain a maximum of 9 per cent of the unexplained variation and often much less. 91 per cent of the variation in reading progress between classrooms remains unexplained by the ratings produced by practical/professional experience. This unexplained variation *may* be attributable to the teacher as well. All that can be said however is that it is not explained by the data presented here.

What do these results suggest in substantive terms? Do classes of children who are taught by highly rated teachers make more progress in reading than classes who are taught by poorly rated ones? The evidence in this review suggests that the effects are small or trivial. For example, the reading progress of classes of children taught by Morris's 'A' grade teachers would seem to be no greater than that of those taught by her 'E' grade ones. Somewhat more optimistically, if we knew how to make teachers who were rated in the bottom fifth of Gray's sample as effective as those who were rated in the top fifth, then we could expect their classes to make, on average, about 1–3 standardized points (about a month of reading age) more progress than at present. It should be noted, however, that even this gain might be occurring by chance and that to make this gain meaningful it is necessary to understand exactly why the teachers differ in effectiveness.

Downing (1975) has warned that there is a danger of the Bullock Report encouraging the 'blind to lead the blind' with respect to the development of children's language at the secondary stage. The same strictures would appear to be in danger of applying at the primary stages as well.

On the basis of the evidence presented here, then, I conclude that further development of the 'knowledge, intuitions and skill of individual teachers', at least as these are currently defined, will lead to at best trivial improvements in measured reading standards or the reduction of reading failure.

Discussion

These results will strike many as so strongly counter-intuitive that they will tend to dismiss them out of hand. Yet, it should be pointed out, those who have followed and accepted the discussion of research on methods to date will find that the studies reviewed here confirm many other, well-known relationships with respect to children's reading development. It requires a certain ingenuity to establish plausible reasons for accepting those results which conform to the conventional wisdom whilst, at the same time, rejecting those which do not.

It may be that the 'teacher', when compared with the other explanations that have been considered by researchers and practtioners, is a relatively good explanation, especially when the focus is on factors that schools can influence. Nevertheless, recent years have seen a considerable number of pessimistic studies concerning the effects of schooling on children's cognitive development. These have ranged from the preschool years (Tizard 1975) to the secondary school (Ainsworth and Batten 1974). Given the central role of reading in the educational process it would, in some ways, have been surprising if studies of reading had produced markedly different results.

The most significant feature of this review, however, is not so much the research evidence as the gap between the account that is generated by research and that built up from practical/professional experience. It is this which requires explanation and it is in this area that suitable explanations are in short supply.

There is an unfortunate, if sometimes justified, tendency for research and practical/professional perspectives to be seen as mutually exclusive. As Bullock complained (page 554): 'Many research studies have been, and continue to be, rather remote from the practical experience of teachers in the classroom.' Researchers, whilst accepting the comparative 'narrowness' of their approach, point to the extent to which their measures appear to approximate the judgments practitioners make. On the other hand, the latter emphasize the extent to which this 'narrowness' tends to exclude potentially important factors. However, to view either approach as definitive is to misunderstand the nature of the relationship between research and practice, which, as Cohen and Garet (1975) have suggested, is perhaps best viewed as a 'dialogue'.

What implications can be drawn from this discussion for bringing the two accounts closer together? First, researchers should undertake studies which correspond much more closely to the various dimensions of classroom practice which teachers employ. This would require far closer analysis of the actual teaching individual children receive, in order to relate it to their reading development. There are so many aspects of the teaching relationship that remain to be investigated that it is doubtful whether a single study could begin to encompass them.

Rather, researchers should consider developing an overall framework for research studies which would enable direct comparisons to be made between studies which varied in terms of size and complexity. For example, an agreement to include at least one reading test measure in common in all future projects would represent a significant step forward. Coordination of such projects on a long-term basis would represent a considerable contribution to the process of building up a reliable body of knowledge on the teaching of reading. An excellent model for this type of coordination has already been demonstrated in the USOE's Cooperative Research Programme in First Grade Reading (Harris 1966) which, despite the criticisms made earlier in this paper, provided a sophisticated basis for addressing the central questions on methods with which it was concerned.

For practitioners, the most pressing concern must be to examine the extent to which reading progress plays a prominent role in their evaluation of effective teaching. Start (1974) reports that in a survey of 1,000 teachers concerning the 'five ways in which they would be able to tell a good teacher from a weak teacher', fewer than one in twenty-five raised the direct criterion 'whether children learned'. My own experience, during three years of discussion and classroom observation, confirms this impression. Whilst I encountered a good deal of monitoring of children's performances in reading, I found few indications that schools or teachers were using this information to monitor their own performances.

As a result of this examination, practitioners may decide that it is impossible, either in theory or practice, to isolate, and hence take into account, the factors that go towards making up effective teaching, let alone to decide what weight to place on reading progress as opposed to other aspects. If this decision is made, then the logical consequence would appear to be that an indirect and implicit theory of effectiveness is preferred to one which is direct and explicit. Whilst the former corresponds more closely to the present pattern of assessment than the latter, its effect on reading attainment seems much more uncertain.

The renewed focus on the teacher as the central feature of the educational process is long overdue, especially in the field of reading. To make further progress, however, it will be necessary to subject our stereotypes of 'good' teaching to far more searching examination than has typically been the case.

References

AINSWORTH, M. and BATTEN, E. (1974) *The Effects of Environmental*

Factors on Secondary Educational Attainment: A Plowden Follow-up
Macmillan, for the Schools Council

AVERCH, H. *et al* (1972) *How Effective is Schooling? A Critical Review and Synthesis of Research Findings* Santa Monica, California: Rand Corporation

BOND, G. and DYKSTRA, R. (1967) The cooperative research program in first grade reading instruction *Reading Research Quarterly* 2 5–142

CANE, B. and SMITHERS, J. (1971) *The Roots of Reading* NFER

COHEN, D. and GARET, M. (1975) Reforming educational policy with applied social research *Harvard Educational Review* 45 17–43

DES (1975) *A Language for Life* (Bullock Report) HMSO

DOWNING, J. (1975) Theoretical overview *Reading* 9, 2, 7–13

GETZELS, J. and JACKSON, P. W. (1963) 'The teacher's personality and characteristics' in N. L. Gage (Ed) *Handbook of Research on Teaching* Chicago: Rand McNally

GRAY, J. (1975) *Teacher Decision-making and Reading Progress* Sussex University, unpublished thesis

GRAY, J. (1976) Teacher competence in reading tuition *Educational Research* (to appear)

GRAY, W. (1931) Reading *Review of Educational Research* 1 247–60

HARRIS, A. and SERWER, B. (1966) *Comparison of Reading Approaches in First Grade Teaching with Disadvantaged Children: The CRAFT Project* New York: City University of New York (USOE Cooperative Research Project, 2677)

HARRIS, A. *et al* (1968) *A Continuation of the CRAFT Project Comparing Reading Approaches with Disadvantaged Urban Negro Children in Primary Grades* New York: City University of New York (USOE Project No. 5–0570–2–12–1, ERIC ED 020297)

HARRIS, A. (1969) The effective teacher of reading *The Reading Teacher* 23 195–204

MORRIS, J. M. (1966) *Standards and Progress in Reading* NFER

MOYLE, D. (1974) A letter from the President of UKRA *Reading* 8, 1, 2–4

ROSENSHINE, B. (1971) *Teaching Behaviours and Student Achievement* NFER

SOUTHGATE, V. (1972) *Beginning Reading* University of London Press

START, K. (1974) Establishing children's learning as the criterion for teacher effectiveness *Educational Research* 16 206–9

TIZARD, B. (1975) *Early Childhood Education* NFER

Denis Vincent

In their quest for statistical and 'psychometric' excellence test producers have sometimes lost touch with teachers and reading specialists. The intention of this paper is to draw attention to methods of assessment which might prove more appropriate to the ways in which reading is currently taught and to techniques which could help bring testing up to date with reading theory.

It would have been equally useful to discuss ways in which teachers could make better use of existing test materials, but for the time being this topic has been set aside. Instead, the paper will concentrate on the application of test research in fresh areas such as the cultural and affective aspects of the reading curriculum, the potential value of checklists as opposed to tests, the need to develop informal clinical techniques into more rigorous means of assessment, and criterion-referenced testing.

The standardized test

Traditonally a reading test has been a normative or 'standardized' set of reading tasks which can be used to measure the spread of ability in a group of children and to determine whether a child is average for his age, or how far above or below average he happens to be. The production of tests or 'instruments' of this kind has become a highly developed science. Much energy and technical expertise has been devoted to ensuring that such tests present a statistically accurate, reliable and representative picture of a child's reading ability relative to others of his age.

What the purchaser of such a test is really paying for is the skill and expense involved in standardizing the test – administering it to a 'representative' sample of children in order to establish how children of varying ability perform on the test. The virtues of the traditional reading test are mainly statistical and the technical improvements which have been made in reading testing over the years have had more to do with the way reading is measured than with the reading process itself. The emphasis has been upon the form of the test, not its content.

As a result, many technically advanced, or at least 'respectable', tests remain burdened with a primitive or naive conception of how reading is taught or learned. There are many educational questions which can be answered through standardized test scores, but they are of a general and administrative nature and have more to do with the strategy of running a school or LEA than the tactics of teaching reading. This trend has thus rendered testing remote from the business of teaching. Reading tests have been developed along the same lines as intelligence and selection tests, although they were really meant to serve quite a different purpose, and as a result reading tests impinge on the teaching of reading only indirectly or occasionally. Over the years, a great deal of research expertise has thus been concentrated into the production of a highly refined instrument, which nevertheless has only limited application in the classroom.

Hopefully the following discussion will indicate both how the technology of test development could be more usefully deployed than hitherto and how teachers of reading might themselves become usefully involved in the production of the next 'generation' of reading tests.

Cultural and affective criteria

Formal assessment in reading tends to be confined to reading as a cognitive skill, rather than as a matter of culture and feeling. Schools assess their reading 'standards' by testing how proficient children are at various verbal problem-solving activities, perhaps involving mechanical problems of phoneme-grapheme correspondence (e.g. word-recognition tests) or more advanced ones of syntax and semantics (e.g. sentence-completion tests). Evidence about what books children read voluntarily and their attitudes to reading activities is not normally sought when there is a general concern about how well reading is being taught. The same is true of the debate about 'national' reading standards. The Start and Wells (1972) test-based survey of reading standards is usually regarded as the definitive work on this question. Yet the findings of Whitehead *et al* (1974) on *what* children read seem equally pertinent and are every bit as illuminating and provocative – only the narrowest and most mechanistic view of what is meant by reading would exclude them.

In fact, most teachers are as much concerned with reading as a literary activity and with the affective aims of teaching reading as they are with developing cognitive reading skills. It follows that any scheme of assessment should reflect the former as much as the latter. It is strange though, that although the basic expertise for doing this is available, so little has been done to capitalize upon it.

There is no reason why attitude scales, interest inventories and questionnaires about reading habits should not be developed for use in schools, alongside the traditional attainment tests. Admittedly, for schools to approach assessment in this way would be novel. However, this is an important domain to which the technology of assessment could be fruitfully applied.

Checklist-based assessment

The standardized test is an 'objective' measure; that is to say, it eliminates the judgment of individual teachers from the process of assessment. The virtues of this are readily appreciated: teachers have a vested interest in the results of assessment and their judgments will always be coloured by subjective bias. A test which relied upon asking the teacher what, or how well, she thinks each child can do would thus seem to be a foolish device. Why should we take the opinion of a teacher on how well a child can read when we can go straight to the child and find out by direct testing? Research shows, for example, that teachers' judgments of children's reading attainment are biased by such considerations as social class. Accordingly, researchers have largely excluded the teacher as a source of information about a child's reading ability and have concentrated on the construction of objective tests, rather than search for those areas where the teacher's judgments are less erroneous, or endeavour to devise means of diminishing or controlling such subjective bias. However, tests which rely on the judgments of a subjectivity-prone observer have flourished in other areas, such as the assessment of personality and intelligence, and there are signs that techniques requiring teachers' observations and judgment are becoming more important in the teaching of reading.

In particular, interest is being shown in the notion of the checklist – a series of questions about what the child can do, which the teacher has to answer, either on the basis of what she already happens to know about the child, or by giving the child some kind of informal test suggested by the checklist.

The outstanding advantages of the checklist approach to assessment is that it can embody a great deal of expert knowledge about reading. A less experienced teacher can thus be guided in a structured and comprehensive way to look for the things that more experienced and expert teachers look for. In short, the checklist can combine and condense a great deal of expertise in a form which can conveniently be used by anyone willing to make the effort.

The technique is also a flexible one. It can be used on an intensive diagnostic basis as in *Framework for Reading* (Dean and Nichols 1974), or as a large-scale screening device, as in a checklist evolved by psychologists in the London Borough of Croydon (Bryans and Wolfendale 1973). It may also form a means of monitoring progress in reading attainment. Herbert Kohl (1974) describes a chart for such a purpose, which he devised as a radical alternative to the standardized objective test.

New techniques

A number of techniques are currently being used – or at least recommended – as informal means of assessment of both reading attainment and reading difficulty. Some are overdue for development into sound and reliable routine assessment procedures, others are already beginning to attract such treatment.

Of the latter, cloze procedure is an outstanding example. The technique has already engaged much test-oriented research and may eventually be developed to the same degree of technical perfection as has been achieved with multiple-choice testing, although it is to be hoped it will prove more useful within the classroom.

Some standardized cloze tests have indeed been published, for example the GAP and GAPADOL tests, yet they perform exactly the same function as traditional tests. Cloze procedure promises more than this, possibly a means of identifying comprehension strategies or the linking of test performance and readability.

Two other types of technique also merit serious consideration as a basis for test development – the Informal Reading Inventory (IRI) and the error analysis sytems proposed by Goodman (1969) and Clay (1972a).

The IRI was developed as a clinical and unstandardized assessment method based on materials selected by the teacher herself. The methodology of the IRI has developed into a fairly elaborate procedure (e.g. Johnson and Kress 1965) but relatively little hard research has been conducted into its validity. Teachers thus have to take most of the established guidelines for devising and interpreting IRIs on trust. What little research there has been suggests that some of the criteria used are arbitrary and inaccurate. A study by Roberts (1976), for example, suggests that the criterion for a 'frustrational' reading level needs serious reappraisal.

Teachers find IRIS useful, but it seems a pity that the details of the technique should be based more on mythology than science and that so little empirical evidence is available to help IRI users interpret their results.

New thinking about the interpretation of oral reading errors should itself be a valuable contribution to the refinement of assessment through IRIS. The work of Marie Clay and the Goodmans has demonstrated that oral misreadings are not uniformly 'bad', that oral fluency does not have a simple linear relationship with the maturation of reading attainment, and that lapses in fluency may be associated with the development of more advanced reading skills.

The outcome of such work must surely be a radical revision of our approach to testing. Misreadings may need to be weighted according to their positive or negative significance, and information should be gathered about the nature of individual differences in patterns of oral reading errors. It may ultimately prove possible to establish developmental continua for oral errors similar to those found in other areas of cognitive functioning. Fully developed, such schemes would render the traditional reading 'age' scale redundant. A child would be placed upon a maturational continuum as a result of the way he reads, rather than just of the mechanical efficiency and accuracy of his reading. Most importantly, individual progress could be expressed concretely, in terms of any new and more mature reading strategies that have been acquired, rather than in 'months' or 'points of standardized score'.

Criterion-referenced assessment

The notion of a test which directly measures what has been learned, as opposed to how much better/worse a child can read in comparison with his peers, has an intuitive appeal. This is the purpose of criterion-referenced tests, which seek to provide a qualitative picture of attainment as opposed to the quantitative one provided by traditional tests.

Information about what a child can do, what a child has learned, is usually of much more immediate use to the teacher who actually has to teach the child than a reading age or standardized score. Criterion-referenced testing aims to provide just such information.

To produce such a test three main tasks have to be completed:

1 the identification and specification of the skills to be taught or

material to be mastered
2   the production of test tasks which involve the performance of the specified skills or mastery of the materials
3   validation to ensure that the test tasks do really cover the skills specified and the establishment of test scores associated with mastery of the specified skills and materials.

Some aspects of reading lend themselves fairly well to this treatment. There is, for example, considerable agreement about both the content of phonics and the skills involved in the mastery of phonics. Indeed most phonic tests have in practice performed a criterion-referenced function. However, McLeod and Atkinson (1972) provide an explicit example of a phonic criterion-referenced test. Their test involves a series of oral word-recognition tasks which have been systematically chosen to provide comprehensive coverage of phonics. For each phonic configuration tested there is an accompanying remedial worksheet. The whole approach is comprehensive and systematic, allowing not only for the assessment of general phonic skills – vowel blending for example – but also for identification of specific and perhaps isolated elements which have not been learned – perhaps just one particular vowel blend.

In criterion-referenced testing much depends upon the credibility of the first test-specification stage. This is fairly easily accomplished for phonic skills, but other aspects of reading are less easily laid out in the fashion of phonics. 'Comprehension' for example, is an area which has attracted much armchair analytic work, but research has yet to verify the existence of the many subskills which are alleged to be involved in it. As a result, the criterion-referenced tests which have appeared in this area have been open to question. The *California Prescriptive Reading Inventory*, for example, claims to test ninety different subskills, many of them connected with comprehension, while the *Instructional Objectives Exchange* of Los Angeles produces a set of comprehension tests for over twenty subskills. While such tests have the virtue of thoroughness they present a picture of reading which is highly misleading, for there is no real evidence for many of the distinctions they make between subskills.

In fairness, it must be pointed out that criterion-referenced testing is often conceived as an integral component in a highly structured reading programme. The tests are intended as indicators of whether a piece of material has been mastered, so that the pupil may go on to the next piece of work in a sequence, or whether more instruction at his present level is required. Many criterion-referenced tests thus have no application outside a specific set of materials or a particular curriculum.

This highly structured and sequential process of teaching and testing may not recommend itself to teachers who prefer not to work within the confines of a prescribed curriculum, or prefer to define their own teaching objectives, or to work with a wide range of materials and techniques in response to the immediate needs of their pupils.

There are two possible alternative ways in which criterion-referenced testing could therefore develop. In the first place, tests could be designed to measure performance in dimensions which are wide ranging and generalizable, rather than minute and specific. For example, in the *Progressive Achievement Tests* of Reading Vocabulary and Comprehension (Elley and Reid 1975) two main skill areas are identified – the size of the reader's vocabulary and the level of readability of prose he can comprehend. The test tasks are based on material roughly representative of each vocabulary and readability level, and validation exercises have been carried out to ensure that the scores obtained really do predict the size of a reader's vocabulary and the level of readability he can comprehend (e.g. Elley 1971). These two dimensions are ones with general, rather than specific and limited application. The test scores measure what the reader can or cannot do in situations which are not tied to specific teaching units or materials.

Secondly, teachers may find it useful to initiate their own small-scale criterion-referenced schemes in which they define what it is they hope to teach, draft appropriate test materials and (most importantly) explore the validity and generalizability of their test results. For example, does a child who performs test task X_1 successfully also perform similar tasks X_2, X_3 and X_4 in situations outside the immediate test one? Also, do children who are known to have mastered a particular skill gain consistently higher scores on the criterion tests the teacher has composed?

For criterion-referenced testing to be effective, therefore, more work needs to be done on the identification of credible content areas to be tested, and in the validation of the tests. Some of this is a matter for research to pursue. However, criterion-referenced testing is so closely bound up with the aims of teaching that much more exploration must be done by teachers themselves into exactly how they can use such testing and the kinds of skills which can be meaningfully specified, taught and assessed in this way.

Item banking

The traditional test situation requires that all children to be tested must attempt the same test if they are to be compared with one another. This concept has now been supplemented by that of item bank testing. By this, tests are produced to meet the needs of particular individuals or situations by drawing suitable questions (items) from a larger pool or 'bank'. All items in the bank are statistically related to one another. As a result, two largely different tests could be selected and given to two different groups of readers, yet directly comparable scores would be obtained. For example, test items with content specific to the particular reading scheme a child had been following, could be included in each test. It may prove technically possible that questions need not even be drawn from the bank, but could be devised by the teacher.

Central to item banking is the concept that success in attempting a test item is an outcome of, (a) the difficulty of the item, (b) the ability of the person attempting it. For a bank to be created, all the items must tend to measure reading equally effectively in readers of all ability levels. It would not be appropriate to go further into the underlying theory at this time, but it will suffice to note that the essential outcome is a means of measuring a person's ability which is independent of particular questions. It follows that items which are subject to particular bias would be excluded, as they would tend to measure knowledge or skills found in only a minority of children. Should reading tests prove to fit the model of attainment implicit in this, much greater flexibility and freedom of choice could be introduced into assessment. Teachers could tailor testing to the language, methods and content which prevail in their own schools by drawing test questions of their own choice from the bank. At the same time they could be confident that what they were testing was indeed part of some larger characteristics called 'reading' and not the outcome of, say, rote learning or memory of material in a particular reading scheme. Much of the centralization and conformity associated with the traditional 'set piece' test would thus disappear.

At present most of the thinking about item banking has been in terms of its application to large-scale assessment and national surveys of attainment, and its usefulness in classroom assessment has yet to be explored. However, it is a new technical possibility which could usefully be applied in many of the areas for development suggested previously. This paper has been concerned with the new directions test development might take. The ideas are suggested as an answer to some of the objections of teachers who are impatient of established reading tests. The cause of many of the difficulties which arise in the use of traditional standardized tests can be traced back to a failure on the part of the test constructors to appreciate that their instruments are really of more use for administrators than teachers. In fact, there is much more that can be done to encourage more constructive use of traditional tests, but the tests of the future will have to show much greater awareness of the requirements of the reading teacher and the reading curriculum. Materials such as Marie Clay's *A Diagnostic Survey* (1972b) and Don Labon's *Assessment of Reading Ability* (1972) exemplify work already begun along these lines, in that they serve rather than submerge the teacher.

References

BRYANS, T. and WOLFENDALE, S. (1973) *Checklist and Guidelines for Teachers No. 1* Reading and Language Development Centre, London Borough of Croydon

CLAY, M. M. (1972a) *Reading: the Patterning of Complete Behaviour* Auckland: Heinemann Educational Books

CLAY, M. M. (1972b) *A Diagnostic Survey* Auckland: Heinemann Educational Books

DEAN, J. and NICHOLS, R. (1974) *Framework for Reading* Evans

ELLEY, W. B. (1971) *Development of a Set of Content-referenced Tests of Reading* New Zealand Council of Educational Research

ELLEY, W. B. and REID, N. C. (1975) *The Progressive Achievement Tests* (Reading Vocabulary and Comprehension) University of London Press

GOODMAN, K. S. (1969) Analysis of oral reading miscues: applied psycholinguistics *Reading Research Quarterly* 1 9–30

JOHNSON, M. S. and KRESS, R. A. (1965) *Informal Reading Inventories* Newark, Delaware: International Reading Association

KOHL, H. (1974) *Reading, How To* Penguin

LABON, D. (1972) *Assessment of Reading Ability* Chichester: West Sussex County Council

MCLEOD, J. and ATKINSON, J. (1972) *Domain Phonic Test Kit and Workshop* Oliver and Boyd

ROBERTS, T. (1976) 'Frustration level' of reading in the Infant School *Educational Research* (to appear)

START, K. B. and WELLS, B. K. (1972) *The Trend of Reading Standards* NFER

WHITEHEAD, F. *et al* (1974) *Children's Reading Interests* (Schools Council Working Paper No. 52) Evans/Methuen Educational

Note

The inventories mentioned on page 187 are not generally available in this country. The *California Prescriptive Reading Inventory* (1972) is published by CTB/McGraw-Hill, Delmonte Research Park, Monterey, California. The *Instructional Objectives Exchange Comprehension Skills* K6 (1973) is published by IOX, Box No. 24095 Los Angeles, California.

Part 6

International perspectives

Right to Read – mid-point progress

Ruth Love Holloway

Some time ago I attended a fashionable Washington dinner party where after dinner the host challenged his guests to name five people who have had the greatest influence on the modern world. The names put forward by my fellow dinner guests surely merit consideration for such a list, and indicate how truly difficult it is to narrow the list to five. They included great political philosophers, like Lecke, Jefferson, Marx and Mao Tse Tung who helped to create the framework under which much of the modern world would govern itself. The list included, also, great political leaders, like Churchill, De Gaulle, Lincoln and Franklin Roosevelt who shepherded their countries through some of the most turbulent and consequential moments of the modern era. Great tyrants like Hitler and Mussolini also were cited for the chaos they spawned and the destruction they wrought. Great moral and spiritual leaders like Mahatma Gandhi and Martin Luther King were named because of their efforts to remind the modern world that a civilization is only worthy of the name if it universally recognizes and protects human dignity. The contributions of science were represented by names like Albert Einstein, Enrico Fermi, Madame Curie. Henry Ford was cited because his introduction of the assembly line into modern manufacturing transformed the industrial process and paved the way to a mass consumption economy.

The list could go on. But when it came my turn, I realized that no one had yet named a man or woman whose contribution to the modern world in large part made the contributions of all these others possible. Without this achievement, the achievements of all the others would be diminished, and in some cases, not possible at all. The man – Johann Gutenberg, the fifteenth-century German printer, who invented movable type, and began the process of popularizing it. Gutenberg's accomplishment can hardly be overstated.

We tend to take for granted how the development of movable type has shaped the world we know today. Yet try to imagine the consequences if movable type had not been developed. There would be no newspapers or journals to keep us aware of what was happening in our own countries nor in the world around us. There would be no books to remind us of the lessons of history or to celebrate our greatest hopes or dramatize our worst fears. The ability to read would be an elitist privilege and most of us, imprisoned in ignorance, would be in almost all things at the mercy of the few.

Instead, we live in a world where the development of movable type has enabled most of us to learn to read, and upon that singular fact, much of our success and fulfilment as human beings now rests. For to exercise effectively our rights as citizen or consumer, we must have access to information about the issues and the capability to comprehend and act on that information. The ability to read gives us that. To perform effectively as employer and employee one must be able to understand instructions or report results. The ability to read gives us that. No matter in what aspect of human endeavour – political, economic, social or religious – the ability to read is a crucial and enriching asset.

For millions of Americans, however, that asset does not exist. The tragic fact is that more than a century since our society adopted the principle of universal free education, nineteen million adult Americans are functional illiterates. Simply stated, that means they cannot read even marginally well enough to function effectively in our society. Not only can't they read a newspaper, they can't read the test necessary to get a driver's licence. Nor the instructions on a bottle of medicine. Nor the terms of a loan agreement. They are imprisoned in ignorance, their inability to read is a towering barrier on the road to fulfilment and success, and unlike the situation in the fifteenth century, they are now the few at the mercy of the many.

Compounding that sad fact is this one: at the outset of this decade there were seven million elementary and secondary school students with severe reading problems. In some large cities, an estimated 40 to 50 per cent of school children are underachieving in reading. In other words, approximately one-tenth of our people are functional illiterates or potential illiterates. No matter how you look at the fact, it represents a major social and economic problem for our society, and one which has gone unrecognized for too long. However, only in a free and open society can people admit their problems and work honestly towards their solution.

That is the reason *Right to Read* exists. Though we are a division of the United States Office of Education, within the Department of Health, Education and Welfare, *Right to Read* is more than a government programme. It is a movement whose goal is to wipe out illiteracy in the United States in this decade.

Let me state that another way. The purpose of *Right to Read* must be understood in a larger context than merely teaching people to read or read better. For the inability to read is a disastrous social handicap and a source of tremendous economic dislocation. The inability to read frustrates effective participation in a society where the ability to read is presumed. Those who cannot read are likely never to realize their full potential for productivity and usefulness, and thus constitute a sorrowful waste of human resources.

So truly the purpose of *Right to Read* is to redeem valuable human resources and help them achieve their potential. *Right to Read* is not prescriptive. We have not attempted to establish any level of reading ability or vocabulary usage as acceptable or not acceptable. Rather, the only reference for our success or failure is the individual who participates in *Right to Read* and whether he or she achieves a reading ability commensurate with his or her goal. And those goals vary greatly, from simply being able to function better on the job, to becoming a more effective homemaker, to a desire to be able to seek advanced education.

Thus, our goal broadly stated, to wipe out illiteracy in this country by 1980 really translates into millions of individual goals focused on the dream of productive participation by all Americans in our society, culture and economy. To help those Americans realize that dream, *Right to Read* was organized by James Allen. Our first task was to develop a strategy to approach the problem in all its aspects. For example, we concluded early that we must reach out to people with reading difficulties where they are, and not expect them to come to us. Thus, we needed both to strengthen reading programmes in our schools and related community institutions, like libraries, as well as address the needs of adult illiterates in the places where they work. We also had to be concerned about the millions who possess the skills of reading, but do not use them.

We established too that we must discover the most effective ways of dealing with reading difficulties and teaching people to read. We knew no one single method would work for everybody, because a variety of backgrounds and circumstances are involved in producing non-readers. Fortunately, a good deal of research on reading and teaching reading already existed. So our job was to ensure that the research came off the shelves and got put into practice where its effectiveness could be measured.

Finally, we knew that we could never do the job by ourselves, no matter how large a staff we had. Our function in Washington is to provide policy guidance, technical assistance and a little money; but in a larger sense, our role is to be a catalyst. In order to provide the kinds of opportunities for reading improvement that people can and will use, we have to get educators and community officials, parents and the private sector excited about and involved in *Right to Read*.

Midway through the decade, I am pleased to report that our prospects for success are good. We have financed twelve model reading programmes in schools throughout the country, trying to find out in rural, urban and suburban settings which processes and practices in reading work best and what makes them work. Each model programme has been designed to have a high degree of transferability, so that successful programmes can be shared in similar communities and situations elsewhere. Moreover, we are moving swiftly to have the results of these model efforts implemented in school systems throughout the country.

Our approach is pronouncedly to work within the established educational system and to seek a commitment at the highest level to *Right to Read*. For example, the state superintendent of education is the head of the *Right to Read* programme for his/her state; the local superintendent of schools the leader of *Right to Read* in his community; the principal, the director of *Right to Read* in his school. Only with the commitment of the men and women at the top of the educational hierarchy can we be sure that a total and thorough effort is made to underscore reading as the essential educational achievement.

I cannot stress this point enough. Socrates once said, 'The foundation of every state is the education of its youth.' Well, the foundation of education is the ability to read and comprehend what is read. Without reading skills, achievement in the arts, humanities, sciences and social sciences is limited indeed. That is why commitment from the top is fundamental. *Right to Read* must be a comprehensive school effort, and not just the narrow province of a reading teacher or reading specialist. In fact, the most successful *Right to Read* programmes are those that marshal all the related community resources to deal with the problem.

The parents and family of a youngster with a reading difficulty need to become involved, not only because of the supportive efforts they can make in the home to what a child is learning in the classroom, but also because frequently a child with a reading difficulty will be symptomatic of a family with inadequate reading skills.

Libraries can establish special reading programmes and clinics, both for youngsters and adults, as companions for more formal reading instruction.

As of today twenty-seven state governors have issued official proclamations committing their state to the *Right to Read* movement and recognizing the goal of achieving universal literacy in our country by 1980. School systems in forty-nine states are implemening *Right to Read*. We are on our way to ensuring the right to read for American youngsters.

But many of those who most urgently need to upgrade their reading skills have already passed through the educational system. Their needs and their circumstances are very different from the young person for whom the classroom is an everyday environment. Thus, our *Right to Read* approach is different. In so far as possible, the *Right to Read* effort for adults seeks to work with people in the places where they are most familiar – on the job, in their communities, even in the home. To this end, we have been meeting with corporate leaders and executives to gain their commitment to *Right to Read* and their coöperation in establishing *Right to Read* programmes in offices and factories. The response has been truly encouraging, because enlightened business leaders know that *Right to Read* will be a sound investment in the future productivity and accomplishment of an employee.

Our emphasis for adults is for them to choose reading materials to work with that reflect their desired reading goal. If their goal is simply to perform better on the job, they may choose to work with training manuals or technical materials. Or they may have other aspirations and choose to work with anything from newspapers and periodicals to the plays of Shakespeare. But it is the individual who wants to read who ultimately must chart the course and set the destiny of the programme.

I fear, because I am somewhat encouraged about our efforts to date, that I may leave you with the impression that achieving our goal will be an easy task. Let me assure you it will not be, unless the cooperation that has been evidenced already continues and the national commitment remains steadfast. In a sense, the national *Right to Read* effort is a coordinated endeavour whose success depends upon the involvement of all segments of society, public and private, professional and non-professional.

Those of us working full-time in Washington, and those already involved in *Right to Read* in communities across America, can do much to inform the public that there is a nationwide reading problem and make *Right to Read* truly a collaborative effort and national movement. Let me describe a few such projects:

We can do much to identify what changes are necessary to accomplish the goal.

We can do much to assist those who need to change to do so.

We can do much to identify the existing resources, public and private, which can be brought to bear on the problem.

And we can do much to demonstrate, through the establishment of reading programmes, effective techniques for the elimination of reading deficiencies, and, therefore, the increase of reading competencies.

But we shall not ensure that in the next decade no American shall be denied a full and productive life because of an inability to read effectively unless the commitment of time and talent by many Americans equals the need.

The national *Right to Read* effort will be labour-intensive. There is no escaping that, for often the most effective way to teach reading is one-to-one. And schools, as well as community institutions like libraries, already experience manpower and budget difficulties every year. Clearly, public service manpower is essential to the mission of *Right to Read*. For a trained volunteer will be a vital member of the *Right to Read* team, offering the kind of special attention and personal encouragement often needed to overcome reading inadequacies.

Where will this 'literacy corps' come from? Well some are already at work. Retired persons, parents, college students, business men and women. Many more are needed, and I believe many more will come forward. Our colleges alone graduate 800,000 young Americans every year who are prime candidates to devote several hours of their week to assisting others in reaching towards the goal they have already attained.

With that kind of commitment, the *Right to Read* movement will not fail. And when we achieve the goal of wiping out illiteracy, we will have done much more. For the inability to read effectively is often a symptom, the tip of an iceberg. In some cases, we will have broken a cycle of illiteracy in a family which too often parallels a cycle of poverty. In some cases we may pierce a web of social maladjustment that too often results in delinquency and even crime. In many cases we can restore hope of a successful and rewarding career. In others we can provide special instruction for the child with specific learning disabilities. But in all cases we shall enrich our culture and endow our economy with revitalized and promising human resources.

In 1976 we celebrate the 200th anniversary of the birth of the American republic. To me, the significance of that celebration is not the commemoration of the historical fact that a ragged army of colonists defeated the greatest empire of its time. The significance of the celebration lies in the fact that we instituted a system of government based on the consent of the governed. The shot heard round the world was not one of musket-fire, but this: 'We hold these truths to be self-evident, that all men are created equal and endowed by their Creator with certain inalienable rights, and among these are life, liberty, and the pursuit of happiness.' Even as our history has been anguished at times by the struggle to perfect our system of government to ensure that all men hold equal title in law to the meaning of those words, we try to become a beacon to the world of what free men and women can accomplish.

It is surely fitting now, in our bicentennial decade, that we make the effort required to ensure that all Americans, when they look on those words, 'life, liberty, and the pursuit of happiness', can read and understand them. Only then will the principles and goals of *Right to Read* be a reality.

22 The reading and writing abilities of Swedish pupils: a survey of the development from Grade 1 to Grade 12

Hans U. Grundin

In a previous paper (Grundin 1975a) I presented the outline of a fairly large-scale Swedish study of the development of reading and writing abilities during the comprehensive and the upper secondary school years; that is, from the ages of seven to nineteen. This study was planned and carried out during the period 1971–5 at the Linköping College of Education.

The project comprised two major parts:

1 a survey of the development of certain reading and writing skills in the comprehensive and upper secondary schools
2 an attempt to establish – by means of, among other things, an inquiry among senior teachers of Swedish – to what extent pupils leaving school had reached satisfactory levels of reading and writing skills.

The survey of skills development was made by means of testing, on two occasions, with one year's interval between the testings, about 2,600 pupils in Linköping. The same tests and instructions were used on both occasions, and each subtest was used at as many grade levels as was deemed feasible, in order to facilitate comparisons between grades. In Grades 6 to 12 inclusive exactly the same test battery was given to all pupils.

The inquiry among senior teachers of Swedish, concerning minimum satisfactory performance levels in pupils leaving school, was addressed to practically all such teachers in the country; that is, about 950 teachers. More than 700 of those teachers completed and returned the questionnaire.

In the present paper I will briefly summarize and comment upon the most important results of this study. The full report of the study has been published in Swedish, with a summary in English (Grundin 1975c; background details and information on the tests used can be found in Grundin 1975a).

The general picture of the development of reading and writing abilities

The general trend in the development of reading and writing abilities is illustrated in Figure 1 (below), which summarizes the results of five subtests. The slope of the line connecting two points of measurement indicates the growth rate during that particular year. Differences like the one between, say, the Grade 4 mean 1972 (x) and the Grade 4 mean 1973 (O) reflect sampling errors, in that they are means for different samples from two consecutive year groups.

Figure 1   General development of reading and writing ability, Grades 1–12

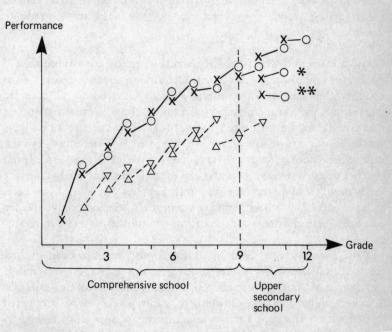

x : Normal class mean, 1972   △ : Special class mean, 1972
O : Normal class mean, 1973   ▽ : Special class mean, 1973
* Semi-academic course   ** Vocational course

The figure shows the development for normal class and special class pupils in the comprehensive school (Grades 1–9). In the upper secondary school the development is shown for three different types of study courses: the academic, including Grades 10–12, the semi-academic and the vocational, including Grades 10–11.

Growth in the abilities studied is, on the whole, continuous from starting school to the end of the upper secondary school. The growth rate decreases markedly, however, with increasing pupil age. There are no clear indices of stagnation or regression – except among pupils in the vocational courses in the upper secondary school; these pupils seem to have reached their maximum ability level by the time they leave the comprehensive school. It is noteworthy that these pupils also were the only ones who did not take Swedish as a subject during the year of investigation.

The growth rate among special class pupils is generally similar to that of normal class pupils in the corresponding grades. In some cases, the differences between the 1972 and the 1973 samples of special class pupils are quite large (e.g. in Grades 3, 4 and 8). This reflects not only sampling errors, but also the fact that the criteria for referring pupils to special classes may vary from grade to grade.

Growth rates at different ability levels – are the gaps widening?
As Figure 1 indicates, the growth rate among special class pupils is roughly the same as that among normal class pupils. This is an interesting and rather unexpected finding. It is normally assumed that any mental growth rate is slower for below-average individuals and more rapid for those above average; that is, differences between individuals increase with age (cf. Ljung 1965 and Olson 1959). If the gap between normal and special class pupils remains fairly constant for a number of years, this may indicate that the school has been at least partially successful in its attempt to provide compensatory education for children with learning disabilities or similar handicaps.

The growth rates at different ability levels have also been studied for each subtest. The results show that the gaps between ability groups remain fairly constant in some skills and increase moderately in other skills. The school seems to some extent to be successful in preventing the gaps from widening, but it does not manage to close those gaps – it cannot even make them more narrow. Most educators would, I believe, agree that the school must try to compensate for various handicaps and disabilities. This probably goes even for those who want society to be different, so that handicaps are not produced to the present extent. Yet few educators are likely to be of the opinion that it should be the objective of the school to close entirely the 'performance gaps' between groups of children at different ability levels.

Performance differences among classes in the same grade

It is a well-known fact that the performance level in any school subject may vary considerably from classroom to classroom. It is rarely possible, though, to compare the differences among classes in the same grade with differences between grades. Such comparisons can be made – and have been made – in the present study. The results show a considerable overlapping between grades in terms of class means from Grades 3 and upwards. This means that a weak class in Grade 4 is below the top classes in Grade 3. And in the higher grades the overlapping is even greater: a weak normal class in Grade 9 can perform at a level which is equivalent to the overall mean for Grade 6! And in vocational classes in Grades 10 and 11 the class mean may be very close to Grade 7 or even Grade 6 means.

These differences among classes have, of course, important implications for the teaching of reading and writing. But the differences are also likely to influence greatly teachers' conceptions about what is the normal performance level in a particular grade. If a teacher's experience is limited either to 'weak' classes or to classes with a high performance level, his judgment about what should be expected of the average pupil may be very much biased (cf. discussion below and in Grundin 1975b).

Performance and socioeconomic status

The effect on academic performance of social or socioeconomic handicaps has been demonstrated in numerous studies. The findings of this study support the view that there is a substantial correlation between the socioeconomic status of a pupil's family and the pupil's reading and writing performance. It has also been possible to study the size of the performance differences between various socioeconomic groups in comparison to the differences between grade levels.

The average growth curves for SES Group 3 (mainly working-class children) and SES Group 1 (upper-middle-class and upper-class children) are particularly interesting to compare. Throughout the comprehensive school year those curves are approximately parallel; that is, the gap between SES Groups 1 and 3 is already considerable after one or two years in the school, but after that it remains fairly constant. The size of the difference between SES Groups 1 and 3 is very considerable: the mean difference is in general equivalent to the difference between the overall means for Grade 6 and Grade 9. In other words, the working-class children seem to lag three academic years behind the upper-middle-class children in terms of reading performance. To what extent this is a genuine handicap in reading ability and to what extent it reflects the fact that middle-class values and norms largely dominate our school system cannot be determined on the basis of the test data available here.

On the whole, then, the comprehensive school seems to leave the gaps in terms of performance between different socioeconomic groups unchanged. The differences existing after the first school year – and presumably already there when the children start school – still exist when the pupils leave school eight years later. It is an objective of the modern comprehensive school to help compensate for the socioeconomically-determined learning handicaps experienced by large groups of children. The Swedish comprehensive school is obviously far from fully successful in this respect. It is possible, though, that it is more successful than immediately appears, since the gaps between the socioeconomic groups can be expected to grow wider and wider, if no compensatory attempts are made. The fact that the gaps do not widen with increasing pupil age may, therefore, indicate that the school is partly successful in its efforts to compensate for socioeconomic handicaps.

Functional reading ability among school leavers

There is in Sweden no commonly accepted definition of functional reading ability or functional literacy. These concepts have, in fact, only recently been used in Swedish discussions about reading. There seems to be no international agreement, either, as to what constitutes functional literacy. Expressed in grade level equivalents, functional literacy can mean, apparently, anything from reading ability at Grade 4 level to ability at Grade 9 level. In my opinion, reading ability at the level which is normally reached after six years in the Swedish comprehensive school constitutes a reasonable criterion of functional literacy in a society which relies heavily, like most industrial or post-industrial societies, upon the printed word for communication of information. It should be noted that in Sweden pupils normally leave Grade 6 at the age of 13.

To what extent do Swedish pupils fail to meet this criterion – or other criteria – of functional literacy? In Table 1 (page 207), data about three different criterion levels are included: the Grade 3, Grade 4 and Grade 6 criteria. For each category of school leavers, the percentages of pupils who have *not* reached the criterion levels before leaving school at the age of 16 are indicated.

Table 1 Percentages of school leavers whose performance on certain tests is below different criteria of functional literacy

Criterion	Test	Grade 9	Upper secondary school		
			Vocational	*Semi-academic*	*Academic*
Grade 3	RC	3.4	4.0	0.8	0.0
mean	SPL	3.6	11.9	0.0	0.0
	COPY	0.6	0.0	0.0	0.0
Grade 4	RC	6.4	9.0	3.1	0.0
mean	SPL	7.8	16.6	1.4	0.2
	COPY	1.9	0.0	0.0	0.0
	RR	4.3	14.2	0.5	0.0
Grade 6	RC	16.3	27.7	8.8	1.4
mean	SPL	18.2	43.6	4.3	1.8
	COPY	12.0	34.3	2.9	0.5
	RR	20.6	42.8	15.5	3.7
	RC–MC	13.1	32.9	6.0	2.6
	PRW	14.0	18.9	1.6	1.6

Key RC   : Reading comprehension, cloze type
     RC–MC: Reading comprehension, with multiple-choice questions
     SPL   : Spelling
     COPY : Handwriting (copying of prose text)
     RR   : Reading rate
     PRW   : Practical reading and writing skills

About 95 per cent of the pupils leaving Grade 9 – including special class pupils – have reached or surpassed the Grade 3 and Grade 4 criteria. And some 85 per cent have reached – or surpassed – the

Grade 6 criterion. Consequently, some 15 per cent of those leaving the comprehensive school have *not* surpassed the Grade 6 criterion of functional literacy. Thus, a substantial proportion of our young people leave school with reading and writing abilities that can be considered insufficient in view of the demands of the society in which they are going to live and work.

(*Note*: Since the 1975 UKRA Conference, accounts of my research have been fairly widely publicized. Unfortunately, the term 'functional illiterate' has been used – for example in the *Times Educational Supplement* (Duckenfield 1975) – as a label for those who reach adulthood with reading and writing abilities not exceeding the Grade 6 level. 'Functional illiterate' – a phrase coined in this context by a Swedish journalist – is a misnomer, as there can be nothing functional about lacking an ability. To use this phrase in the present context is also – and that is more serious – misleading, since it conveys the idea that a person reading only at Grade 6 level is almost illiterate. And this is, of course, far from true, since the average thirteen year old has quite well-developed reading and writing skills. The average difference in ability between a thirteen year old and a sixteen year old is also much smaller than the average difference between, say, a ten year old and a thirteen year old (cf. Figure 1 above).)

Teachers' estimates of minimum satisfactory performance levels for school leavers

A survey of the actual development of pupils' reading and writing abilities can tell us nothing about whether we should be satisfied or dissatisfied with the present situation. In order to shed some light upon this problem we carried out an inquiry where senior and experienced teachers of Swedish were asked to indicate – for each test employed in our survey – what, in their opinion, was the minimum level of performance an average pupil leaving school should reach, before he should be considered to have given proof of satisfactory ability. In other words, teachers were asked to indicate, for each test, what score they believed constituted the minimum satisfactory performance level.

Not unexpectedly, this proved a very difficult task. A number of teachers refused to make any judgment, as they considered the task impossible. Many teachers also found if difficult to make the necessary distinction between what they believed pupils *can perform* and what they thought pupils *ought to be able to perform*. I have discussed these problems in a paper in *Reading Education* (Grundin

1975b), to which the reader is referred for a more detailed exposition.

There are great variations between teachers' opinions regarding the estimates of minimum satisfactory performance levels for school leavers of each category (comprehensive school, upper secondary academic, semi-academic and vocational). This leads to considerable overlapping between categories of school leavers. Some upper secondary school teachers demand less of a Grade 12 pupil in an academic course than other teachers demand of the average Grade 9 pupil! And vice versa: some comprehensive school teachers demand more of the average Grade 9 pupil than other teachers demand of the average Grade 12 pupil! Such wide differences in teachers' judgments have, of course, far-reaching implications for any attempt to evaluate the results of the school's reading and writing instruction by means of inquiries among teachers.

In spite of the great variations between teachers' judgments, there is fairly good agreement between the average demands – or expectations – of teachers, on the one hand, and the average performance level of the pupils, on the other. This is particularly true of pupils in Grade 9. It must be emphasized, though, that this does not necessarily mean that most teachers are satisfied with the performance level of the average school leaver. A teacher may be dissatisfied and yet accept, reluctantly, the present situation – perhaps simply because he does not believe that any marked improvement is possible. In other words, it is impossible to tell to what extent our questionnaire replies reflect resignation rather than genuine satisfaction.

Consequences for educational research and practice

As regards the need for future research, my findings above all point to the importance of studies of functional literacy: what can be expected or demanded; how can we teach – or help pupils to learn – the skills they need? The studies needed are not simply empirical studies of abilities and teaching or learning outcomes. We also need analyses of a more philosophical nature, where the value systems underlying various kinds of evaluation of reading abilities are studied and made 'visible' and where the implications of various ways and means of evaluating reading ability are spelled out in great detail.

For educational practice, the findings discussed here should have consequences primarily within the following areas:

1   The formulation of objectives for reading and writing instruction. More specific and precise formulations are needed, preferably with reference to a widely acceptable definition of functional literacy.
2   The organizational and instructional prerequisites for a continuous, systematic training of reading and writing abilities throughout the school years. These prerequisites must be carefully analysed, particularly with reference to the higher school stages.
3   The allocation of instructional resources to various subjects. It should be considered whether the total effect of schooling could be improved by devoting more resources to the training of basic communication skills.
4   The education and further education of teachers. All teachers, but above all teachers of Swedish, should be better equipped to help their pupils to develop basic reading and writing skills.

The conclusions that can be drawn from this Swedish study of the development of reading and writing abilities from the ages of seven to nineteen are, in several respects, similar to those of the British Bullock Committee Report (DES 1975). In particular, both my study and the studies and analyses of the Bullock Report point to the need to redefine the teaching of reading, so that it is made clear to all those concerned that there must be a continuous effort throughout the school years. My conclusions therefore fully endorse the third of the Bullock Report's main recommendations (page 514): 'Every school should devise a systematic policy for the development of reading competence in pupils of all ages and ability levels.'

References

DES (1975) *A Language for Life* (Bullock Report) HMSO

DUCKENFIELD, M. (1975) Sweden: Reports reveal alarming illiteracy *Times Educational Supplement* 14 November, 14

GRUNDIN, H. U. (1975a) 'The development of reading, writing and other communication skills' in W. Latham (Ed) *The Road to Effective Reading* Ward Lock Educational

GRUNDIN, H. U. (1975b) Judgment in the evaluation of reading ability *Reading Education* Summer 20–6

GRUNDIN, H. U. (1975c) *Läs-och Skrivförmagans Utveckling Genom Skoloren* (The development of reading and writing ability through-

out the school years. In Swedish with a summary in English.) In
the National School Board series *Utbildnings-forskning* No. 20.
Stockholm: Liber Läromedel

LJUNG, B. O. (1965) *The Adolescent Spurt in Mental Growth* (Stockholm
Studies in Educational Psychology, 8) Uppsala: Almqvist and
Wiksell

OLSON, W. (1959) *Child Development* (second edition) Boston:
D. C. Heath and Company

23 Intervention to prevent school failure: the resource teacher programme, a support service within the school

Marjorie J. McLean

The setting

Most of the comments and observations in this paper are made with reference to the Winnipeg School Division No. 1 and to the Province of Manitoba. The following facts should give some idea of the size, nature and location of this school division:

1 Greater Winnipeg is one of the largest cities in Canada – after Montreal, Toronto and Vancouver. It has been described as the industrial centre of the mid-west, midway between the Atlantic and Pacific Oceans.

2 Greater Winnipeg, a little more than 100 years old, with a population of 642,000, is the capital city of the Province of Manitoba.

3 The Province, with a population of 1,028,000 people, is divided into fifty-one autonomous school divisions, twelve of which are within the Metropolitan Area of Winnipeg.

4 The school division of Winnipeg No. 1, the largest of the divisions, services the inner city of the metropolitan area which has a socioeconomic range from very low to very high and a pupil population of about 39,000.

5 Winnipeg has always been the home of a variety of ethnic groups, and the range and diversity has increased dramatically within the last few years. Recent population figures reveal, (a) that at least sixteen national associations exist to promote the language and culture of each group, (b) that the major ethnic groups represented include:

Ukrainian – 85,000; German – 80,000; English – 62,000;

Scottish – 30,000; Jewish – 24,000; French – 21,000; Portuguese – 20,000; Polish – 18,000; Italian – 15,000; Hungarian – 11,000; Indian-Metis – 11,000; Irish – 8,000; Other Slavic Groups – 8,000; Asiatic (Chinese, Japanese, Vietnamese) – 7,000; Spanish American, Chilean – 5,000; Philippines – 4,000; 1,200 additional Vietnamese people are expected to arrive in August (1975).

As one would expect, these factors have had considerable impact upon the nature of the educational programme.

Government

Historically, in Canada, education has been a Provincial matter with elected local school boards. This means that support and direction from the Canadian Federal Government is minimal, although federal funds are available for specific programmes. Manitoba is one of the few provinces that does not maintain a system of government-supported separate church schools. This is still an unresolved political question. At this point in time, a shared school-services concept has been developed.

From apparent necessity, the Manitoba school system grew from a pattern of tightly centralized control. A centralized Provincial curriculum, external examinations at upper grade levels, a regulated grade system, and a centralized supervisory system provided by a team of inspectors defined and maintained the educational standards. Two of the factors related to such control had to do with the availability of well-trained teachers and the extent of teacher-training opportunities.

Gradually, the province has moved from this position of central control, and in the last decade has done much to support independent curriculum development. Schools divisions have paralleled, in varying degrees, this move towards greater autonomy for schools and clusters of schools.

Decentralization

What has the trend towards decentralization meant for schools within a division? To be more responsive to local needs, the Winnipeg School Division, for example, has been subdivided into three smaller areas. Each area now has a superintendent and a consulting team to help to focus more specifically on the needs of varying communities. Parents in community groups are becoming much more aware of ways in which they may help to bring about changes in schools and to participate in the developing programmes.

Changing needs and services

As part of a response to needs identified by parents, the resource teacher programme was introduced by the Winnipeg School Division No. 1 in 1969.

The leaders of the local Association for Children with Learning Disabilities became very active in seeking more comprehensive school services for their children. Their belief was that children with special problems were not receiving the kind of education and attention to which they were entitled. No longer were these parents willing to accept a rigid grade system that did not seem to allow for significant differences in learning. They were willing to have their children placed in segregated special classes only as a last resort. Their request was for comprehensive service to their children within the regular class.

These needs had not been ignored by Winnipeg through the years, but availability of trained personnel and appropriate funding were two of the major reality factors that had to be considered. The school division through the Child Guidance Clinic did provide diagnostic and remedial service on a limited basis. The clinic offered a multidiscipline approach through its departments of speech and hearing, social work, reading, psychology and psychiatry. Along with this, remedial reading programmes and a carefully devised system of special classes had been set up in an attempt to ensure that children with special needs had full opportunity to learn. In order to receive appropriate help, some children had to leave their home school to attend sessions at the clinic or classes in another school.

The clinical and remedial reading services were well suited to the nature of the educational programme at that time. Every attempt was made to help the child reach the level that would enable him to fit back into the regular class. Gradually, however, some teachers and helping personnel began to work out different ways of coping with the individual styles of learning within the regular class. Programmes were geared more often to the needs of the child rather than to the demands of a grade level.

The resource programme, then, was introduced at a time when many important influences were being brought to bear on education. Clinical personnel, educators, parents and politicians were becoming much more involved in discussing individual differences in children, especially with regard to learning problems. The concept of the 'at risk' child was developing. Steps were taken within schools to give more attention to the very young child in terms of early intervention to prevent learning difficulties. Continuous progress became more acceptable to many.

Gradually, volunteers and paraprofessionals formed a more integral part of the educational team. Innovative grants were set up by administration to encourage teachers to consider other ways to design and plan for a wide range of instructional needs. The result was that teams of teachers began to work together to devise more appropriate instructional approaches and learning environments.

The resource teacher programme

The resource teacher programme began with about twenty-nine teachers serving fifty-eight elementary schools. Their initial function was to be available on a regular basis within schools to provide service to those children with learning problems or those who were thought to be 'at risk'. The procedures involved preliminary assessments, consultation with the teacher and remediation. If further assistance seemed to be warranted, referrals were made to the Child Guidance Clinic. The change in emphasis in this programme had to do with thinking beyond the concept of a reading problem to that of a learning problem. Resource teachers began to pay more attention to language, to movement, to the processes of learning, as well as to specific achievement areas such as reading, writing, spelling and mathematics.

Follow-up by the resource teacher was arranged on a flexible basis. Often children were taken out of classes at set intervals for direct instruction. As experience was gained, however, some resource teachers began to move into the classroom to work with the child or a group of children in ways acceptable to the teacher. When this happened, the teacher and resource teacher were likely to be in closer contact about specific aspects of the programme.

Where possible, resource teachers worked with volunteers to help them be more effective within the school. Alone, or in conjunction with teachers, they set out suitable tasks for practice or instruction and assigned specific students to the volunteers. The volunteers included elementary and high school tutors, peer tutors, university students, community helpers, parents and senior citizens. This part of the work added a new dimension to the helping service within schools, and also brought about changes in attitude of parent, child and staff.

Currently in the resource programme, at the conclusion of the sixth year, the staff consists of forty-five elementary teachers in fifty-eight schools, twelve junior-high teachers, and three physical education resource teachers. The physical education resource teachers provide a service coordinated by Physical Education and Special Education. This service has been linked to that of the resource teachers to give them a contact person within each school who will be available to respond to programme recommendations. The thrust of this part of the programme is at the primary level (including nursery/kindergarten) to make certain that movement activities are specific to the needs of children who may have special problems.

One resource teacher has been attached to the Learning Assistance Centre for children with emotional difficulties. Since these centres are based in various schools, the resource teacher becomes a key person in terms of providing consultation about achievement levels and appropriate instructional materials. A liaison function with a child's home school and with other teachers and resource teachers becomes possible.

An ongoing programme of inservice training is designed by and for resource teachers each year. The school division has been most generous in providing for regular meetings and in funding specific workshops. The series of programmes varies from year to year, but usually consists of a balance of local participation and external leadership. One year the total focus was on the study of language. Other programmes have included workshops on topics such as evaluation and remediation, comprehension and the art and science of questioning, learning styles and processes, movement and rhythm, materials and methodology, and communication and interpersonal relationships.

Through these meetings, private studies, conferences and school staff development programmes, the resource teachers have developed a wide range of competencies in a relatively short time.

Programme review
To give further impetus to the resource programme in Winnipeg and in the Province of Manitoba, the Department of Education reviewed the resource teacher function in terms of the delivery of service throughout the province. This resulted in a comprehensive statement of resource service, designed to be more effective in providing support at the school level. In general, the statement is quite compatible with the direction in which the Winnipeg School Division is moving, and is providing a guide for future development.

The definition of resource service in this new statement identifies the functions of consultation, collaboration and direct service. The

Departmental preference was to consider these in a hierarchy, but most of the field personnel felt quite strongly that at this time the components should be viewed on a horizontal plane with freedom to deliver the service at the level most suited to the particular situation. The emphasis in the new statement is in terms of a support system for the teacher. The resource teacher is tending to be seen as a person who is knowledgeable about programme planning and the range and nature of available resources.

Value

As resource teachers have moved away from a strict direct remedial reading approach, the value of the service appears to have been enhanced. More and more, the resource teachers are working with other teachers in a variety of ways to develop instructional approaches that have more meaning for the diverse school population.

One junior-senior high school recognized the need to reduce the number of students coming to any one teacher in a day. Four core subject area teachers and the resource teacher worked out a programme for 150 students. The resource teacher is well informed about the aims and goals of the programme and moves in and out of classrooms to assist with specific students.

In a large city-centre elementary school the population comprises a complete range of ethnic groups. Volunteers and helpers of varying backgrounds pour into the school. The resource teacher has become a kind of coordinator of 'the helping people'. He makes certain that the helper and the teacher or child to be helped are well matched. Among the helpers are senior citizens known to the school as 'grand-friends', students from the faculty of education, clinical personnel who are available to conduct small therapy groups, physical education personnel who provide additional gross motor programmes, and aides or helpers with knowledge of languages other than English.

In another school a special situation exists where the elementary and junior-high resource teachers are in different school buildings within the same area. They have worked out a system of cross-age volunteer tutoring using the services of older students who have problems. The junior-high resource teacher is able to deal with behaviours important to successful tutoring with younger children; the elementary resource teacher defines the task, offers support, and keeps in touch with her junior-high colleague.

Although the resource programmes vary from school to school, basic guidelines provide the parameters for developing a comprehensive service. In all schools, the principal is the key person who sets the tone and is available for consultation as needed. Staff members are recognizing the value of having available to them on request someone with special skills and knowledge who is able to assist in working out more appropriate learning opportunities for children.

24 An evaluation of the reading programmes in Lagos State secondary schools

Oladele Taiwo

Introduction

Nigerians as a people have yet to develop the habit of reading for pleasure. They either do not read at all or are such poor readers that they cannot enjoy what they read. In a situation in which the language of the home is usually different from the language of the school, in which books are only just becoming available in the right number and quality and where there is so much traditional respect for the printed word, it is not altogether surprising that the habit of reading for pleasure has not been easy to cultivate.

The reading programmes in Lagos State secondary schools are directly affected by the situation in the society at large. If homes are crowded and provide an uninspiring atmosphere for study, if books and journals are few and good parental examples are hard to come by, if the home employment of the child is usually strenuous, time-consuming and unacademic, then a situation is created which retards rather than stimulates the reading habit. Where illiteracy is common and entertainments are largely communal, there is a natural tendency to capitalize on the oral traditions and collective cultural activities of the people, at times at the expense of reading. Only activities which tend to promote a sense of togetherness are encouraged. In this context, sitting down alone to read a book for pleasure may appear unnatural or even antisocial. Rural areas afford the quiet but not the motivation. Where the motivation exists in the city, other social factors militate against the cultivation of good reading habits. The result is the familiar picture painted by Paul Edwards (1963):

In 'English-speaking' West Africa not many people make a habit of reading just for pleasure. For one thing not many know enough English to read it fluently, and those who can read in the vernacular tongues have only a few books to which they can turn. But even those who are able to read in English and who can afford to buy books are not, on the whole, very interested in doing so. The reading that does go on above the level of the daily newspaper is mostly of texts for examinations, or books about the reader's profession. People seem to feel as puritanical about reading as they do about medicine, as though nothing can be any good unless it hurts. There are parents who refuse to let their children read fiction on the ground that reading stories is a waste of time that should rightly be spent on serious study.

Reading programmes

Given this social background, it is not surprising that reading for pleasure is accorded such a low priority in Lagos State secondary schools. A recent research study in twenty-seven schools shows that attention is concentrated on intensive reading and that the need for balance between intensive and extensive reading is often overlooked. (This research study, sponsored by the University of Lagos, was undertaken by me during the academic year 1974/75 into the Reading Programmes in Forms 1–3 of selected secondary schools in Lagos State. This paper embodies some of its findings.) There is a tendency to focus attention in this case, as in other aspects of school work, on drills and practices considered immediately relevant to the child's next examination. The value of reading for personal growth is largely ignored. Yet in the African setting, where there is so much to learn, reading for pleasure could be a potent instrument of education, an infallible means of widening the child's horizon and exciting his imaginative experience.

Because the approach to reading is so utilitarian, traditional methods are still employed in the teaching of the two aspects of reading which dominate school work – intensive and extensive reading. A brief description of the situation as it applies to the schools visited might be helpful.

Intensive reading

This takes about 80 per cent of the time and provides the core of the whole programme. Most schools devote at least three hours a week (out of a total of five or six for English) to intensive reading. Passages for comprehension, or summary exercises, are derived from a set book or, in a few cases, a number of books. The passages in the books deal with a variety of topics and backgrounds and are usually of increasing length and difficulty. The centres of interest they represent include in order of popularity:

Culture and history
Domestic life
Education
Science and technology
Health and social studies
Business and commerce.

The questions on the selected passages are one or other of the following types:

1 Involving basic comprehension of facts, using techniques such as:

   (a) multiple choice
   (b) sentence completion
   (c) identification of phrase(s) or sentence(s) which are the key to comprehension
   (d) paraphrase of the key phrase(s) or sentence(s)
   (e) 'open' or traditional questions
   (f) interpretation of a graph or table or diagrammatically presented material based on the passage.

2 Involving analysis of the content – how it is organized within a paragraph or through a series of paragraphs.
3 Involving the student in making deductions or seeing the implications of a number of facts or arguments.
4 Involving the use of the subject-matter of the passage or an aspect of it as the basis of some general discussion.
5 Traditional summary work which involves the whole passage or part of it.

Some types of questions are more popular than others. For example, types 1(c), (d) and (f), 2 and 3 listed above are not commonly found in popular textbooks and are therefore used only occasionally in class. It is left to a few dedicated and qualified teachers to devise their own questions of these types and apply them judiciously. Where this is done, the pupils benefit greatly. Even where children have to rely mainly or entirely on the traditional types of questions, like 1(b) and (e), 4 and 5, some improvement still results from the consistency of the practice and the enthusiasm shown by the pupils and their teachers. Nearly all the teachers interviewed emphasized the important role of intensive reading in any reading improvement programme. This belief provides the motivation for the professional help they give to the pupils in this connection. Although they adopt methods and approaches which are mainly traditional, they certainly execute this aspect of the reading programme with zeal and, in many cases, professional competence. So the deficiency here is not so much what is taught or how it is done, but the almost total reliance which teachers place on the intensive reading skill to the partial detriment of other skills.

Extensive reading

The research study devoted a lot of attention to this important but largely neglected skill. Questionnaires were served on the twenty-seven schools investigated on this particular aspect. Questions ranged from the importance attached to extensive reading in the reading programme, the kinds of books read, the relative emphasis placed on prose, drama and poetry to the relevance of the background of authors and books, the importance of the teacher's approach and suggestions for making the whole programme more effective. The replies to many of these questions are illuminating. Only a summary of them with a few quotations can be given in a short paper of this kind.

Prose is the most popular literary form taught in the schools. All twenty-seven schools place emphasis on prose. Next comes drama. Poetry is usually given a low priority. Some of the reasons adduced for this are interesting:

1 'Most of the primary school products come from illiterate homes, and primary school curriculum and teaching are such that these pupils can hardly express themselves intelligibly in English. Therefore they haven't got the language exposure necessary for understanding Poetry.'
2 'I will teach Prose first because children should go from known to unknown. In African culture storytelling is a nightly form of relaxation and as such I assume that pupils are familiar with people telling stories or giving news. Prose is also simple and straightforward so that pupils can easily grasp the plot of a story.'

The average number of books read every year is four, and the list usually includes books by African and non-African writers. The reading of Shakespeare's plays is on the decline but Lamb's *Tales from Shakespeare* is still popular. Usually a class concentrates on an anthology of poetry, but at best only a few poems are read a year. The background of the author is no longer the great issue that it was a few years ago, even though programme planners still show a mental preference for books written by Africans or against the African background. This preference does not appear to be wholly justified, as the following responses to a particular item of the questionnaire would show:

1   'Pupils prefer books written by African authors because the subjects that African writers write about are usually within the experiences of the pupils, e.g. *The Drummer Boy, No Longer at Ease* and *Abiku* whereas foreign authors write often about situations that are outside the pupils' experiences, e.g. snow, winter, poppies etc.'

2   'Pupils prefer books written by Africans because African authors picture the culture and customs of particular ethnic groups and those cultures and customs are similar to what the pupils observe in their own tribes or clans.'

3   'Children from nursery/primary schools feel at home with books written by foreign authors. Others don't really mind the author. Provided the experiences they read about are familiar to them and appeal to their imagination, they will read whatever they are made to read . . . My pupils have responded better this year to *Pride and Prejudice* than the class last year did to *Cry, the Beloved Country*.'

It would appear therefore that the method of presentation is far more important for the achievement of the teacher's objectives than the authorship or the background against which the selected books are written. Teachers suggested several ways of making the presentation more attractive to the children and of enhancing the value of extensive reading. Some of their replies make interesting reading:

1   'From Form One pupils should be encouraged to spend more time on supplementary reading. A library can be set up in each class so that pupils will bring private books there for the others to borrow. We might also start a Readers' Club in the school.'

2   'First and foremost, I will choose very good, straightforward and interesting books for children in the lower classes . . . Secondly,

I shall be a real master of the books I teach so as to be able to answer children's questions and explain some difficult aspects of the books. Thirdly, I shall give summary notes after each chapter or Act. Fourthly, I shall arrange film shows on these plays, especially on Shakespearian books.'

3 'By having a literary and debating society. By having many literature books which are African in scope in the school library. By making students read at least a literature text book a week from the library and to record the contents. By choosing leaders among the students to supervise literature groups.'

These suggestions are important in the way they point to the problems confronting the schools and the reading programmes. The main problems appear to be the following:

1 At the time the pupils start secondary-school work, their reading ability is poor and the reading habit has not yet been cultivated. Their understanding of English is faulty. The opportunity for application is also limited.

2 The school library, where one exists, is usually only open for the pupils' use during school hours. This prevents the pupils from making full use of the library at their leisure. The school librarian may not be particularly well qualified for his work and is therefore usually of little help to the pupils.

3 Class libraries are few and not always well organized. They function only when the teacher provides the necessary leadership. Because of lack of supervision the books do not go round enough during the week. At worst, the books simply vanish.   ,

4 Little provision is made for remedial work. The backward child hardly receives any special help. He therefore tends to lag behind the rest of the class. The absence of reading improvement courses reduces the effectiveness of the reading programmes.

Observations and suggestions

The three most important components of a successful reading programme are: parents, teachers and the right books. The responsibility of the home is great. Not only should parents provide a strong moral, spiritual and intellectual foundation for the child, they should also ensure a peaceful and decent environment which enables the child to develop his natural talents. The ability to read is so basic to all education that it can hardly be successfully acquired without the active support of parents. Gertrude Whipple (1967) tells us in an article how this can be done:

Parents emphasize the importance of reading by reading, by being seen reading newspapers, books and magazines, and by reading to children. This tells the child that reading is important, because the people who mean the most to him, his parents, do it. Parents who permit the radio and television to dominate the home atmosphere all of the child's waking hours are not helping a child find a time to read or time to be read to.

It is obvious from what was said earlier on that most parents in Lagos do not give the kind of support the child requires to improve his reading skills.

The teachers play a more successful role. About 80 per cent of the teachers interviewed are qualified for their job. Apart from a good first degree, many of them hold a post-graduate diploma in education. Those who are not graduates have recognized teaching qualifications. However, only a few teachers have taken specialist courses in reading and none of them qualifies to be called a reading specialist. In the absence of specially devised reading improvement courses, reading is usually taught as an integral part of English. Given the time allocation to reading and limited expertise and resources, it will be unrealistic to expect more from the teachers.

My research shows that books do not present an insurmountable problem. The book trade in Nigeria has grown tremendously in recent years and has been given a boost recently by the establishment of a Federal Government-sponsored Book Development Council. The proposed universal primary education in 1976 will make a great impact on the production and distribution of books. As books become available in large numbers, it is frightfully important that the right ones are selected for the reading programmes in schools. At present there is no noticeable difference based on sex or locality in the selection and use of reading material. This can hardly be avoided in a situation where reading lists are prescribed by some central authority, like a government, a voluntary agency or a religious body. Even where, as in Lagos State, the reading lists sent to schools are presented as mere suggestions to help the teacher, they still influence very heavily the final selection of books by the schools. One looks forward to the time when individual schools and teachers will feel free to compile their own lists without reference to an external body. Then it will be possible for the list of books in the reading programme to reflect the particular needs of the different kinds of schools, the rural and urban nature of their

H

environment and the peculiar needs of boys and girls.

Of the three components discussed above, the home constitutes a serious deficiency which good teachers and right books cannot adequately make up for. But there are also other basic weaknesses in the school reading programmes which must be quickly rectified. To start with, only two reading skills are emphasized, in some cases to the utter exclusion of others. Of these two, only the skill of intensive reading is taught. It is generally assumed that all that is required of a child for him to cultivate the habit of extensive reading is practice. In fact, as all reading specialists know, it is just as important to teach the skill of extensive reading as it is to teach that of intensive reading. For this purpose the child would require different kinds of material – extracts from books, reference works, stories, biographies, newspapers, letters, notices and directories, to mention a few. The child should be taught the skill of extremely rapid reading – skimming and reading the gist – for the purpose of locating information like names, dates, places or giving the substance of a passage or book. It is only when these skills are imparted early to the child that he stands the chance of developing sound reading habits as he grows up.

There is a clear indication of the need for the establishment of reading centres and clinics. The centres should devise various reading improvement courses. In the context of Lagos schools the aim of such courses should be:

1 To help eliminate many or all of the child's mechanical defects in reading – word-by-word reading, poor visual perception, vocalization and sub-vocalization, excessive eye fixation, finger pointing and head movement, regression and slowness in word recognition, which are some of the common faults.
2 To help identify and control other more serious causes of reading disabilities like auditory defects, inefficient motor control, low mental ability, physical defects, emotional difficulties, environmental or educational deficiencies. Serious cases should be referred, as necessary, to the medical doctor, educational psychologist, health visitor or welfare officer.
3 To help organize and coordinate research into various aspects of reading, concentrating on neglected areas like listening comprehension and how to increase verbal facility, auditory discrimination and attention span. An important area of research may be to find out to what extent the personality attributes and disorders which affect a child's reading speed are the function of heredity

and environment. For reasons which are partly traditional and partly modern, there is a great need in the context of Nigeria to do fundamental research into the reader's attitude. For, as Unoh (1972) says:

> If the reader is the kind of person who tends to be too careful, too afraid to take any risks in life, and too afraid lest he makes any mistakes; or if he is the kind of person who has great respect for written words, who feels that to be fair to an author one must read his publication word-for-word, then the chances are that he will have some difficulty in attempting to read fast. He will probably have far too much respect for individual words as vehicles of thought, to risk losing the train of thought by skipping any word!

> Research might throw light on how the Nigerian could reconcile his traditional respect for other people's property, in this case the printed word, with the modern necessity to use a book or a reading passage freely and for various purposes.

There is yet another area to which research can make a tremendous contribution – the tendency to use the written word as a traditional symbol. Nigerians, like most Africans, use symbols for every kind of purpose. There is hardly any kind of activity into which some measure of symbolization is not introduced. Be it a funeral or naming ceremony, a ritual performance or wedding, the various objects used are symbols for the celebrant's desire for peace and prosperity. Of immediate relevance to reading is the use of symbols to send messages and in incantations, ordinary speech and catch-words. When a Nigerian child reads slowly, regresses, does excessive eye fixation, is he at that stage pausing to decipher the symbol from what he has read? When we complain, for example, that the child in a Lagos State school has difficulty with the return sweep when reading, could it be that he is taking his time to unravel the symbol presented by one line before moving on to the next or is it, as reading specialists would say, a plain case of eye-muscle difficulty? This is a point on which only fundamental research can throw an intensive searchlight. For, if the truth might be faced, the African, states R. Bastide (Olabimtan 1974):

> . . . sees in everything which is given to his senses something other than he sees – he deciphers the other, that is to say the sacred, through the mineral, the vegetable and the animal. It is

not the word of man that refers to and circumscribes objects; it is objects that are 'words' for the African.

The findings of research studies should be made available to schools. The schools too must be willing to experiment with different ways of making books available to pupils in the right number and quality. For example, the experiment with book boxes carried out by the British Council in primary schools in Lagos (*Read for Success* 1969) ought to have been repeated. Secondary schools too will benefit from such an experiment, which will ultimately have a salutary effect on the adult community. The place of the home should be strengthened, so that it can play its assigned role in the matter of providing a sound foundation for reading. Given government support, a meaningful programme and the active cooperation of the school and home, it should be possible for Nigerian society at large to recognize reading for pleasure as a potent instrument of achieving national solidarity and international peace and understanding. The reading programmes of Lagos State secondary schools have to be greatly improved, if they are to make any noticeable contribution to these laudable objectives.

References

EDWARDS, P. (1963) *West African Narrative* Nelson

OLABIMTAN, A. (1974) Symbolism in Yoruba traditional incantatory poetry *Nigeria Magazine* 114 35–42

THE BRITISH COUNCIL (1969) *Read For Success* Lagos (Unpublished report)

UNOH, S. O. (1972) *Faster Reading Through Practice* Oxford University Press

WHIPPLE, G. (1967) 'Inspiring culturally disadvantaged children to read' in R. Staiger (Ed) *New Directions in Reading* New York: Bantam Books

25 The teacher as the most important variable

Frances T. Caust

It is my intention to describe an innovation in teacher education which began when the South Australian Education Department (Primary Division) established the Reading Development Centre in 1972.

Background

South Australia covers a wide geographical area (380,070 square miles) and has a population of just over one million people, 800,000 of whom live in or near Adelaide, the capital city. The student population in our schools is nearly a quarter of a million. There are approximately 15,000 teachers, 6,118 of whom are in the Primary Division (1974 figures). Education has always been centrally administered from Adelaide, but regional administrative autonomy is being established.

The problem

Growing concern with literacy standards was expressed by teachers, principals of schools, administrators, parents and employers. Traditionally in our state, reading has been seen as the initial concern of the infant teacher who educates the beginning reader, and as the subsequent concern of the remedial teacher who educates the primary-school child who has failed in the normal classroom. This approach is inadequate, because it does not provide all practising teachers with the knowledge, opportunity or responsibility to provide for the needs and abilities of the majority of children in our schools.

Initial teacher training for the teacher who would be responsible for seven to twelve year olds, has done little to alleviate the problem. In 1971 the student-teacher received from 0–20 compulsory hours preparation in the teaching of reading during a three-year course

(Caust 1971). In 1974 the student-teacher received from 0–30 compulsory hours (Crisp 1974).

This has occurred despite the view now emerging that *all* teachers, regardless of specialization, are teachers of reading and should be prepared and supported accordingly.

The demand by practising teachers for more support and assistance in their teaching programme and the known inadequacy of teacher preparation, were factors which led the Primary Division of the South Australian Education Department to establish the Reading Development Centre in 1972. An old city school was provided, with plans in hand to restructure the interior of the school to meet the needs of an inservice centre.

The establishment of the Reading Development Centre

At the beginning of 1972 I was appointed as Principal of the centre with the following charter:

1 To be responsible to the Director of Primary Education for the development and running of the Reading Development Centre.
2 To assist classroom teachers to improve their competence to teach reading in a manner that provides for the differing abilities and needs of children.
3 To assist the classroom teacher and the school to diagnose and remedy reading difficulties except those that require a specialist's attention.
4 To assist heads of schools and staff to introduce reading programmes to provide for the differing needs and abilities of children.
5 To visit schools to assist in diagnosing weaknesses and suggesting alternatives and to give support to their introduction.
6 To give guidance and support to reading innovation and experiments in reading.

In order to achieve these aims it was necessary:

1 To provide inservice education in reading at the centre and in schools.
2 To develop at the centre a large display of reading schemes, ancillary and audiovisual material, diagnostic and testing materials, reading reference books, reports of South Australian, Australian and overseas research findings, innovations and experiments in reading.

3 To develop at the centre appropriate advisory services.
4 To develop the competence of advisory teachers appointed to the centre.
5 To give information on reading materials and methodology at infant, primary and secondary levels.

The work of the Reading Development Centre

The above brief outline indicates the task to be undertaken. The Reading Development Centre was to be an inservice centre, information-giving and advisory on request. With the overall objective to assist the classroom teacher to meet the differing needs of children in reading, it was necessary to consider where to begin. The first term of 1972 was spent in identifying needs, planning and organization. The following is a short account of some of the key areas in which we are working, and some related considerations.

Resource schools

Early in 1972 meetings were held between teachers, principals, inspectors and administrators and the concept of the 'resource school' evolved. Resource schools are schools nominated by inspectors of urban districts with the cooperation of school principals and staff. The schools nominated undertake to ensure that *all* teachers in the school, including principals and librarians, attend the inservice course at the Reading Development Centre.

During and following the inservice course, teachers from these schools are given regular advisory teacher support, usually one day a week for a school year. Assistance is given to the school to continue its own inservice programme with current and new staff. Our aim is to encourage each resource school to become independent of the centre's services so that new resource schools can then be established.

At the end of the inservice course it is hoped that each teacher will be more adequately informed of:

1 the nature of the English language and the analysis of the language for the teaching of reading
2 the nature of the reading process
3 the different approaches to the teaching of reading
4 a rationale for selection of reading schemes
5 diagnostic procedures
6 useful reference material

7   school and classroom organizational options.

Each school is encouraged to maintain and update reading reference materials and is expected to act as a resource centre for other schools in the district. Resource schools often try out new reading materials to ascertain their suitability for South Australian schools.

In 1975, there has been a concerted effort to consolidate the work done in the resource schools. As further support, the advisory teachers have helped to organize and run further inservice sessions for the total staff in their own schools. The schools have also organized inservice for teachers in their district on the 'Resource Book on the Development of Reading Skills'. This inservice work is assisted by their advisory teacher.

Other schools

Resource schools provided the nucleus for inservice courses. However, when the centre became operational in the second term of 1972, the inservice programme was repeated three times a week. The repeats became necessary as teachers from other schools, guidance officers, teachers in special education and others wished to participate in the course. So from the beginning, parallel inservice help was offered to schools other than resource schools.

Whilst carrying through the daily inservice programme, the requests for longer courses for credit led to a night course being established in 1973 (sixty contact hours) and a correspondence course for country teachers in 1975. These two courses are the first of their kind in Australia to be offered for credit in the teaching of reading, to practising teachers in normal teaching situations.

With country schools the concept of resource schools was not appropriate, because of long distances between schools. One week per term, all other work stops at the centre while we undertake a week's inservice work with country teachers. The appointment of regional advisory teachers in reading and the correspondence course have been greatly appreciated by country teachers.

Preparation of advisory teacher staff at the Reading Development Centre

Teachers appointed to the Reading Development Centre are chosen carefully from open advertisment. All are competent practising teachers who are seconded to the centre for at least three years, and who have had at least three years, preferably five years, teaching experience. New appointees have one term of induction before they each undertake responsibility for three resource schools. The aim has been to balance staff with infant and primary trained teachers. Currently we have one secondary teacher, as our service to secondary schools is limited, and is only one of the options available to secondary teachers. Our librarian was also seconded to us by the Secondary Division.

Advisory teachers need experience in the whole range of children's development and need to become familiar with practices in many schools. All new staff follow a common induction programme and then assume responsibility for both infant and primary classes, regardless of their previous training and experience.

One morning a week is given over to *staff* inservice work in which we:

1 continually assess our own procedures
2 assess new reading materials
3 examine new reading research.

Regional advisory teachers undergo the one term's induction programme and have regular planned inservice sessions at the Reading Development Centre in Adelaide for their continuous professional development.

Nature of inservice work
In our work with teachers the point of view of the centre has been straightforward. Our aim is to meet the needs of teachers; that is, we are a service organization. Practising teachers and centre staff seek solutions to problems by working together. Survey information indicated that many teachers wanted and needed:

1 information about the reading process
2 opportunities to exchange ideas and information with other teachers
3 structure within the school to facilitate cooperative and productive learning
4 more effective communication with children, parents, administrators, consultants, etc.

Most teachers were concerned to develop:

1 confidence in their ability to effectively teach reading to a class of children with a wide range of reading attainment; that is, in a normal classroom situation

2 overall objectives and a sense of direction
3 strategies to move towards these objectives.

As a result of these surveys, the centre decided to focus its attention on the need to convey to teachers in a structured way the following knowledge:

1 the skills which a child needs in order to master the reading process
2 all *known* variables which affect a child's reading progress
3 organizational options open to teachers
4 materials available to assist the teacher to meet these needs, including teacher-made materials.

It was clear that not only was it important to plan the content of inservice courses carefully, but also to consider the way in which the content was presented. In this area, practising teachers and centre staff seek solutions to these problems by working together. We make it clear to teachers that we can organize courses in a logical way, but that they too are responsible for suggesting modification to meet their needs; for example, teachers rapidly concluded that the lecture system is often ineffective, so we have arranged to supply written material whenever this is more appropriate. Seminars and workshops are usually preferred.

As teachers are the successful products of an education system and probably never experienced difficulty in learning to read, as well as having forgotten the initial process, ingenuity is needed to place teachers in learning situations where the task relates to reading but is difficult to master. For example, we use the mirror drawing of a star, and decoding unknown graphemes with known phoneme correspondence; that is, a simulated 'reading' lesson.

In both exercises we establish a traditional classroom atmosphere in which the teachers themselves are the students, attempting to master new skills under pressure from authoritative teacher figures. Here the variables which influence learning in a social situation are dramatically highlighted.

Individual children in a class are often experiencing difficulty at a task which the busy teacher may miss. Therefore, much use is made of individual children on tape and video, performing a reading task which may be in any area of the curriculum. Teachers can then watch and listen, record and then discuss where they think the difficulty lies and between them suggest appropriate teaching/

learning strategies.

The areas of spoken language, listening skills, reading and writing are all treated developmentally.

A group of thirty teachers, infant, primary and secondary, attend inservice work at one time. Most teachers have said that they benefit from mixed groups as they gain greater insight into the problems which face teachers at different levels of our school system.

We are conscious of the individual needs and differences of teachers. If we expect teachers to be able to meet the individual needs of children in reading, then we should be able to meet the individual needs of teachers in inservice study. We aim to use inservice courses on reading in the same manner in which it is expected that teachers will teach reading in the classroom. This is an extremely difficult task, which highlights the difficulty of the teachers' own task. Each situation, each teacher, is different, but by working together we are gradually establishing models and finding out what does and does not work.

Involving teachers in devising their own curriculum
In attempting to determine the services that the centre could most usefully offer, it became obvious that we needed to define more specifically the problems that teachers experience. Such defining is constantly undertaken with teachers who state the difficulties they have with inadequate resource material, etc.

Repeated requests from teachers for reading games and activities that teachers find successful led, in 1972, to a collection of games and activities from infant schools throughout the State. These were collated and printed by the centre in the form of a booklet, *Reading: Word Recognition and Listening Activities*. A revision of this booklet is now complete and has been adapted for use in both infant and primary grades.

In August 1973, teachers from resource schools, with staff from the centre, cooperated to produce a book aimed at meeting the stated needs of classroom teachers in the area of reading. The result was the production of the *Resource Book on the Development of Reading Skills*.

One inservice film, *The Teaching of Reading in Upper Primary Grades,* was completed in 1974. In 1975 we have made *Motivation: A Reason to Read*, in conjunction with the South Australian Film Corporation.

The concern expressed by teachers, particularly beginning teachers, about the inadequacy of preservice preparation in the area of reading and the need to greatly expand inservice facilities for all teachers at all levels of teaching, led to a one week residential conference to consider the 'problems, practices and perspectives on the teaching of reading in South Australia'. This report and its recommendations has now been published and we believe will have far-reaching influence. Representatives of preservice and inservice preparation, teachers, administrators and research workers in South Australia took part in this Conference.

Communication in reading education

The Education Department has many and varied persons and agencies which focus on the school and the teacher. These include inspectors, guidance and special education branch, libraries branch, research and planning branch. Communicating with all concerned bodies is an ongoing task for the centre and one that we regard as essential to its efficient and productive functioning.

In 1972 we listed these various bodies and planned a series of meetings. We explained what we were attempting and why, and sought cooperation when necessary. Advisory teachers in reading take part in inservice work in science and physical education, to show how reading is essential to all areas of the curriculum, the readability of texts, and so on. In the same way speech therapists, educational psychologists, librarians and others assist in our courses. Close cooperation with universities and colleges of advanced education is necessary. Representatives of colleges take part in the planning and assessment of our credit courses and assist in our inservice programme. We in turn assist colleges in their courses, on request.

Our initial contact with parent bodies was at schools, talking at parent meetings. The interest of parents was so great that we now have open afternoons once a month and one night meeting a term to discuss aspects of reading education. These meetings are always fully attended with a maximum number of fifty per session.

The growing interest of teachers and others led to the formation of the South Australian Reading Association in 1973. This association has between 500 and 600 members, regular meetings are held and a journal is published four times a year. It is the South Australian Reading Association that has sponsored the first Australian Reading Conference in Adelaide from 27–31 August, 1975. From this conference we intend to form an Australian Reading Association. It is hoped that a national organization will provide a focus and form for further advance in reading education and literacy standards.

The current position

Resource schools (*1974*)	Number
Infant and primary	25
Secondary	4
Catholic	1
Independent	1
Total number of resource schools	31

Teachers involved in inservice

It is estimated that in 1973 25 per cent of the teaching population of primary teachers, that is, 2,005 teachers, had between a half day and eleven days inservice study. Following a survey undertaken in 1974, it is estimated that 45 per cent (3,278) of the present teaching population at primary level had from one to sixty hours inservice training.

Staff at the Reading Development Centre 1975

Principal
2 Vice-Principals
12 Advisory teachers – metropolitan
9 Advisory teachers – regional
5 Teachers on part-time release
1 Librarian
2 Teacher aides
3 Clerical assistants

Figure 1 (page 238) shows the current programme of the Reading Development Centre.

Conclusion

It has not been possible in this short paper to fully acquaint you with all the activities undertaken by the centre. For example, I have not been able to give you details of the retrieval system used for information on research in reading, materials available and so on. However, since the Reading Development Centre has been operating, we have learned that teachers in South Australia need and welcome supportive help when it is available in a non-directive and working partnership.

It has long been recognized that the knowledge and training of teachers is critical to successful student learning in all areas of the

Figure 1   The current programme of the Reading Development Centre

Aim: To assist teachers to meet the needs of children, in reading, in their classroom.

Intention: To be an inservice centre for teachers and information-giving and advisory on request.

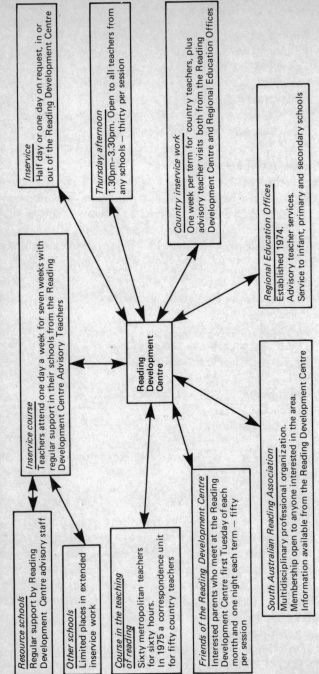

Resource schools
Regular support by Reading Development Centre advisory staff

Other schools
Limited places in extended inservice work

Inservice course
Teachers attend one day a week for seven weeks with regular support in their schools from the Reading Development Centre Advisory Teachers

Inservice
Half day or one day on request, in or out of the Reading Development Centre

Thursday afternoon
1.30pm–3.30pm. Open to all teachers from any schools – thirty per session

Country inservice work
One week per term for country teachers, plus advisory teacher visits both from the Reading Development Centre and Regional Education Offices

Regional Education Offices
Established 1974.
Advisory teacher services.
Service to infant, primary and secondary schools

Course in the teaching of reading
Sixty metropolitan teachers for sixty hours.
In 1975 a correspondence unit for fifty country teachers

Friends of the Reading Development Centre
Interested parents who meet at the Reading Development Centre first Tuesday of each month and one night each term – fifty per session

South Australian Reading Association
Multidisciplinary professional organization.
Membership open to anyone interested in the area.
Information available from the Reading Development Centre

Reading Development Centre

curriculum. In South Australia the preservice preparation of teachers in reading has been inadequate. However, regardless of their quality, preservice programmes cannot maintain the teacher in the job. A teacher's professional preparation consists not only of pre-service work and activities but of a continuous inservice programme. Perhaps the ideal is for such inservice programmes to be offered within and between schools.

We have still much to learn about ways of supporting teachers in their efforts to meet the literacy needs of their pupils. The South Australian Education Department is committed to the challenge in the belief that the employing body has the responsibility to provide the ways and means which allow teachers to increase and share their competence and experience in order to further the development of literacy skills in their students. Our Education Department, in making this commitment, does so because of its understanding of the basic problems facing teachers in assisting children to acquire reading skills.

References

CAUST, F. T. (1971) Unpublished survey

CRISP, G. D. (1974) 'Reading development survey, 1974' in *Problems, Practices and Perspectives on the Teaching of Reading in South Australia* (Report of Conference R98) Adelaide: South Australian Education Department

Part 7

A Language for Life

Donald Moyle

This paper is an informal report of conference seminars introduced by John Downing, Coleman Morrison and Donald Moyle and responded to by colleagues from a variety of educational backgrounds and responsibilities, including some members of the Bullock Committee. As such, therefore, the views expressed are not all those of the compiler.

In total, *A Language for Life* was widely praised as a thoughtful and helpful volume, but some of the recommendations were challenged – and as one would expect, there was a good deal of disagreement concerning matters of detail. The group was unanimous in their disappointment that the Secretary of State prefaced the report with a statement to the effect that no extra finance would be available to aid the implementation of the committee's recommendations.

Initial preparation of teachers – course content and time allotment

The report proposes that all intending teachers should take an integrated course which would include all aspects of language from the development of language, concept formation and the nature of language to classroom organization and methods and materials for language and reading teaching. Such an immense content is a forbidding prospect and to proceed even at the most elementary of levels it is difficult to see how the ground could be covered in the 100 to 150 hours of contact time which the report suggests should be devoted to the work. It would seem that perhaps the enthusiasm of members of the committee may have run away with them when they were working out their two sample syllabuses, but that their courage failed them when they had to consider how much time could possible be alloted within the total initial preparation course. Within the colleges there are many competing claims for time and priorities have to be established. In this respect, there are still many college tutors who are not convinced of the necessity of giving a large slice of the available time to work in the area of language and reading. Those who are so convinced must take on the responsibility of spreading their conviction.

One possibility for overcoming the time difficulty would be to follow the example of California and increase our standard course lengths from three and four years to five and six years. Longer does not, of course, necessarily mean better; but it would bring about the possibility of having worthwhile courses to extend students' understanding of the nature of language and the manner in which learning takes place.

It must not be forgotten, however, that initial teacher education is aimed at the production of effective teachers and not at the creation of linguists or learning theorists. At the moment, all too few students seem to amalgamate their learning from theoretical courses, professional courses and practical work among children. It is always a hope, of course, that theory and practice will inform and develop each other, with the effect of aiding the development of effective teaching strategies.

Consideration might be given to re-orientating initial teacher preparation by basing the student in one school for the duration of his course, say for two days each week. His/her task, with the help of tutor and teacher, would be to find the needs of the children and then seek out the knowledge and understanding necessary to plan work to achieve the satisfaction of these needs. Again, there are many difficulties involved in such a change. It would be difficult to write a syllabus for such a course, or to examine performance by traditional means. Further, the schools might not be too happy at the prospect of the permanent attachment of students. Students, in their turn, may object to working in only one school during their course.

There is an obvious danger in the idea of an integrated course, in that tuition may be given at such a level of generality that the student is left with a very poor idea of how he may organize work or teach specific skills within the classroom. Whilst it is easy to agree to the notion of viewing all the language arts as closely related, it is also essential that the student is aware of the activities which can be used to guide a child from one level of development to another. Tutors could become so busy talking about linguistics and learning theory that the necessary expertise in the teaching of reading could become a very minor part of a 'language in education' course. To overcome such a possibility, it would appear necessary to divide the course into a number of units covering the various areas, but this equally carries the danger of the student not fully appreciating the essential unity of language and its use in education.

Specialist teachers and their preparation

The Bullock Report proposes that every school should have a 'language in education' specialist whose task would be to oversee the school's work in the area of language, advising on matters of school policy and providing a support service for the other teachers. Such specialists are envisaged as having the help of area advisory teachers. These advisory teachers would each have a specialism such as reading difficulties or the teaching of English as a second language. Finally, within each local education authority a post of Adviser for English should be established whose major task would be the coordination of advisory services for language work in schools.

These are interesting suggestions and have been welcomed quite widely, not least because they give the opportunity for some sort of career structure to emerge in the language and reading field, which has been missing in the past. It is depressing, however, that after making very great demands for the recognition of language and reading in initial teacher preparation, the committee's suggested periods for the training of specialists are so tiny. The suggestions are for a course of approximately thirty hours for specialists within a school, one term for advisory teachers and one-year courses for advisers in English.

While realizing the problems involved in providing courses of any great duration for at least one teacher from every school, it was felt that such brevity of training could add little to the teacher's existing knowledge, competence and understanding. Further, if all teachers complete a major course of 150 hours in their college years, they are unlikely to respect thirty further hours of training as a qualification for a specialist post. The role of specialists within the schools who have a function across all areas of the curriculum is a difficult one and it would seem essential that they, at least, commence the task from a training background which is respectable in the eyes of their colleagues.

It might be better to reverse the suggestions for the training of specialists and to ask for one-year courses leading to a diploma level qualification for the specialists within the school. Those who wish to become advisory teachers might follow a further one-term course in a narrower field of study, whilst the adviser in English would be expected to have completed a master's degree in a relevant area. All would of course be expected to have appropriate and successful teaching experience.

Two major problems arise in providing courses at advanced level. Firstly, the cost of seconding so many people would be forbidding and secondly, there is a grave shortage of people with the expertise to become tutors of advanced courses. One possible way out of this dilemma might be to provide course materials of the type produced by the Open University. Instead, however, of teachers enrolling merely as individual students, they could be brought together in groups. Regional Language in Education Centres could draw together all those people in their area who could make a tutorial contribution and guide the groups through their course of study. Assuming a mixture of day release and evening courses, it might be possible to meet the demand for trained specialist teachers in some six or seven years.

The report has little to say concerning the content of such courses and there is a danger that courses of too broad a nature may leave the specialist unable to give advice and help of a detailed nature to the class teacher. It might be more fruitful, in view of the needs of the schools, to base the studies in the mastery of written language and then view spoken language work for its impact and interaction with the written.

Whatever the content orientation, it will certainly be necessary to give a good deal of attention to the mechanisms by which the specialist can inform and influence the practice of teaching colleagues within the school. To date, the British teacher has valued independence very highly and this is an important feature of our educational system which the use of specialist teachers should not be allowed to destroy.

The schools
The provision of material resources within the schools is unlikely to be greatly enlarged within the coming two or three years. There are, nevertheless, many suggestions within the report which could be implemented without extra finance.

One such idea is that each school staff should work out a policy for language and reading within their school. Such a task is reasonably easy in general terms but is no easy matter when the details of competencies and attitudes and the methods by which they are to be achieved have to be agreed.

In some senses the report is not helpful in giving teachers and schools a lead in the formulation of a policy, for it is ambivalent and inconclusive in many of its attitudes and directions. Possibly this was the result of the many diverse opinions represented upon the committee.

There is, for example, a considerable contrast between the sections dealing with reading and those dealing with language. In the former, there is appeal to research evidence, a laying out of clear objectives and detailed discussion of teaching strategies. In comparison, the sections dealing with the teaching of English lack clarity and proceed only at the level of generalization. School staffs will find it difficult to amalgamate the two on the basis of the suggestions given by the committee.

Yet the task must be fulfilled if we are to improve the quality of the use of language among children. In order that this can be achieved, teachers will need to look elsewhere for the information which will help them to give the same sense of direction to the use of spoken language that the report makes available in the field of written language.

Apart from Froome's note of dissent, there appears to have been a general affection within the committee for the language-experience approach. However, at two points even this commitment wavers. Firstly, in the areas of materials and methods there are contradictory statements. In one place the suggestion is made that all structured materials and formal approaches to the teaching of both oral and written language should be jettisoned at the earliest possible date. At another point, however, the committee suggest that they saw 'good work' being undertaken by a wide variety of teaching methods and with the use of materials of different types and quality. Here, a stronger lead would have been welcomed by teachers.

There seems also to be some confusion of language-experience with the use of the child's own language. The latter can be helpful, but equally can be as unreal and boring to children as phonic drills. Language-experience, as an approach, insists that an experience cannot be satisfactorily completed unless language is involved. In this way, language becomes an integral part of the activity and not an appendage to it. Thus, the writing of a letter to ask for some information can be seen as necessary communication to the child, rather more than the writing of a report on a visit for the teacher to mark.

The school must succeed in overcoming the ambivalence which is present in the report. A policy is not going to be helpful unless it is clearly stated, understood and implemented. Yet the policy must not become a fetter which limits the inspirations and imaginations of teachers. To this end, there must be room for the expression of each teacher's individuality within the framework and also the opportunity for regular evaluation and modification of the language policy.

It is somewhat easier to see how a policy can be worked out and how the language in education specialist can have a clear function at the primary school stage, than it is at the secondary stage. Here the curriculum is normally orientated to subject specialisms and the divisions of subject matter and the work of departments is often very marked.

It would be unrealistic to expect the English department to take the sole responsibility for the development of language and reading work. English has a content of its own and this must not be lost by the teachers spending most of their time on the development of language skills. Equally, if all departments are to take the responsibility for the development of language and reading in their own subject area there could be a lot of boring repetition of skill work. In some way the division of labour must be achieved, for especially at the higher levels of comprehension, the child needs a knowledgeable guide through the concepts and thinking strategies within the subject area. Equally, the skill-learning must not be divorced from the areas where the skills can be usefully employed, or a transfer problem may arise.

The contributors

Asher Cashdan M.A., M.Ed., F.B.Ps.S.
Senior Lecturer in Educational Studies
The Open University

Frances T. Caust B.A., Dip.Ed.
Principal, Reading Development Centre
South Australian Education Department

Peter Dickinson
Author of *The Changes* and many other books for children and
adults

John Gray B.A., M.Ed.
Research Fellow, Centre for Educational Sociology
University of Edinburgh

Hans U. Grundin Ph.D.
Department of Educational Research
Teachers' College of Linköping
Sweden

Ruth Love Holloway Ph.D.
Director, Right to Read Effort
Washington D.C., U.S.A.

Helen Huus B.A., M.A., Ph.D.
Professor of Education
University of Missouri-Kansas City
U.S.A.

Ronald W. Johnson
Senior Adviser
Cheshire Education Authority

Kenneth Jones M.Ed.
Coordinator of Special Education Courses
Redland College, Bristol

Eric A. Lunzer M.A., Ph.D.
Professor of Educational Psychology
School of Education
University of Nottingham

Tom MacFarlane Dip.Ed.
Curriculum Development Leader for Adult Literacy
Manchester

Marjorie J. McLean B.A., B.Ed., M.Ed.
Assistant Coordinator, Special Learning Difficulties
Winnipeg School Division No. 1
Manitoba, Canada

Julia MacRae
Managing Director, Hamish Hamilton Children's Books Limited
London

Michael K. Molloy Dip.Curric.Stud.
Senior Lecturer in Education
St Joseph's College
Belfast

Joyce M. Morris B.A., Ph.D.
Language Arts Consultant
London

Donald Moyle M.A., L.C.P., L.T.C.L.
Reader in Education
Edge Hill College
Ormskirk

Lenore D. Parker Ed.D.
Associate Professor
Lesley College
Cambridge, Massachusetts, U.S.A.

Anthony K. Pugh B.A., M.Phil.
Staff Tutor, Faculty of Educational Studies
The Open University

Bridie Raban
Teacher at the Reading Centre
Bristol, Avon County

Michael Raggett
Publications Marketing Officer, ILEA
(formerly with Ward Lock Educational)

Jessie F. Reid M.A., M.Ed.
Senior Lecturer, Centre for Research in Educational Sciences
University of Edinburgh

Sam L. Sebesta B.A., M.A., Ed.D
Professor of Elementary Education
University of Washington
Seattle, U.S.A.

Vera Southgate M.A., B.Com.
Senior Lecturer in Curriculum Studies
Faculty of Education
University of Manchester

Oladele Taiwo M.A., Ph.D.
Head of Department of English
College of Education
University of Lagos, Nigeria

Nicholas Tucker B.A.
Sub-Dean, School of Cultural and Community Studies
University of Sussex

Denis Vincent M.A., B.Ed.
Research Officer
National Foundation for Educational Research
in England and Wales
Slough

Gordon Wells B.A.
Research Fellow, School of Education Research Unit
University of Bristol